Proce(
Pseudo Society

First Series
1986~93

Proceedings of the Pseudo Society

First Series
1986~93

edited by
Richard R. Ring and Richard Kay

MEDIEVAL INSTITUTE PUBLICATIONS
College of Arts & Sciences
Western Michigan University
Kalamazoo, Michigan
2003

Library of Congress Cataloging-in-Publication Data

International Congress on Medieval Studies.
  Proceedings of the Pseudo Society : first series 1986-93 / edited
by
Richard R. Ring and Richard Kay.
        p. cm.
Parodies of academic arguments presented to the "Pseudo Society", an
audience devoted to fun at the annual meeting of The International
Congress on Medieval Studies.
Includes bibliographical references.
  ISBN 1-58044-048-7 (pbk. : alk. paper)
 1. Middle Ages–History–Humor. 2. Middle Ages–Humor. I. Ring,
Richard Raymond, 1942- II. Kay, Richard. III. Title.
  PN6231.M48I58 2003

   940.1'02'07–dc21

   2003000690

Donald E. Queller
in memoriam

CONTENTS

Introduction
Richard Kay
1

DE MAJORIBUS NOSTRIS JUTI (May 1976)

Jutish Studies: Introductory Remarks
Dennis W. Cashman
7

Saint Wythelas, Mother of the Jutes
Jo Ann McNamara
11

The Jutes and the Bayeux Tapestry
R. Dean Ware
15

What Happened to the Jutes: A Possible Sexual Explanation
Vern L. Bullough
19

PRIMAE NOCTIS INVENTIONES (May 1986)

Inventing the Past:
The Methodology of Pseudo History
James A. Brundage
33

The Account Books of Saint Francis of Assisi
John F. McGovern†
37

A Newly Discovered Medieval Redaction of a
Previously Lost Manuscript of Soranus Which Amplifies
the Abbreviated Translation of Caelius Aurelianus
Vern L. Bullough
41

Medieval Technology and the Chastity Belt
James D. Ryan
47

The End of the Bayeux Tapestry
R. Dean Ware
51

Leonardo's Latest Invention
Richard Kay
55

INVENTIONES APUD AHA (December 1989)

Inventing Our Motto:
Introductory Remarks at the AHA
R. Dean Ware
65

The Engendering of the Franks:
The Methodology of *Urkonstruktionismus*
Jo Ann McNamara
69

The Name Game
Thomas F. X. Noble
75

The Badman of Bossy-sur-Inept:
Memoirs of a Medieval Peasant
Richard Kay
81

The Pseudo Society at the AHA: Comments
James A. Brundage
89

ALIAE INVENTIONES PRAECLARIORES (1987-93)

Peccata Papae: The Secret Diaries of Pope Innocent III (1987)
James A. Brundage
97

"Or/ordure": From Gold to Garbage, or Deconstructing
the Anglo-Norman Romance *Topas et Pleindamour* (1987)
William Calin
107

Isidore of Seville's Saintly Interventions in Medieval Combat:
The *De interventibus bellicis calamitosis* (1987)
James F. Powers
113

Joinville's Secret History (1988)
Charles T. Wood
125

Boethius on King Arthur: A Newly Discovered Text (1988)
Maureen Fries†
135

Libri pontificales extravagantes (1989)
Thomas F. X. Noble
143

The San Gimignano Dossal and a Note on a
New Discovery about the Pescia Dossal (1989)
William Cook
147

Newly Discovered Danteana from the Biblioteca Bengodiana (1989)
Christopher Kleinhenz
157

Artorius Rex Britanniae from a Contemporary Witness (1991)
Richard C. Hoffmann
175

The Lost Letters of Charlemagne's First Wife,
Autostrada, Also Called Desiderata or Desideria (1991)
Richard R. Ring
181

On the Discovery of a Lost Manuscript of Chrétien de Troyes:
Toward an Appreciation of Its Vast Importance
for the Study of Medieval Literature and Culture (1992)
Evelyn Birge Vitz
189

Sue Doe's Society: A Recent Archival Discovery (1993)
Janetta Rebold Benton
201

Registrum inventionum omnium, complectens
annos 1986–2002, una cum relationibus de Jutis anno 1976
203

Contributors
209

Proceedings of the Pseudo Society

INTRODUCTION

Richard Kay

At the risk of evoking hoots of laughter, let me begin by assuring the reader that this introduction is not a joke. Unlike the papers that follow, its task is to instruct rather than to entertain, lest the origins of the now legendary Pseudo Society be wholly forgotten by an audience devoted to fun.

The International Congress on Medieval Studies is an annual event that takes place on the campus of Western Michigan University in Kalamazoo. The amount of serious scholarship on offer in any given year is simply staggering: by 2002 the number of presentations has grown to about sixteen hundred; when the Pseudo Society began in 1986, the number stood near nine hundred. Perhaps human nature cannot sustain such massive gravity without recourse to some countervailing levity; if so, it took only four hundred papers to provide the first reaction in 1976.

In that year Dennis Cashman was inspired to invent a preposterous organization for a nonexistent specialty—The American Committee for Jutish Studies—and he happily persuaded a team of witty scholars to present Jute-related parodies of academic arguments. Originally he had enlisted Dean Ware, Vern Bullough, and Fred Russell, whose names were given in the printed program, but by show time a flyer announced the addition of three more papers, only one of which, by Jo Ann McNamara, was actually presented. The special session took place on 3 May 1976, at the unlikely hour of 9:45 P.M., in Room 104, which overflowed with an audience of three dozen, including one genuine and disappointed student of Jutica. The program was a crazy success, still fondly remembered by those present, and now preserved in part for posterity in the present collection. Understandably, however, the ACJS never met again, for the original presenters had exhausted their theme: any further jokes about Jutes could only be lame and anticlimactic.

1

Although the niche vacated by the Jutes remained unfilled for ten years, a need was nonetheless perceived, as is evident from several attempts to alleviate the mounting pressure of serious communications. Since at least 1981, the art historians were airing their "nutty notions" at the Old Stones Society in papers of five minutes or less that were speculations rather than spoofs. Other historians were less orderly: in 1982, during a joint session with the Medieval Academy of America, a few of us commandeered a room and held a spontaneous "rump session" at which Tim Runyan delivered an impromptu lecture on "The Constitutional Implications of the Jury Rig." Though symptomatic of the irrepressible need for historical satire, this romp would have been an isolated incident were it not for the emergence of a new and appropriate social structure.

Beginning in 1983, the management of the Kalamazoo conference had found it convenient to subcontract the organization of sessions, either to individual entrepreneurs or to sponsoring groups. Many of the latter were well-established institutions, such as the Dante Society of America, but now a new breed began to appear on the program as sponsors: for example, the Tristan Society, the American Cusanus Society, the International Machaut Society, and more frankly, Spenser at Kalamazoo. The raison d'être for these ad hoc societies was simply to sponsor one or more sessions at Kalamazoo on a subject of common interest to some coterie of specialists. Although these factitious societies undoubtedly served (and still serve) a useful purpose, because they had none of the usual trappings of formal organization—such as a constitution, officers, members, and dues—their lofty titles seemed pretentious and faintly ludicrous.

It was in emulation of these ad hoc societies that the Pseudo Society was conceived and named in 1985 to fill the gap left by the passing of the Jutes. As was our custom, a group of convivial historians lingered together after the smorgasbord banquet, draining our collection of carafes. As one such gathering blends with another in my memory, I cannot be altogether certain who was present that night, but surely among us were Jim Muldoon, Jim Ryan, Tom Blomquist, David Wagner, and Jack McGovern. We lamented the absence of any entertainment between the banquet and the dance, deplored the Jutes' short shelf life, and resolved to found a more durable ad hoc society devoted to spoofs of medievalists' scholarshit. The name for this, the ultimate factitious society, was, I believe, my own invention.[1] We outdid one another in suggesting ridiculous and even outrageous topics—such as "The Eighth Liberal Art," "Saint Oxymoron, Patron of Archdeacons," and "Attila's Last Night"—together with suitable rascals to announce the discoveries.[2] Several papers were volunteered on the spot, and I was commissioned first Master of the Pseudo Society. Thus armed and enabled, I organized an inaugural session in the ordinary way with the distribution of the following letter, dated 1 September 1985:

> Dear ———:
>
> This is your opportunity to become a Charter Member of the (literally) fabulous Pseudo Society! Otto Gründler has now approved the enclosed proposal for our first session at the 21st International Congress on Medieval Studies (8–11 May 1986) and I am hoping that you will agree to give one of the papers.
>
> I suspect that many scholars have long been hoping that some lost document would eventually turn up that would settle a long-standing dispute (e.g. the minutes of Philip the Fair's privy council). Here is your chance to announce the *inventio* of such a source and to point out the consequences. . . .
>
> I commend to you Aristotle's remarks on the relative advantages of poetry and history (1451b1–10).[3]

With the Old Stones Society as a model, the first program was overloaded with seven communications and a substantial preamble. Echoing the Pseudo Society's titular dedication to *inventio,* the conference program, with remarkable prescience, entitled our first session, "Inventing the Past." The society's first spoofing bee took place on 10 May 1986, and the harvest, collected there and in this volume, was prodigious.

The continued success of the society was assured by Dean Ware, who organized sessions for the years 1987 through 1989, from which most of the remaining papers in the present collection have been selected. After a fallow year, in 1991 Rich Ring assumed the mantle of Master of the Revels, in which role he continues to preside.

Although at Kalamazoo the Pseudo Society continues to flourish on its native soil, an attempt was once made to transplant it to the less-receptive environment of the American Historical Association. In 1989, Don Queller, our longtime fan, arranged for a special session of the society at the AHA in San Francisco, and these papers are also included in the present collection. Mine, however, is not the one I first proposed, entitled "The End of History: Derrida, Deconstruction, and Superficial Profundity/Profound Superficiality," which, to my amazement, the AHA Program Committee rejected because it felt that some might be offended by satire. As you shall discover from the screeds in the present anthology, no such scruples—or indeed hardly any at all—have inhibited our revels at Kalamazoo.

The present volume is dedicated to the memory of the late Don Queller, who first proposed that the proceedings of the Pseudo Society be published and then enthusiastically facilitated the project. Most of the papers in this collection were originally selected and assembled by Dean

Ware, who then passed the project on to Rich Ring. Eventually Rich tired of the sound of one editorial hand clapping and consequently he added another, my own, on the cozy principle, "Manus lavat manum." Now, friends, it is your turn to applaud our efforts, so loudly (and profitably) that our publisher may decide that the comedy, far from being over, is to be continued by further volumes of the society's proceedings.

NOTES

1. I certainly provided the original Latin title: "Societas fontibus historiae Medii Aevi inveniendis, vulgo dicitur 'The Pseudo Society,'" the Latinity of which was subsequently improved by Karl Morrison to read "vulgo dicta."

2. The Pseudo Archive preserves my record of these deliberations, which fills eight sides of some four-by-six cards.

3. *De poetica* 9: "The distinction between historian and poet is not in the one writing prose and the other verse . . . ; it consists really in this, that the one describes the thing that has been, and the other a kind of thing that might be. Hence poetry is something more philosophic and of graver import than history" (trans. Bywater).

DE MAJORIBUS NOSTRIS JUTI
(May 1976)

JUTISH STUDIES: INTRODUCTORY REMARKS

Dennis W. Cashman

It is appropriate that the first plenary session of the American Committee for Jutish Studies be held here at Western Michigan University, for it was here, in Kalamazoo, that the committee was established last year. To say that the birth of our organization was the result of a legacy of distrust born of generations of suspicion, outrage, betrayal, and hardship would be no exaggeration. The bias and oppression which plagued the lives of the Jutish people themselves have now been inherited by those who have devoted their scholarly careers to the study of Jutish civilization.

To be specific, the American Committee for Jutish Studies came into being when a number of our founding members concurrently and spontaneously realized that the basis for the palpable discrimination they had suffered for so many years resulted not from any accident of birth, creed, sex, or race but rather from the particular nature of their scholarly specializations. The occasion for this recognition was the forcible ejection of four Juticists from the dinner of Anglo-Saxonists held here on 5 May 1975. This ugly incident served to underscore what many of us have long recognized: that there is a heavily funded, carefully orchestrated, internationally coordinated conspiracy intended to intimidate and hence to silence any who would call attention to the Jutish contribution to Western Civilization. We are not yet certain what organization is responsible for this campaign to muzzle the Jutes, but we know that it *does* exist and we—all of us—have felt its effects. Paranoia, you may think, but in this the era of Watergate, assassination plots, and so forth, think again!

Consider some random examples:

1. We hear a great deal of Hengest and Horsa, but virtually nothing of Halftreac and Lefrac, without whom the 446 expedition to England must surely have failed. Why the oversight?

2. Sympathetic scholars long ago proved that the Jutes were the inventors of the roof, a convenience unknown to the Angles and Saxons. Without Jutish carpentry, the armies of Hengest and Horsa would have perished from exposure. Yet where is this accomplishment noted?

3. One of our members has shown that—though they were badly damaged by the Vikings, and again during the invasions of World War II—there is very good evidence that the original grove of Calvados trees planted in Normandy by the migratory Jutish people still stands, neglected and unacknowledged. Why has no graduate student been encouraged to exploit this clearly fruitful research possibility?

4. There is a New England tradition that, until recently discovered by anthropologists, the Abnaki Indians of northern Vermont were one of the seventy-three lost Jutish tribes. That, too, is a tale which remains to be told.

5. Art historians have shown that the very high degree of naturalism so characteristic of early medieval art (particularly the art of the Merovingians), though clearly of Jutish origin, is invariably ascribed to the Picts. Why have none come forward to de-Pict this art?

6. All of you have undoubtedly heard of the *Liturgica Jutica,* the famous liturgy in which the Introit comes at the end *(exeunt intrantes).* And yet, this unique text remains unedited.

The examples might be multiplied, but the point should by now be clear. This is more than coincidence: the agonies of the oppressed, fugitive Jutish people continue in our own day, shared, as it were, by their modern admirers. I invite you to look at your conference programs. There are two sessions devoted to Old English, full of attention to *Beowulf* and the Anglo-Saxons but wholly silent about the contemporary and superior *Song of Wartley Heath* by the pseudo-Mudward, the classic account of Halftreac's battle of the bogs against the retreating "Roman" armies. Similarly, there are two sessions on Germanic literature, but not a single paper on the *Ulthrupsaga,* the tale which provides the clue to the process of the conversion of the Jutes by Saint Withelas. And perhaps most blatant of all, we find listed Session 48: "Early Germanic Folk," with frequent references to Angles, Saxons, Frisians, and (curiously) Alemanni—but not a word about the Jutes.

Is this a conspiracy of silence? Are there some on the program committee of the Eleventh Conference on Medieval Studies who would have preferred to see the American Committee on Jutish studies stifled, or better yet—denounced? We cannot say for certain, but there is a wealth of evidence which, though circumstantial, is nevertheless persuasive. Here we sit, beginning our session at ten in the evening instead of during a regular daytime slot. The peculiar scheduling was due, we are told, and I quote, "to an administrative error." At this very moment, Lady Ellen of Tarawvaithe, mistress of dance for the Middle Kingdom of the Society for Creative Anachronism, is holding forth in a neighboring room. Could it be that the organizers of this conference, by tinkering with the content of our session (several of the papers to be presented tonight were somehow not listed in the program) and by scheduling us at this hour, are seeking to cast doubt on the sincerity of our purpose? If so, they will be sorely disappointed. We are very aware that the malice of the ancient foe knows no bounds. And we note the "coincidence" that the Germanic surnames "Gründler" and "Sommerfeldt" are most common in Saxony, and rarely if ever encountered in Jutland. Another "accident" perhaps, but we are on our guard. The Jute, as we say, is on the other foot, and the implacable march of Jutish studies will not be stopped!

Before getting on to our presentations I would like to share with you some excerpts from two communications I have lately had. The first is from Sir Harry Snapper Organs, K.B.E., emeritus Professor of Jutish Studies at the University of Harwich in East Anglia.

7 Warley Heath Road
Harwich, East Anglia
England

The Chairman
American Committee for Jutish Studies
One Dupont Circle
Washington, DC 20003
U.S.A.

Dear Professor Cashman:

Though my wounds and the recent devaluation of the pound regrettably prevent my attendance at the first annual meeting of the ACJS, I am immensely gratified to learn that your group has undertaken the too-long-delayed rejuvenation of the supposedly obscure Jutes. As you know, I have devoted my life to just such a resurrection, and my early retirement from the University has permitted me to focus my efforts during the past five years.

I am hopeful that the organisation of your committee heralds an end to the unfortunate excesses so characteristic of the Germanic school of Juticists—excesses which have in the past frustrated the hopes and prayers of all who advocate a moderate solution to the Jutish problem.

I am,

Yours sincerely,
H. Snapper Organs

Professor Organs had planned to be with us today but was "accidentally" shot two weeks ago while searching for the Fenland Anonymous in the moors of southern Yorkshire. His assailant, a local farmer named John Saxonby, explained to Scotland Yard that he thought he had taken aim at a badger. It has been determined that Professor Organs was shot from a distance of less than thirty feet. Still, Saxonby was released from custody. The professor is on the mend, thankfully, and I have forwarded our heartiest good wishes to him in his convalescence.

The other letter comes from Doctor Heinrich Dreimalgänger, longtime director of the Institut für jutisch Geschichte in Kiel.

93, Jutischweg Allee
Kiel 60W9
Germany

The Chairman
American Committee for Jutish Studies
One Dupont Circle
Washington, DC 20003
U.S.A.

Dear Professor Cashman:

Your strenuous efforts on behalf of the heroic Jutish *Volk* do not go unnoticed here. Centuries of unjust tyranny and calculated harassment have made us wary of self-proclaimed champions, whatever their country of origin. As you know, we have been stabbed in the back altogether too many times.

Nevertheless, we welcome the foundation of your committee. The new lands of America may yet provide our salvation. The pseudohistory preached by Organs and the other English revisionists has for too long distracted the attention of serious Juticists. We look to you to correct this inequity.

Heinrich Dreimalgänger
Institut für jutisch Geschichte

We will now proceed to our papers. I am sure that you will find them stimulating and novel, and that you will have questions after the presentations.

SAINT WYTHELAS, MOTHER OF THE JUTES

Jo Ann McNamara

Historians were content for far too long to consign Saint Wythelas, the Mother of the Jutes, to the realm of legend. Around the turn of the century, she was relegated to the sole proprietorship of literary critics interested in the folkloric elements in the *Saga of Ulthrup the Sudden*.[1] Archeologists working on Continental sites, however, have now exposed crucial material which must lead historians to a serious reconsideration of this vital source that may go far to solving the problem of the disappearance of the Jutes from English historiography.[2] At the onset, I would like to dedicate this paper to the memory of that staunch hero of Jutish Studies, "Fuzzy" Lovell-Grovelle, whose career was so brutally damaged by the controversy arising out of his disinterment of the lost Jutish army on the shores of the Rhine.[3]

The Fenland Anonymous's *Vita Withelae* should no longer be considered a hagiographical fantasy. Nor should Wythelas herself be dismissed as an ancient vegetation goddess disguised as a Christian missionary. The work is a reliable account of the life of a remarkable person whose ordeal in preserving the Jutes from immediate extinction, despite the ultimate cost to a proud people, has been tragically misunderstood. The chronological difficulties which have hitherto troubled scholars in this work can largely be solved by the newly discovered South Gyrvian connection.[4] A close study of the South Gyrvian redaction of the *Anglo-Saxon Chronicle* shows that there were, in fact, two contingents of Jutes penetrating the swamp—one under Halftreac and one under Lefrac—who were unknown to each other until their accidental encounter in the Fens. With this knowledge, many of the difficulties in the manuscript can be cleared up.[5]

The stumbling block to a serious study of Wythelas has always been the central miracle of her sexual transformation.[6] Once dismissed as a meaningless racial memory of some lost ritual drama, this miracle, I propose, can now be seen as a truthful account of a central event in the Jutish life cycle. The evidence from the grave of the eleven thousand will substantiate this thesis with some cautiously offered support from more traditional sources, such as Gregory the Great's account of a similar miracle, which may conceivably relate to a lost branch of the Jutes in Italy.[7] It is my hope that this revisionist view of the *Life of Wythelas* will open new horizons to the ever-growing number of young scholars who are beginning to devote their attention to the Jutes.

The story, as everyone in this distinguished audience will recall, begins abruptly in the middle of a battle.[8] The two groups of Jutes, believing that they had encountered the Anglo-Saxon invaders of their marshy realm, were embraced in deadly combat. As their characteristically down-turned feet, usually so well adapted to swamp travel, gained purchase in the mud, they were gradually being sucked into the unstable bog when a mysterious figure appeared, hanging by her feet from a great tree and having in her hand a standard with which she transported the combatants one by one from the quicksand. This was, of course, the Jutifer. The failure of later medieval chroniclers to understand the significance of that implement caused them to believe that the Jutish army was, in fact, a group of simple women. The propensity of later scholars to misread Jutish sexual philology caused them to translate the word *instortingfart* as "virgin" and to maintain later in the Ursula legends that the Huns had massacred eleven thousand virgins rather than eleven thousand Jutes led by Wythelas across the North Sea. We can now see that what happened was very simply that in the course of flinging the Jutes out of the swamp, Wythelas underestimated her own strength. As they were cast into the sea and swept toward Germany, the Jutish army underwent the transformation effected by the brandishment of the Jutifer.

Wythelas, we must believe, had little choice but to use the Jutifer in this undecorous manner. She had to act quickly to save them, even if it put them at risk in the tides of the Wash.[9] This material is, of course, all too familiar to you. I must apologize for wearying you with its repetition. But it is this abrupt intervention which links the South Gyrvians to the eleven thousand. In the wake of this disaster, the surviving Jutes were scattered in many directions. They can be traced only by the presence of false jutifers among their grave goods, which testify to their forlorn efforts to restore the balance in their sexual ecology. Moreover, Wythelas had, in the panic of the moment, repeatedly brandished the Jutifer over herself, and this precipitated the uncontrollable procreative seizure that is so powerfully recorded by the Anonymous.

Let us now return to the Fenlands and that beleaguered band of Jutes memorialized by our anonymous hagiographer. When Wythelas arrived in their midst, they had long been established in that felicitous environment. Fragments of old songs indicate that "Wythelas" may have been a generic name for those persons who presided over the annual mudsucker festivals, brandishing a jutifer as they swang through the trees. Our Wythelas may have been the last of a line of sacred swingers who guided her people through the rites of passage so essential to their survival. During her ordeal of unrelenting labor, her attempts to brandish the Jutifer widdershins left her in a hermaphroditic condition that she could not correct unaided. It was only the arrival of Patrick, with a pair of snakes, that solved the crisis. Thereafter the grateful Wythelas submitted to baptism and began the preaching career that offered the Jutes survival in a heavenly kingdom as repayment for their fatally marred genetic future on earth.

With the obscurity typical of Jutish sources, the South Gyrvian redaction says only that her preaching swayed the Jutes and that they tilted into the bogs to be baptized. With the Irish connection, however, we are on firmer ground. For nothing could be clearer than that the great Hibernian apostle brought some Jutes with him into Ireland. The miracle recounted by Gerard, abbot of Lismore, of the resurrection of a dead princess as a boy, who thereafter enjoyed a long reign, clearly refers to a Jute.

For Wythelas herself, however, the way was not so smooth. The Anonymous recounts her many miracles with enthusiasm. He cannot praise her sufficiently for driving the hippopotamus out of England or for the parting of the marsh gas. But he leaves us frustrated when it comes to that crucial act, the transformation of the Jutifer into a religious symbol. Did Wythelas herself abandon the brandishment? Was it an error in the process that started the Jutes evolving backwards into the little people remembered in Fenland folk lore? Or did her attempt to repair the damaged instrument simply fail, leaving her stranded in incomplete female guise? Was it a mistaken zeal for the Christian ideal of virginity that caused her to refuse the necessary fertilization? Or, at last, does the answer lie in the deeper recesses of the human mind, to be penetrated one day by psychohistorians investigating suigenophobia?

We only know that the ancient Jutish penitentials, attributed to Wythelas herself, severely condemned the brandishment of the Jutifer. We know that its persistent—indeed necessary, though risky—continuation by the Fenland Jutes was repeatedly condemned by Anglo-Saxon clergy for many centuries to come as witchcraft or worse. Perhaps, having suffered the unspeakable fate of becoming the Mother of the Jutes, Wythelas strove to save others from a similar destiny.

NOTES

1. *Ulthrup* 8.28, where Ulthrup finds Wythelas hanging from the sacral tree.

2. Sir F. A. R. T. Lovell-Grovelle, "Preliminary Report on the Grave of the 11,000," *Jutish Studies* 258 (1935), 119–05 mapped the course of the new scholarship by establishing the fact that the 11,000 were the Jutish army rather than the legendary troop of virgins who accompanied Ursula. His brilliant identification of the Jutifer as the standard carried by the chieftain who had inadvertently led his army out of the Fens to be swept away in the Wash to their eventual lonely grave on the shores of the Rhine was the key to the study of the same standard in English swamps: "The Significance of the Jutifer in Establishing Jutish Migratory Patterns," *Jutish Studies* 245 (1939), 540–25.

3. This tragedy of modern scholarship has been tenderly traced by his student and successor, Jutith Fenway, herself reputed to be of Jutish origin, in *The Desanctification of Ursula* (Ely: The Bogvolk Press, 1956).

4. Mordecai Phantast, "The Fenland Background of Ulthrup the Sudden" (in press).

5. Interestingly enough, this theory was simultaneously advanced by two scholars working in ignorance of one another's discoveries: Sturdevant Ffondruff, "East Anglian Place Names and the Invasion of Halftreac," in the *Cambridge History of the Jutes* (Cambridge-atte-Wash, 1943), pp. 682–704, and Avantgard Ffrudnoff, "Lefrac, the Wandering Jute," in the *The New Oxford Jutish History* (Oxford-on-the-Fens, 1944), pp. 450–572.

6. Lovell-Grovelle, "The Jutifer as Key to the Sexual Characteristics of the Jutes," *Jutish Studies* 224 (1945), 235–18.

7. In my earlier consideration of this problem, "Not Jutes but Jewels," *Jutish Studies* 201 (1963), 110–98, I believed that Gregory had encountered only two Jutes who had probably been brought to Rome by slavers.

8. Once dismissed as a common topos, this combat has now been identified as the Battle of the Bogs, so movingly recounted by pseudo-Mudward in the *Song of Wartley Heath.*

9. Though I now believe that they survived in greater numbers than previously suggested. See my "Orlando, Last of the Jutes: An Homage to Virginia Woolf," forthcoming in *Feminist Issues in Jutish Studies.*

THE JUTES AND THE BAYEUX TAPESTRY

R. Dean Ware

It is a distinct honor to be asked to participate in this first annual meeting of the American Committee for Jutish Studies. I well remember the occasion when my interest was first directed toward the Jutes. In 1956, just twenty years ago, an essay of mine, entitled "Frith and Grith on the Eve of the Conquest," appeared in the Edgar Puddle *Festschrift,* and a distinguished reviewer, among otherwise generous remarks, raised the now all too obvious question, "but what about the Jutes?" This gave me pause. At that time I had to confess a near-total ignorance of this curious nation, but assiduous application to the writings of Jolliffe dispelled that ignorance to replace it with a confusion that inspired me over the next years to devote what time I was able to steal from the busy round of teaching and other fruitless occupations of our profession, to a systematic study of this mysterious people, described aptly by Sir Frank Stenton as "this mysterious people." My paper this evening may be regarded as the culmination of these many years of effort; it ties together the results of several of my earlier investigations, namely: "Cornage and Dreynage: A Medieval Dilemma," published in the *Leekshire Miscellany for 1962;* "Pannage and Soilage: A False Quandary," a paper delivered before the County Cork Peat Society in 1970 during my sabbatical year in Ireland; and "Tillage and Toilage: An Unnoticed Paradox," that appeared just last year in the *Ladies' Home Journal.*

During these years of Jutish preoccupation, my thinking gradually turned from the original prompting question—"What about the Jutes?"—to a concentration on the problem of "Whatever happened to the Jutes?" Every Anglo-Saxonist knows that Angles, Saxons, and Jutes figure equally prominently in the age of invasion and settlement; yet the Jutes play a *diminishing* role as time goes by and ultimately *disappear* from history.

People talk only about the Anglo-Saxons. The Jutes simply *vanish* from view! And then it came to me that the Bayeux Tapestry provided the clue. So let me now fulfill the promise of the title of this evening's address.

The Bayeux Tapestry, as James Bryce once observed, is neither a tapestry nor was it done at Bayeux. It is in fact an embroidery, every warp and weft of which betray it as a product of the Crewel School of Canterbury; in short, it must be an exemplum of Jutish needlework. It is, of course, a wonderful work, the only piece that bears comparison with it being the nearly contemporary depiction of the adventures of Pudor and Pudenda, apparently embroidered at Roué, but surviving unfortunately only in a circumcised form. Although the weight of the Bayeux Tapestry has never been determined exactly, it measures 19 1/2 inches by 231 feet. In contrast to the common notion that a panel or so is missing at the end of the tapestry, its clear Jutish provenance leads me to believe that several panels have actually been interpolated into an original that was only 212 1/2 feet long, or precisely twenty-five Jutish cubits of 8 1/2 feet. I shall not press this hypothesis now, but will simply point out that by omitting those panels that I have identified as spurious, a compelling argument for Jutish design and execution can be made. In its putatively original form, the Bayeux Tapestry depicts six hundred people, two hundred horses and mules, fifty dogs, five hundred other animals, thirty buildings, forty ships and boats, and forty trees, all, *nota bene,* decimal totals. That the number ten was especially sacred to the Jutes cannot, I think, be disputed, made up as it is by adding together their favorite numbers, one, two, three, and four; and the evidence for the use of these numbers in Jutish society and culture is abundant and incontrovertible.

The artistic "Jutishness" of the Bayeux Tapestry now having been convincingly demonstrated, I shall get to the heart of my thesis, and that entails a much more significant departure from received wisdom: that is, the tapestry has nothing to do with the Norman Conquest of England! The conventional attribution derives from several casual resemblances and innocent coincidences, such as the names "Edward," "Harold," "William," and a story of disputed succession and military conflict. I can now lay to rest all such facile identifications and careless assumptions. My paper this evening is the first public exposition of my discovery that the Bayeux Tapestry is not only Jutish in origin but Jutish in subject matter, for all the episodes depicted are otherwise unrecorded events in Jutish history. Moreover, all the figures represented are *life size!* Yes, it is my considered opinion that, when all the evidence is taken into account, the Jutes were really a race of midgets. The corroboration of the Bayeux Tapestry is conclusive. The legendary two-handed battle-ax, for which there is not a shred of archeological evidence, is just a simple hatchet or tomahawk, yet still the wee Jute needed both hands to wield it. And the familiar body-covering kite shield is recognized as oversize only by comparison with the under-sized Jute. But in addition to this, there is gavelkind. Indeed it was my study of this peculiar Jutish landholding system that brought me to yet another stunning realization. Gavelkind, as we all know, is characterized by par-tibility of inheritance, with the inevitable consequence of progressive reduction in size of holdings. In a flash it came to me that the only ration-al explanation for such a practice is that the members of Jutish society were not only small, they themselves were growing smaller from generation to generation. The Jutes pictured in the Bayeux Tapestry, then, had larger ancestors and smaller descendants. They seem to have been normal in size while still in their continental homeland, and they only began to shrink soon after invading Britain. Why this happened, I do not know. One pos-sibility, however, is that living *up* on the *downs* destroyed their sense of direction. But this is sheer conjecture.

What is fact, though, is that the Jutes were conspicuously shorter already by 600 A.D., when their king Ethelbert took a Frankish wife, there-after known as "Big Bertha." The marriage had originally been regarded as a certain *mésalliance*, but after Ethelbert's friends put him up to it, the union was successfully consummated. By 700 A.D. the Venemous Bede is calling the Jutes *eotenas* 'giants', in derisive allusion to their stature. There is also the evidence of toponymy. The earliest place names, where the diminutive *inga* is incorporated, such as "Hastings"—"little Hasty's place"—derive from the late fifth and early sixth centuries, when individ-ual Jutes had begun to downsize but the majority were yet regular size. By the late sixth century, though, *all* the Jutes were smaller and *inga* place names give way to formations on other principles, such as "Rochester"— "Rock-on-casters"—apparently so-called from a large mobile boulder near the site.

But enough of bald, unadorned fact! I shall conclude by asking you to ponder with me the ultimate fate of the Jutes. Already less than a foot high in the eleventh century, the race continued its earthward descent. By the twelfth century, though history does not record it, we can well imagine heroic conflict with the pitiless field mouse, and epic struggles with worms (*wyrms*), now dragonlike in relative size. Finally, no doubt, even ants would have made the Jutes their prey, until a few survivors—can we call them for-tunate?—found microscopic sanctuary. Let us fondly hope that still today, somewhere, proud subatomic Jutes are uttering their fearsome war cry, "Hengisthorsa!"—"my Hengist for a horse"—the meaning of which is not entirely clear.

WHAT HAPPENED TO THE JUTES: A POSSIBLE SEXUAL EXPLANATION

Vern L. Bullough

This paper seeks to answer the question of what happened to the Jutes. It is a problem much more complicated than it seems because of the open hostility to the Jutes expressed in many of the sources. So great was this hostility that Gavin Langmuir in his definitive study of anti-Semitism in the medieval period recorded that English anti-Semitism was much worse than on the Continent because a chronicler in King Alfred's court had confused the word "Jute" with "Jew," writing *Judaeus* rather than *Jutaeus*.[1] This careless slip of a scribe in describing the Anglo-Saxon and Jewish settlements in England led, he said, later Norman chroniclers to attribute all the hostility that was expressed to the Jutes to the Jews. I am convinced by Professor Langmuir's explanation of the confusion of the Jews with Jutes, but unfortunately he never explains what there was in Jutish culture which led to such fear and anxieties that their very name was a sign of opprobrium.

Is it possible that their bad reputation had something to do with the disappearance of the Jutes? In any case it seemed a lead worth pursuing. Fortunately others had been intrigued by this same question, and several explanations have been advanced, some with more merit than others. Alfred Andreas, in a paper which he gave at a colloquium on medieval music at the Philadelphia Pro Musica Society, demonstrated rather conclusively that the term for the modern Jute box derived from an original Jutish musical box, a many-stringed and colorfully arrayed instrument that sounded unmusical even to the ears of the Celtic bagpiper.[2] Professor Andreas, however, was careful to avoid ascribing the medieval anti-Jutism to their unique musical instrument, however much it must have angered their Anglo-Saxon neighbors. Still, since animosities build up gradually, it is important to include this among the variables involved in anti-Jutish prejudice exhibited against them, but other variables also have to be considered.

Emily Coleman in her early studies of infanticide found in some trial records that in certain sections of England parents whose children had disappeared were reported to have given them over to the Jutes.[3] This might simply have been another slur upon the honor and integrity of the Jutes, but there seems more to it than this. Earlier James Brundage, in a monograph on some of the less well known aspects of canon law in the early Middle Ages, had also reported references to Jutish death practices in connection with a heretical group devoted to the worship of Mary Ionis.[4] This last has proven to be a more fruitful source of investigation.

Recent scholarship has found that Mary Ionis was an early cult centered around Saint Mary but radically different from other Mary cults. In fact this cult seems to have been a Jutish version of the cult of Isis with a Christian overlay. Ionis, as all those familiar with studies of Greek folklore know, was the daughter of the king of Argos who was changed into a cow by a jealous Juno. She then became identified with Isis and Hathor in Egyptian history, and in this form re-entered Europe and apparently influenced the northern Germanic peoples. Though the Jutes were converted to Christianity through the efforts of Theodore of Tarsus after their arrival in the British Isles, they did not entirely discard their pagan goddess Ionis but Christianized her as Mary Ionis, and as such she played a powerful role in their funeral ceremonies.

Interestingly, this cult, as Jo Ann McNamara and other feminist-oriented scholars have shown, still holds a great deal of importance for us today. In fact McNamara and her colleagues were able to get a five million dollar grant from the U.S. Food and Drug Administration and the National Institute of Mental Health to study it. They proved conclusively that it was from the Jutish cult of Mary Ionis that we get the word "marijuana." Obviously, McNamara et alia concluded that part of the ceremonies celebrated with the worship of Mary Ionis was the smoking of marijuana, perhaps in ways similar to the peyote cult among the southwestern Indians.[5]

Impressed by McNamara's ability to make medieval studies vital to today's need for new solutions to old problems, the National Endowment for the Humanities gave a similar grant for studies into our drug culture headed by Donald Queller, Warren Hollister, and Mary Daly. Following the path-breaking studies of McNamara's group into the cult of Mary Ionis, they too found the Jutes a rich source of study. It seemed too obvious to link the Jutes with jute (a particular form of hemp), but good scholarship, as every sociologist knows, is demonstrating the obvious. Fortunately they had a good comparative linguist in their group, and they found that the Sanskrit word *johot,* or *jhout,* was originally the name for a tribal group of Indo-Europeans who used the plant in their worship ceremonies.[6] Though, unlikely as it might seem, thanks to medieval studies, we have now found that both forms of cannabis—the Middle Eastern form (hashish) and the American form (marijuana)—can be traced to the Jutes. Since there seem to be two different and independent strands of evidence connecting marijuana and other forms of cannabis to the Jutes, it seems safe to say that the Jutes were obviously users. But what did this have to do with infant mortality?

John Riddle, in his recent study of abortifacients, contraceptives, and similar herbal medicines, added to this knowledge through a chemical analysis of the contents of some jars found at a Jutish grave site inside a cave. The graves had originally been found and recorded by Josiah Russell, who described a series of cave paintings in what must have been a kind of Jutish mausoleum. These paintings showed Jutish mothers holding infants with one arm while rubbing something on their own nipples with the other hand. Russell added that a certain unique jar was always portrayed at the same time. Whether Russell took some of these jars,[7] or whether some of his students did, is not now known, but several were later found by Riddle in the storage room of a North Carolina pharmaceutical museum. They had been shown to him by the director, who knew they were old and that they were somehow associated with medicine, but he did not know exactly what they were. Riddle recognized them from Russell's photographs and had the foresight to have them chemically analyzed. Both contained traces of a mixture of various forms of cannabis, in its marijuana and jutish, or hashish, form. He postulated that this was the original form of the plant which underwent some modifications as it spread in the New World and became slightly different from the old world variety.[8]

It seems clear that the mothers rubbed cannabis on their nipples to help soothe a crying baby, and that the infants liked it, and that some mothers simply put too much on, and the infants had mild hallucinations which caused them both to have acute diarrhea and to feel happy and not cry, and they died of malnutrition. More recent finds have found that mothers also rubbed the marijuana on the gums of teething babies, and so those who survived infancy were again threatened by the treatment for teething.

Would the use of cannabis in its various forms have given the Jutes such a bad name? Could its widespread use have led to the disappearance of the Jutes? The answer to both questions has to be in the negative. We know that the Jutes used cannabis at key ceremonies in their life and not just to soothe infants. Marriages were marked by the use of cannabis and so were funerals. We know that the Jutish funeral practices came to be widely imitated by others, although alcoholic beverages generally, for reasons not yet clear, replaced marijuana in most of western Europe. The Irish wake, according to a recent study by James Muldoon and Dean Ware, is a direct descendent of the Jutish funerary rites.[9] These rites originally took place in a pasture, in deference to the association of Mary Ionis with the sacred cow. Mourners sat in a circle on large rocks and smoked marijuana/hashish. According to some philologists, this is the source of the expression "getting stoned," although others have cast doubt on this interpretation, arguing that since the mourners sat on the rocks, they could not have thrown them. In fact, if they had thrown them, it has been pointed out, the Jutish funeral would have been more lethal than the contemporary remnant, the Irish wake. Moreover, anything so widely copied could not have been regarded by contemporaries as so horrible. Perhaps, however, they simply sat on the rocks and stones until they passed out, which meant they resembled the immovable stones on which they sat. The whole topic is controversial.[10]

As far as infanticide is concerned, there remains the question of how many infants died. The late Professor David Herlihy, in one of his many studies on mortality, has shown that approximately 25 percent of the Jutish infants died within their first year, and an additional 35 percent died before the age of seven.[11] Still some 40 percent survived to adulthood, and while this is a high mortality, it would still enable the Jutes to reproduce themselves if the average family had five or more children born alive. This is a question which will be investigated later in this paper. At this point, however, it can be safely said that cannabis in its various forms and with its various uses does not seem to be the complete answer either for the Jutes' decline or for the anger and fear expressed about them.

When we search the scattered sources for possible answers, a brief hint appears in the *Anglo-Saxon Chronicle*. The anonymous compiler of the Laud version simply recorded that in 449 the Jutes settled in Kent and on the island of Wight. He then added an ominous sentence which appears in only one manuscript (perhaps a latter addition) that he will say no more of the Jutes because they are *maledicti*.[12] But why are they *maledicti*? Another hint comes from Snorri Sturluson, who in one of his *Eddas* mentioned that when the sons of Guðrun were cutting off the hands and feet of King Jormunrekk, he woke and shouted to his men that he would be "juted" if they did not respond at once.[13] Since Jormunrekk's men responded and beat off the sons of Guðrun, the meaning of "juted" remains unclear. This reference appears in isolation, and though I have scanned other literature of the period, the only thing I have found is a possible mention in one manuscript of *Beowulf*, but I only received information about this at second hand and have been unable to trace it down. I would ask Beowulf scholars who read this article to examine their sources for possible further references to "juted" or "Juted," since I must admit my own ignorance of this arcane field.

Since the meaning of "juted" in the *Eddas* is unclear, it has offered scholars from other disciplines a field day. I would like to examine two interpretations to illustrate the dangers of allowing scholars untrained in medieval sources to utilize the medieval period to find answers to their questions. One interpretation was given by the English eugenicist Karl Pearson, holder of the first chair of eugenics at the University of London at the beginning of this century. Professor Pearson was very much concerned with hereditary genius and, conversely, with hereditary feeble-mindedness. To encourage genius, he wanted people with high intelligence to have lots of children and people with low intelligence to be sterilized. Obviously it became important for him to find groups of people who were feebleminded, whom he could use to illustrate the dangers of reproduction of such individuals. He consulted a wide variety of sources, including incidentally the *Eddas,* and believed that Jormunrekk meant that he would be knocked senseless and become like a Jute. From this he concluded that the Jutes were an inherently feebleminded tribal group who had given rise to what he called "the various undesirables" in England. He felt in fact that the Cockney dialect was a Jutish perversion of true Anglo-Saxon English (he left out the Normans and their effect on the language). He also offered other evidence by tracing the migration of a ninth-century Jutish group to present-day Belgium, and found that they settled near Geel. Here they established a church dedicated to Saint Dymphna who, because of the inhabitants, became known as the patron saint of the feebleminded. It was from this Jutish migration, he argued, that Geel became a haven for the feebleminded and those troubled with mental illness. But Pearson was not content with this explanation. He also claimed that the Jutes internally often referred to themselves as "Jukes," and many ultimately adopted the family name of "Juke." He then hypothesized that the famous Jukes sisters who with the Kallikat family were long used as a bad example in eugenics classes were an American remnant of the feebleminded Jutes.[14]

Needless to say that Professor Pearson's thesis is not now accepted, and his historical data has been found to be based upon little more than prejudice against the Jutes, although it took the Holocaust to cause a reassessment of such thinking. Equally unacceptable to modern scholars is the interpretation of the word "juted" by Leopold von Sacher-Masoch, the nineteenth-century historian turned novelist. Though it is sometimes difficult to distinguish his fiction from his history, von Sacher-Masoch claimed that the term "juted" meant "to be tortured" and that the male Jutes were sadists.[15] In light of this assumption, it was probably no accident that von Sacher-Masoch made the hero in his novel, *Venus with Jewels,* a person of Jutish background.[16] Recent scholars, particularly those who approach history from a feminist perspective, have argued that in this respect the male Jutes were not different from the Angles and Saxons, and if sadism in men is defined as domination of women, no western European group would have a good reputation.[17] Other scholars, however, have emphasized the symbiotic relationship between the sadist and masochist, which would imply that if the male Jutes were sadists, the female Jutes were masochists.[18] Still, a close review of the evidence, I think, would not support either von Sacher-Masoch or his critics, and other explanations for the anti-Jutish prejudice will have to be found. I must admit I find it surprising how some scholars will build a whole theory on a simple passing reference, but fortunately neither of the ones I have just cited was a professional medievalist.

Key to this is understanding what Jomunrekk meant by his fear of being "juted." One source which might throw some hint upon it is the early Jutish saints. In tracing these down, and distinguishing Jutish saints from Angle and Saxon ones, I found a rather interesting phenomenon. All the female saints were bearded. The most famous of course is Saint Uncumber, or Wilgafortis. Though according to tradition Wilgefortis was born to a non-Christian ruler of Portugal and his Christian queen, a recently published manuscript from the Bath College Museum (Bath, MS 2) dating from the eighth century, contains the phrase, "Wilgefortis Jute est," which I take to mean that Wilgefortis was a Jute. The story in this manuscript does not differ in any other way from the traditional version. For those of you who do not know the story, Wilgefortis was determined to remained unmarried. Her father was equally determined to have her marry. He betrothed her to a local king (probably from East Anglia), and when she protested that she would refuse marriage, her father ordered her to marry anyway. In desperation she prayed for help, and her prayer was answered by the sudden growth of a long drooping mustache and a silky, curling beard. When her father saw her, he ordered her to be heavily veiled and escorted off to the altar anyway. In the midst of the ceremony, Wilgafortis managed to show her bearded face to her would-be husband, and he immediately broke off the engagement with words reportedly to the effect that he knew the Jutes did that sort of thing but that he really did not think they would do it to him.[19]

Though the story has been described as having the "unenviable distinction of being one of the most obviously false and preposterous of the pseudo-pious romances by which Christians have been deceived or regaled,"[20] Wilgefortis became venerated, and her story traveled across Europe, where she became known by a variety of names, usually derived from the term "*liberata*," as "the deliverer," or "Uncumber," and she became the patron saint of women wanting a divorce. Two other bearded Jutish saints were Saint Galla and Saint Paula.[21] From these accounts, it might be concluded that bearded brides were not uncommon among the Jutes, particularly if we use the scholarly definition of a sample as being two or more cases. But were bearded brides common among the Jutes, and if so what does this mean?

Further light is thrown on this question by various recipes in the *Anglo-Saxon Leech Book,* which uses the term "Jute" (as distinct from Mary Ionis) at least twenty times. Several of these recipes deal with *fistula in ano* (hemorrhoids) and recommend the application of certain powders and salves perfected by the Jutes to relieve the painful symptoms. Other recipes use the term "Jute" as a verb, synonymous almost with penetration, so for example, a person should "jute" this in the anus, or "jute" this in the vagina, or "jute" this in the mouth.[22] Linguists have argued that penetration is not a fully accurate translation and argue that the closest modern English word is "jut," meaning "to project," "to protrude," or as one English dictionary states, "that which has a projection."[23] This would seem logical because it then explains why the Jutes got their name. Before this, it was assumed that Jutland had been named after them, but now it appears that they settled in a place they called "Jutland" from its projection into the Baltic, and they received their name from the place. This is an important clue, because why would anyone settle in a place that even Sigmund Freud recognized had long been a phallic symbol?[24]

With these hints I turned to the penitential literature, and I found— again in a Bath manuscript—a hitherto unpublished penitential dating from the late sixth century or early seventh, which is very similar to the penitential known as the *Preface of Saint Gildas on Penance.*[25] In this newly found penitential, however, instead of "fornication" and "sodomy," the terms used by Saint Gildas, as well as by other early penitential writers, the Bath manuscript uses the word "jute." Anyone who "jutes" and who has previously taken the monastic vow has to do penance for three years.[26]

If this penitential represents some remnants of Teutonic language, then the term "jute" uttered by King Jormunrekk expresses a fear of being penetrated. Further evidence for this comes from the Old Danish word for companion. *Nichtiutenfreund* ("companion") literally translated means "not a Jute," that is, one who can walk behind one and be trusted. With this interpretation all kinds of hidden understandings and implications emerge. Wilgefortis, for example, really wasn't a bearded bride at all, but a normal male following one of the Jutish rituals for marriage. The later transcribers of the Wilgefortis legend, however, found it easier to transform him into a her than to face the issue of homosexuality. This explanation, moreover, easily explains the hostility which many contemporaries had to the Jutes. But there is more to the Jutish tradition than simple male homosexuality. After all, there were also Jutish women. Were they all lesbians? Undoubtedly some were. The most famous I have been able to find, however, is the person known as "John Anglicus," usually known as "Pope Joan," who unfortunately in her womanly frailty gave birth to a baby in the midst of a papal procession. Traditionally Joan is said to have been made pregnant by a Benedictine monk from Spain, who reminded her of her beloved companion Ulfilias, with whom she had traveled to Constantinople. The same Bath manuscript that has given us additional information on Wilgefortis also indicated that both Joan and Ulfilias were Jutes, but adds that Ulfilias was really Ulfilia. This explains why Joan later become pregnant. She naturally thought the Benedictine monk was a female like her beloved Ulfilia, and only much too late did she find herself unnaturally deceived.[27]

Perhaps the terms "homosexual" and "lesbian" are the wrong ones to use, since quite clearly both the male and female Jutes were bisexual. It seems also that the Jutish women were more heterosexual than the Jutish men, and many are known to have served, if only briefly, as prostitutes. This role is commemorated by the heroic Jutish heroine of the ninth century, Syphilides, who rebelled against the subordinated role of women in the Jutish culture, in which men sometimes married other men, and women were kept around only to do the necessary cooking and cleaning tasks, and occasionally to give forth children if they could find a deviant enough male to have intercourse with (deviant by Jutish standards of course). According to the Jutish chronicle, also uncovered at Bath,

Syphilides raised the standard of revolt, demanding greater rights for women and assailing Jutish male prerogatives. In the midst of her nearly successful revolt, the Jutish chronicle reports that she was struck ill and her body was covered with sores. A curse was put upon her by the Jutish men to the effect that anyone who would have truck with her or her descendants would be inflicted with similar sores. It was from her illness that someone coined the word "syphilis."[28]

Inevitably the combination of syphilis, homosexuality, and perhaps other sexual activities attributed to the Jutes gave them a rather evil reputation. They were stigmatized by other Anglo-Saxon groups, and in order to escape this stigma they dropped their identity as Jutes, merging with other peoples. How much can we rely upon these newly discovered Jutish sources? Personally I tend to discount the story of Syphilides as a fraud perpetuated by male chauvinist historians. I do, however, tend to think there is some truth in the homosexuality stories. Unfortunately, to accept them seems to discount the recent work of John Boswell, who argued that there was a greater tolerance of homosexuality during this period than later.[29] I hold that Boswell was wrong, as the evidence of hostility to the Jutes would indicate and as appears in many and varied sources, some of which have been cited in the present study. Rather than combat such charges openly, the Jutes in order to survive went underground, since they were not able to or willing to stand the abuse leveled against them. Though the hostility to the Jutes continued in the later literature, as a group they no longer existed, at least openly.

What evidence exists to indicate that the Jutes, like many of the Marranos in Spain, kept Jutism alive by going underground? Perhaps the best evidence is the fact that surviving documents, recently published, were located deep in a cave at Bath, now known as Old Steam Bath Cave, No. 1. We know that the Jutes traditionally luxuriated in the baths, and part of the medieval hostility to the bath was for its association with the Jutes. The second kind of evidence is the many closet Jutes recently emerging into the light of day and proudly proclaiming their Jutish antecedents. In conclusion, let me assure you that the Jutes remain a rich source of study, and though my hypothesis must still remain tentative, there is evidence to indicate that the Jutes had a strong bisexual tradition. Probably homosexuality was institutionalized among them and was more acceptable at certain times of life, as among the Greeks, after which they settled down and had a family with women they had rescued from prostitution. They were aided in these transitions through ceremonies associated with Mary Ionis. Though all of this seemed quite rational to them, to the non-Jutish world, their lifestyle was a source of fear and hostility; for a period the stigmatization was so great that a whole cult of anti-Jutism appeared. Only now can we really begin a serious study of the Jutes. They have been stigmatized long enough, and the time has come when Jutish studies should move out of the closet and into the classroom. By studying them, we can hopefully better understand our own times.

Notes

1. Gavin Langmuir, "The Jutes: A Source of Medieval Confusion," *Semitica* 5 (1947), 1–55. This view was later seconded by Rabbi Benjamin Maimonides, "Langmuir Has Found a New Source of Anti-Semitism," *Modern Jewish Studies* 142 (1952), 45–49.

2. Andreas later published this paper under the title of "A Jutish Box," *Medievalia et Musica* 4 (1973), 7–8.

3. Emily Coleman, "Infanticide in Medieval English Records," *Studies in Population* 57 (1973), 111–18.

4. James Brundage, "Some Hidden Aspects of Early Medieval Canon Law," *Canonica canonicorum* 108 (1973), 445–51.

5. Jo Ann McNamara et al., "The Origins of the Word Marijuana," part 1, of a 210–part study entitled *Drug Culture Today from a Medieval Perspective* (Washington, D.C.: U.S. Government Printing Office, 1976), pp. 40–42.

6. Donald Queller, Warren Hollister, and Mary Daly, "The Jutes, Jute, and Hemp: A Medieval Social Problem with Modern Implications," *Drugs and Social Problems* 5 (1983), 13–22.

7. I interviewed Josiah Russell about this, and though he remembered finding the cave and writing up the summary, he looked askance at me when I asked him if he had perchance taken any of the jars. Since at the time of his discovery he was on the faculty of the University of North Carolina and since he was accompanied by several of his students in the excavation, it seems obvious why the jars ended up in North Carolina. Fortunately for this paper, some of Russell's students seem to have seen the jars' future value to scholarship.

8. John Riddle, "An Early Form of Marijuana—Hemp in a Jutish Burial," *Cemetery and Pharmacy Studies* 1 (1992), 4–9.

9. James Muldoon and Dean Ware, "A Jutish Funeral and Its Modern Successor," *Funerary and Mortuary Studies* 102 (1989), 5–6.

10. Leslie Domonkos, "A Bibliographic Guide on Medieval Discussions of the Meaning of 'Stoned,'" *Rolling Stones Magazine* 22 (March 1987), 395–560.

11. David Herlihy, "Infant Mortality in Seventh-century England Based upon a Jutish Doomsday Book Previously Unpublished," *Computers and History* 4 (1973), 4–7, table 3. Professor Herlihy's students have continued to do studies on this scholarly find and hopefully the full manuscript will be published sometime in the future.

12. *Anglo-Saxon Chronicle,* Laud Version ("E"), an. 449. Interested students might consult the English version translated by Jane Payne (London, 1953).

13. Snorri Sturluson, *Heimskringla,* trans. William Morris and Eirik Magnusson (London, 1893–1905), *"Skaldskaparmal"* ("Poetic Diction"), passim.

14. Karl Pearson, *The Jukes and the Jutes: An Explanation* (London: Blackgood, 1899), passim.

15. Leopold von Sacher-Masoch, "Das Eddas und Sadism," *SM Jahrbuch* 1 (1890), 40–45.

16. Leopold von Sacher-Masoch, *Venus with Jewels,* trans. Hugh Hefner (Chicago: Playgirl, 1973). The original novel was written in 1878, but it is not as well known as his *Venus with Furs.*

17. Gerda Learnwell, "The Woman as Masochist: A Long Tradition," *Signs and Signals* 14 (1969), 22–33.

18. The best analytic-psychological approach to this problem is by Norman Cantor, "The SM Symbiosis in Medieval Culture and in the Modern World," *Psychology and History of the Future* 1 (1999), 35–90.

19. *Butler's Lives of the Saints,* ed. Herbert Thurston and Donald Attwater (New York, 1956), 4 vols., 3:151–52; *Acta sanctorum,* July, 4:50. The Bath manuscript was reported on in *Bath Manuscripta* 5 (1965), 42–48.

20. *Butler's Lives of the Saints,* 3:151–52.

21. Ibid., 4:36–37; *Acta sanctorum,* Feb., 3:173; Oct., 3:162.

22. Oswald Cockayne, *Leechdoms, Wortcunning, and Starcraft of Early England,* Rolls Series, 3 vols. (London, 1864–66), passim.

23. See, for example, *Webster's New Collegiate Dictionary* (Springfield, Mass., 1959).

24. Sigmund Freud, "The Geography and Meaning of Phallicism," *Collected Works,* 5 (New York, 1920), pp. 50–80.

25. Many of the early penitentials have been translated by John T. McNeill and Helena M. Gamer, *Medieval Handbooks of Penance* (New York, 1938). The prohibited acts are mostly the same.

25. I. M. Gay, "The Bath House Penitential," *Penitentialia* 4, (1969), 7–14.

27. Unlike other Jutish individuals, there is a massive literature on Pope Joan. See, for example, the bibliography cited in Vern Bullough, *Sexual Variance in Society and History* (Chicago, 1976), p. 377, n. 85. For the Jutish aspects, see Lawrence Durrell, *The Jutish Pope Joan* (London, 1975).

28. I realize that this story, reported in *Bath Manuscripta* 7 (1967), 34–48, is very similar to the one recorded by Hieronymus Fracastorius, *Syphilis* (St. Louis, 1911), and originally published in the sixteenth century. I can only surmise that Fracastorius derived his story from an earlier Jutish source.

29. John Boswell, *Christianity, Social Tolerance, and Homosexuality* (Chicago, 1980).

PRIMAE NOCTIS INVENTIONES
(May 1986)

INVENTING THE PAST:
THE METHODOLOGY OF PSEUDO HISTORY

James A. Brundage

It is both an honor and a pleasure to welcome you to the first annual meeting of the Societas Fontibus Historiae Medii Aevi Inveniendis, more familiarly known as the "Pseudo Society," and to introduce to you this evening's panel of distinguished inventors. We are gathered here, as many of you know, to carry on in a somewhat wider, and hopefully more endur-ing, field of enquiry the work of our late lamented predecessor organiza-tion, the venerable Society for Jutish Studies. The Jutes, as we learned at the first and only meeting of our predecessor society, have unfortunately shrunk past the point of insignificance into the uncharted oblivion of non-(or perhaps through a black hole, even negative) existence. We can only hope that, wherever they may be (if indeed they can in any sense be said to be at all), they rejoice in the company of their glorious foundress and patroness, Saint Witless, the Mother of the Jutes. I had thought of asking you to stand for a moment of silence in their memory—I will, however, refrain from doing so for fear that some of you may have difficulty stand-ing at all.

In any event, the Society for Jutish Studies has definitively ceased to exist. Comes now its successor and the inheritor of its proud if short-lived tradition, the Pseudo Society. This society, as its stately Latin title pro-claims, is devoted to creative scholarship, namely the *invention* of long-lost, or at least misplaced, medieval sources. Its purpose consists in providing a forum for the announcement of those *inventiones*, which members of the society or their invited guests may have made since the previous meeting of the society. Since the society has never met before this evening, our speakers tonight have an unusually wide range of discoveries to present to us.

Before I introduce the first of our distinguished speakers, however, I pray your indulgence for a moment in order to prepare you for the slight shock, or even disorientation, that the methodology of these *inventiones* may induce in an audience accustomed, or perhaps inured, to the methods of conventional historical scholarship.

You will notice as we proceed this evening that our speakers have used in their research one or the other of two innovative methodologies, both of them adaptations of techniques popular among our colleagues in the hard and semisoft sciences. These techniques are data enrichment and evidence enhancement.

Although they are ultimately related, these techniques differ in subtle but important ways. Data enrichment involves filling in the gaps, as it were, between known events by defining the parameters of virtual events that *must* have happened in the intervals between the bits that we know about from conventional sources.[1] Data enrichment thus provides us with virtual evidence for virtual events. Although data enrichment is in widespread use by scientists in numerous disciplines, including physics and medicine,[2] and was even practiced by the monk Gregor Mendel, the founder of the science of genetics,[3] medieval historians have hitherto been even more backward than usual in applying this sophisticated and economic technique to their sources.[4] Data enrichment has the great virtue that it enables us to discover historical facts and produce incredibly learned papers about them without spending laborious hours in the discomfort of inconvenient and ill-lit libraries and archives pouring over dusty and illegible documents. Data enrichment is also an exceptionally cheap form of research to support. This makes it virtually irresistible to foundations and other funding sources.

Many of the same benefits accrue from evidence enhancement, but there is, as I mentioned, a significant difference between the techniques. Whereas data enrichment supplies the missing parts, the virtual documents that conventional sources have inconsiderately left out, evidence enhancement is a strategy for selective highlighting of evidence that already exists. Enhanced documents, that is documents transformed by evidence enhancement, enable us to see things that, without this technique, we might otherwise have missed entirely. This is an analog of a familiar and well-established methodology in the physical and biological sciences—all of us, no doubt, have gazed in admiration at splendid photographs from interplanetary space enhanced by false colors so that we could see in them what otherwise couldn't be seen at all and in fact never has been seen by anyone. And toward the other end of the physical scale, most of us have given at least an occasional glance at electron micrographs that have likewise been enhanced in processing so as to make the invisible apparent.[5] Evidence enhancement techniques can also boast a long and illustrious lineage in the history of physical science and were practiced by such eminent luminaries as Newton and Kepler.[6] Applied to historical research, evidence enhancement consists in selectively leaving out the distracting and irrelevant evidence in order to highlight the really important data that supports our theories.

It is, of course, possible to combine the two techniques so as to invent virtual sources that are both enhanced and enriched. This requires a high degree of methodological virtuosity, but several of our speakers this evening have aspired to it and it will be up to you, ladies and gentlemen, to determine how successful they have been at it.

Notes

1. See the classic paper of Henry R. Lewis, "The Data Enrichment Method," reprinted in *Journal of Irreproducible Results,* Selected Papers, 3rd ed. (1986), pp. 239–41, from *Operations Research* 5 (1957) 551.

2. Walter W. Stewart and Ned Feder (N.I.H.), in a major study, unfortunately still unpublished because of fear of lawsuits; reported in *New York Times,* Tuesday, 22 April 1986, pp. 15, 18.

3. William J. Broad, writing in *New York Times,* Tuesday, 23 January 1990, p. B7.

4. The case could be made, however, that Herodotus pioneered in the use of both of these research techniques. Other classical writers—Livy comes to mind, as does the elder Pliny—were also daring pioneers in the use of these valuable methodologies. St. Isidore of Seville, the patron of this society, likewise made liberal use of them. The stodgy successors of these great innovators, particularly since the mid-nineteenth century, have usually been too timid and unenterprising to follow in the methodological footsteps of the great innovators.

5. This technique is indispensable in electronmicroscopy, because without enhancement, as is well known, all electronmicrographs look exactly like all other electronmicrographs; indeed, this is sometimes true even with enhancement. See Albert Heine, "A Drastic Cost-Saving Approach to Using Your Neighbor's Electron Microscope," *The Best of the Journal of Irreproducible Results,* ed. George H. Scherr (New York: Workman, 1983), pp. 107–08.

6. William J. Broad, in *New York Times* (above n. 3) at B5, B7.

THE ACCOUNT BOOKS OF SAINT FRANCIS OF ASSISI

John F. McGovern†

Very little by the way of authentically amusing material surfaces among the early Franciscans. The joy and celebrated jocosity of these *jongleurs* of God really represent slapstick indignities inflicted on self-pride, or constitute grimly serious teaching devices; rollicking guffaws or even the decent giggle were as rare among friars as mysticism is nowadays among dentists. Two new sources which I have uncovered dealing with the early business careers of Francis and his associates explain this absence of humor; prior to their conversion, Francis and his buddies were serious businessmen. Consequently, a twin and tragic inheritance haunted the later development of the friars. They could not escape property and worldly success, though they longed for poverty; they sought the sun of a smiling spiritual abandon yet achieved only the bone-chilling humor of a medieval Louis S. Rukeyser.

Curiously, and again tragically, the double shadows of monetary gain and the quickly checked grin have stalked the pages of Francis's modern biographers. As a group, and excepting accountants and suppliers to the armed forces, they are easily the most humorless and well-rewarded writers of the twentieth century. But let us not be ungrateful for small blessings. The greatest bore of the nineteenth century, Ernest Renan, almost wrote a life of Francis. Instead, he commissioned his apprentice-bore, Paul Sabatier, to perform the task. Forty-seven editions of Sabatier's study appeared from 1893 onward. Pecuniary reward and scant amusement also marked the biographical endeavor of the Dane, Johannes Jørgensen. It is a telling fact that officials of Assisi honored the research of Jørgensen by renaming the city's street known as Via Santa Maria delle Rose to Via Johannes

Jørgensen. The change of name suggests thermal underwear and financial security.

G. K. Chesterton's work stands perhaps as an exception. His 1924 biography of Francis appeared in a revised version in 1957, but I doubt if the volume really made much money. Moreover, while Chesterton's study is humorless, it is highly diverting, packed as it is with bizarre neo-Catholic crankiness. In any event, the recent study by the French writer Julien Green promises to restore Franciscan historiography to its now traditional profitability and dourness. Poet, novelist, and ideologue, Julien Green, now an octogenarian residing in Paris, is one of the most intricate intellectual cuckoo clocks to appear in western Europe since the twelfth-century canonist Laurentius Hispanus. Green, for example, believes that France is a person, a woman with a crown. This kind of metaphysical metastasis puts Green in the same comedy-corner as Charles Péguy and Charles De Gaulle.

Well, to be brief, my two new sources uncover the spiritual ancestry of the double Franciscan taints of pelf and grimness. The first text is a *vita versificata* in the vernacular, and the second manuscript is certainly an early version of the Latin hymn-poem *Dies irae*. Tentatively, I have ascribed both sources to Thomas of Celano (d. 1255), to whom credit is usually given as the author of the *Dies Irae*.

Instead of the feckless and fun-loving life of aspiring courtly knights, these manuscripts make it plain that Francis and his friends before their conversion were learning to be heavy hitters in Italian financial circles. The verse life describes Francis's coterie as "favoring sober dress, early rising, fresh and natural foods." Another text in the verse life asserts that these associates of Francis urged communal governments to take "a sensibly firm stand against coddling beggars." The verse life refers to Francis and his friends as "giovanotto borghese di mestiere," which can only be rendered as "young urban professionals."

The versified life goes on to assert that these Yuppies were infatuated with their account books, especially after devising an investment consortium referred to in one place as "borsali di amore" and in another as "fondi mutuali." I will discuss this early form of lovable mutual funds elsewhere in another paper. Suffice it to say here that the moneys were in fact invested in selected *condottieri* and champions at trials by battle; yet these same investments were drawn up in the form of exchange contracts pegged to the currency fluctuations in Dublin.

The early version of the *Dies irae* is most surprising. Although born in the Abruzzi region, Thomas of Celano must have been a member of the "young urban professionals" in Assisi some time prior to 1206. It is a bit distasteful citing the first and nasty version of the hymn-poem. The first three-line stanza reads:

Bonum meum, bonum tuum
Solvent quinque super unum,
Semper res dant incrementum.

[Good for me and good for you
Paying five for one when due,
That's how our investment grew.]

The sentiment is age-old and sordid to most of you having fifteen or more years to go before retirement. Again one of the most heralded lines of the *Dies irae,* the one which reads: "Tuba mirum spargens sonum," originally went like this: "Aurum laete rotans mundum"—"Gold makes the world go round joyfully."

Thankfully, Francis and his disciples soon found all of this Babbitry and Yuppiness unacceptable. Alas, some of the selfish and unfunny traits continued to haunt some later adherents.

A NEWLY DISCOVERED MEDIEVAL REDACTION OF A PREVIOUSLY LOST MANUSCRIPT OF SORANUS WHICH AMPLIFIES THE ABBREVIATED TRANSLATION OF CAELIUS AURELIANUS

Vern L. Bullough

Soranus of Ephesus, who practiced in Rome during the second century A.D., is best known for his studies on gynecology.[1] He also wrote numerous other works in Greek which have apparently not survived, although some of his works exist in Latin translations, particularly those made by Caelius Aurelianus, a fifth-century physician. Most important of these are Latin versions of *Acute Diseases* (in three books) and *Chronic Diseases* (in five books).[2]

The translations of Caelius Aurelianus are helpful in studying sex in the classical world, especially *Chronic Diseases,* since it includes the most complete discussion of homosexuality in any surviving classical medical text.[3] Unfortunately, as P. H. Schrijvers pointed out, these passages on homosexuality pose particular difficulties, probably because they underwent considerable Christian censorship over the centuries.[4] As evidence for this conjecture, Schrijvers argued that the passage is far more condemnatory of its subject than any other section of the book. In fact, except for these passages, the book is usually descriptive, and nowhere else does the author or translator attempt to draw moral lessons. Schrijvers held that this condemnatory attitude could be remedied simply by removing a half-dozen or so adjectives in the text, which he argued were simply later inserts. With the adjectives removed, the text is similar to others in the book. Readers will have to judge the success of this effort on their own, although his argument is persuasive to me.

It is most likely that this section was revised in the ninth and tenth centuries by various copiers to deal in a negative way with the possible existence of homosexuality in monasteries. This assumption has more merit than might seem to exist on the surface, because of the rather curious history of the manuscript. Virtually the only direct reference to the existence of a manuscript is in two ninth-century catalogues of the monastery of Lorsch, although there is a somewhat dubious reference in Cassiodorus.[5]

The first printed edition appeared in the sixteenth century under two different editors. The treatise known as *Chronic Diseases* was edited by Johannes Sichart in 1529 and issued by Heinrich Petri at his press in Basel; *Acute Diseases* was edited by Johannes Winter (Guinterius) von Andernach in 1533 and issued by Simon de Colines at his press in Paris. In each case, a single manuscript seems to have been used for the edition and then lost.[6] In 1921, and again in 1922, Johannes Ilberg discovered in a library at Zwickau missing leaves (three all told) of a manuscript used by Sichart. They appear to be from a ninth-century manuscript, perhaps the same one referred to as existing at Lorsch. Comparison of the leaves with Sichart's text indicates that his edition, as far as these sections are concerned, is generally faithful and dependable. His deviations are almost all confined to correcting obvious errors of the scribe and substituting the orthography of the sixteenth century for what is found in the three leaves.[7]

Since Sichart reported that he had the help of Joannes Cornarius, the noted physician and philologist, it has been hypothesized that it was Cornarius who brought the manuscript to Zwickau, where the leaves were found. All subsequent editions of the manuscript were based upon Sichart's version, although some editors claimed to have consulted other manuscripts; but Drabkin is suspicious of such claims, since no others have surfaced. For this reason Drabkin used the first edition as the base, although he used paragraph numbers adopted by Johannes Conrad Amman, whose edition was first published at Amsterdam in 1709.[8]

In tracing the steps of Drabkin in his edition of the manuscript, I was struck by the fact that the leaves found by Ilberg dealt with such topics as diseases of the bladder, discharge of semen (gonorrhea?), nocturnal emissions, weakness of the seminal ducts, and priapism, all in some way associated with the male sex organ. From this I hypothesized that there might still be other materials on this same topic at the library at Zwickau, since this happened to be one of the special interests of Cornarius. I therefore went to Zwickau, where not surprisingly I found that Ilberg and Drabkin had done their work well. There were no surviving leaves from any ninth-century manuscript remaining uncatalogued or unidentified. I did find some books by Cornarius in the library, but they too had long ago been catalogued and described. Though one dealt with prostate problems and another with what we now call dysmenorrhea, there was nothing that could be identified as coming from Caelius Aurelianus. Apparently Elizabeth Whipplehoff, the librarian who was working closely with me, sensed my disappointment, and eager to help, she indicated that there were some papers of the Cornarius family that I might want to look through, although she indicated these mostly dated from the eighteenth century. She added, however, that some of these papers dealt with sex.

"Sex" was the magic word to me, and I asked her to bring them out. She brought out two bundles which had been carefully catalogued, either by the family or by a librarian when the family donated them. The two bundles had a brief annotated list of contents, and though the second bundle was indexed (in German) as including a "sex manuscript," I could not find it in the papers. Before I could mention the missing manuscript to Elizabeth Whipplehoff, she had appeared at my side with a separate, locked box. She explained that the manuscript had been put in a lockbox early in the twentieth century, and she had only become conscious of this because a shelf note referred to it, which she had seen when she checked the box in which the two bundles had been stored. When I opened the box (which she had already unlocked), I found a fifteen-page manuscript in what I took to be an eighteenth-century hand, with detailed illustrations of the sex act interspersed among the text. As I investigated further, I found that three pages of it corresponded to those found by Ilberg, but after discussing these topics, the anonymous author had quickly gone on to deal with sexual intercourse.

Even though the manuscript was clearly an eighteenth-century one, I was intrigued enough to continue my examination of the bundles of Cornarius papers to see if I could find any explanation. In them I found a note by a descendant of the sixteenth-century Cornarius, a well-known Zwickau artist named Kinsey Cornberg (died 1760). Kinsey Cornberg had written that in going through the family papers prior to giving them to the library, he had found fifteen manuscript leaves of a medical manuscript owned by his great-uncle Joannes Cornarius, which were obviously part of a much longer manuscript, and they included a chapter entitled "De secretis." Cornberg, knowing of his relative's connection with the edition of Caelius Aurelianus, assumed that these leaves came from that manuscript. He had compared the first three leaves (probably the ones that Ilberg later discovered) and found that they were very similar, although he could not find anything in the book remotely resembling "De secretis." Kinsey Cornberg wrote that he carefully made two copies of the manuscript in his own hand, including their illustrations. He added, however, that he had modified the illustrations to conform with modern anatomical data and his own artistic inclinations. He emphasized, however, that the text was accurate and that the theme of the illustrations had been the same. Wanting to share his work with someone, Kinsey Cornberg had shown one of his copies to a friend, whom he badly misjudged. The friend was so shocked that he gave a copy to the local minister, who had not only burned the manuscript but reported the existence of an obscene manuscript to the officials of the canton, who had then demanded the original. Cornberg had reluctantly complied but, with their permission, saved the three leaves lacking any illustration or discussion of the sex act. It was these three fragments which were discovered by Ilberg in the twentieth century.[9] Kinsey Cornberg, however, had never made known his second copy, and it was this copy which eventually made its way to the library at Zwickau. The story is "do-able" and reasonable, and it certainly fits in with what we know. Apparently when the papers were turned over to the library, the curator saw the sexual illustrations and simply locked up the manuscript, although being a good librarian he had made a notation of where the sex manuscript might be found.[10]

I would argue for the authenticity of the story, although I am not certain the fragment was originally part of the Caelius Aurelianus manuscript. Though it seems logical that Caelius Aurelianus would have included a discussion on sexual intercourse, since he included a discussion of homosexuality, the material is much too similar to that found in the *Kama Sutra,* copies of which had only come into Europe through Islamic Spain.[11] Certainly there were Arabic treatises from the ninth and tenth centuries which deal rather specifically with sexual positions.

From this, I have re-created a scenario in which a monk, after a pilgrimage to Jerusalem, returned to Lorsch at the end of the eleventh century with information about a book some of the pilgrims from Islamic lands had shown him and allowed him to copy. Though some of his fellow monks had been shocked by his book, they were also interested, if only for scholarly reasons, and decided to preserve it by adding it to the one book in their library, Caelius Aurelianus, which had any kind of discussion on such topics. They had lovingly copied it and illustrated it, giving the various positions titles which must have amused them. I wish I could have seen the original folios with some of the comments that must have been written upon them by monks. When the manuscript was originally printed, the editor had not dared to include the section on sexual intercourse, and instead he had given the section to his friend and adviser, who probably intended to publish it eventually. Somehow it never became possible to do so, and the manuscript came down with the family papers and ended up in the library in Zwickau. His great-nephew had become interested, but once he ran into public opposition had concluded that there was no hope of publication, although he obviously hoped that the text would be published someday in the future, as witness his own "updated" illustrations.

Kinsey Cornberg must have been somewhat of a man about town, since he notes that although the manuscript says a particular position is possible, he cannot imagine that it is. All told, twenty-five positions are listed and described and illustrated. I plan to bring out an illustrated edition of these in the near future, and the Medieval Institute at Kalamazoo has consented to publish them. My publishers, however, have warned me about going into too much detail about what is included, and so with this in mind, I would simply like to whet your appetite with translations of some of the titles of some of the positions. Among them are "Exploring the Holy Places," "The Way of Muhammed," "The True Cross," "The Hand of Satan," "The Last Supper," "The Stations of the Cross," "The Trinity," "The Bishop's Desire," and "The Mother Superior."

I can still imagine the monks getting together and thinking up the names for these positions. All we can say is that when the monks turned their talent to the subject of double entendres, they would be a match for any of us today. Hopefully my book will be out soon, so that you can read in more detail about the manuscript, which after several centuries will be finally published with illustrations by Kinsey Cornberg.[12]

NOTES

1. Soranus, *Gynaeciorum libri quattuor,* ed. J. Ilberg, *Corpus medicorum Graecorum,* 4 (Leipzig: Teubner, 1927), is the authoritative one; an English translation by O. Temkin, *Soranus' Gynecology* (Baltimore, 1956) is excellent.

2. Caelius Aurelianus, *On Acute Diseases and on Chronic Diseases,* ed. and trans. I. E. Drabkin (Chicago, 1950). It is regarded as the authoritative edition. Some additional Latin fragments of Caelius Aurelianus's Latin versions of Soranus have also been found. See *Caelius Aurelianus Gynaecia: Fragments of a Latin Version of Soranus' Gynaecia from a Thirteenth-century Manuscript,* ed. Miriam F. Drabkin and Israel E. Drabkin (Baltimore, 1951).

3. *Chronic Diseases,* book IV, sec. ix, par. 131–37 (pp. 900–05 in the Drabkin edition).

4. P. Schrijvers, *Eine medizinische Erklärung der männlichen Homosexualität aus der Antike* (Amsterdam, 1985).

5. Drabkin, p. xii. See Cassiodorus, *Institutiones divinarum et humanarum litterarum* 1.31.2, ed. R. B. Mynors (Oxford, 1937). English trans. by L. W. Jones, *An Introduction to Divine and Human Readings* (New York, 1946).

6. Drabkin, p. xii.

7. Drabkin, pp. xii–xiii.

8. Drabkin, p. xiv.

9. The Zwickau records include a record of a public burning of obscene materials in 1726, and these might have been the materials.

10. I am also certain that there was a word-of-mouth tradition about the manuscript and that each generation of librarians had gone through the locked box as part of their initiation into the library.

11. In fact, we have a fourteenth-century manuscript from Spain written in Catalan which deals with the same subject matter. This was discovered by Guy Beaujouan, and it bears the evocative title, *Speculum al foderi,* literally, "A Mirror for Fuckers." See Danielle Jacquart and Claude Thomasset, *Sexuality and Medicine in the Middle Ages* (Princeton, 1988), p. 135.

12. The working title of the book is "The Christian Way of Sex: A New Look at the Middle Ages."

MEDIEVAL TECHNOLOGY AND THE CHASTITY BELT

James D. Ryan

It is my great pleasure to report that a stroke of luck has brought success to years of intermittent but diligent research; the true origin of the girdle of chastity has been brought to light. Although it has long been believed that the chastity belt surely *should* have had its beginnings in the medieval period, there was no documentation for such a medieval genesis until now. Rather, the physical and textual evidence concerning the *ceinture de virginité* strongly suggest a fifteenth-century origin, perhaps in Renaissance Italy.[1] If this be true, the *freno della lascivia* was another of the fruits of Humanism, one additional credit to that great age of intellectual refinement during which men's minds were refocused on the beauties of this world.[2] This lack of witness to the medieval origins of the chastity belt sharply contrasts to the abundant proof concerning its later development and proliferation. Literary and other evidence clearly document both its appearance in France in the mid-sixteenth century and its ultimate spread throughout the rest of Europe. The *Keuschheitswächter,* or as it was also known, the *Italienisher Schloss,* was probably most widely employed in the seventeenth century, as the many surviving examples of German manufacture attest, with its use persisting in Spain, among other places, at least into the 1880s. Prior to the publication of this *inventio,* however, there has been no credible evidence advanced for its fabrication or use in the medieval period.[3]

Undaunted by the lack of documentation, chastity-belt scholars have managed to conclude that medieval man played a key role in transmitting the seminal ideas on which the *cintura di castità* was later constructed. In the generally accepted scenario, crusaders learned in Outremer of eastern practices such as female infibulation, the suturing closed of a wife's *labia majora* to assure conjugal fidelity while the husband was abroad on business. Subsequently, they carried such exotic fancies home to Europe, where they civilized them through the application of technology. Voilà, the *Frauengürtel* was born.

Although a lack of evidence has not deterred the eminent scholars of chastity and its guarantor cited herein, I found this lacuna most disturbing. When making obeisance to the muse, I promised Clio diligent pursuit of historical truth and devotion to documentation. Even more important, however, was my concern for the future of medieval studies. Everyone knows that the medieval period was characterized by bizarre and bestial brutality, and in that aspect lies much of its appeal to the sophomoric *mentalité*. Intellectually benighted *chevaliers* quested about, excitedly seeking grails and indulging themselves in rape and rapine, pausing occasionally to pray in Romanesque or Gothic cathedrals, confident in the knowledge that a securely locked *Weberverschluss* protected both their honor and the wife they left at home. Such images provide medieval romance with substance. Should any of these popular icons be called into question, whither the attraction of medieval studies for future generations of undergraduates? Frankly, the lack of documentation concerning medieval chastity belts appeared to me as a threat to the well-being of our discipline.

I reveal with delight that the medieval period's reputation has been redeemed; the *Keuschheitsgürdel* had its origin in the eleventh century, even before the Crusades, and can safely be attributed to purely European barbarism. Although the evidence is still but fragmentary, its airing is justified at this juncture. The key to the puzzle was found in an unlikely place: an aside in a footnote in Richard Lefebvre des Noëttes's classic study on horsepower in the Middle Ages.[4] Commenting on early representations of the horse collar, Lefebvre des Noëttes noted that, in some manuscript illustrations, the collars appear to have been put on the wrong end of the horse.[5] He, and others, have failed to grasp the significance of certain crude but technically accurate manuscript illustrations.[6] In an effort to breed bigger draft horses in the promiscuous atmosphere of the common pasture, medieval man, perhaps by the dawn of the eleventh century, had invented chastity belts for mares. Illustrations from the early twelfth century appear to show the use of similar devices on cows, in the obvious attempt to upbreed draft oxen as well.[7] Here was a technological revolution of the first magnitude, but it was only a beginning. The medieval mind was not slow to carry this *inventio* over into the realm of human relations.

Evidence for the application of leather *Treuschutz* to humankind is again pictorial. Perhaps the texts are silent because clerical scribes found the matter too delicate, or too mundane, for inclusion in their *opera*. Whatever the circumstances, we can discern, in illustrations of late twelfth-century female apparel, radical changes in fashion. Can the introduction of voluminous skirts best be explained as an attempt to cover the cumbersome bulk of an elaborate leather harness, worn as an undergarment? One can only hope that historians of fashion will give this question the serious consideration it deserves.[8]

Although my investigation is still incomplete, it is now possible to posit a new line of historical development. The chastity belt is not an import into Europe, but a homegrown marvel of technology. The Crusades did play a part in the story, but merely by stimulating the adoption and dissemination of the device, still a relatively primitive leather harness in the High Middle Ages. The transition from leather to iron doubtless occurred in the fourteenth century, at the hands of the armorers of northern Italy. This connection at last makes explicable the hitherto fabulous tale concerning Francesco II of Carrara, tyrant of Padua, the so-called inventor of the *freno della lascivia*.[9] At most, he played a small part in its refinement. There are still significant problem areas, most notably the question of locks, at which love learned to laugh in the sixteenth century.[10] Such problems now appear minor, however, and we can all take comfort from the fact that the chastity belt has been restored to the Middle Ages, where it no doubt originated in the fertile mind of the ever inventive medieval male chauvinist.

NOTES

1. All sources agree that the earliest extant example of a *Venusband* dates from the *Cinquecento*. See note 8 below. While there is a considerable written corpus on the subject of *ceintures de chasteté*, for some reason, much of this material has been published privately, anonymously, or under a nom de plume, and it is not always readily accessible on scholars' shelves. Exceptions to the rule among the works cited below notwithstanding, the scholarship employed for most of this ilk is lamentable. Lacking either critical apparatus or the spirit of critical enquiry, they borrow freely from each other and differ more in their extravagant (sometimes lurid) prose than in factual content. Often provocative, they seldom evoke much mental stimulation. For a representative sample, see: "E. M." [Valerie Busnelli?], *La cintura di castità: Notizie storiche* (Rome, 1881); Dr. Canfeynon [J. Fauconne?], *La ceinture de chasteté: son histoire, son emploi, autrefois et aujourd'hui* (Paris, 1904); F. Grapow, *Der Keuschheitsgürtel* (n.p., 1911); anon., *Padlocks and the Girdle of Chastity* (New York, 1925); and Dr. Eric John Dingwall, *The Girdle of Chastity: A Fascinating History of the Chastity Belt, Illustrated* (London, 1931).

2. It is somewhat surprising that Jacob Burckhardt did not include a discussion of this appliance in *The Civilization of the Renaissance in Italy* (1860), where it would surely have rounded out either Part 4 on "The Discovery of the World and of Man"

or Part 6, "Morality and Religion." Renaissance studies have suffered because generations of puritanical historians have failed to correct this oversight.

3. It may be noted in passing that numerous examples of chastity belts, particularly from the seventeenth century and later, survive in museum and private col-
lections. The device enjoyed even wider popularity as an icon in the popular imagination, probably most especially among males. It was given a variety of names in
all European languages, as this report should make clear.

4. Richard Lefebvre des Noëttes, *L'attelage et le cheval de selle à travers les âges: contribution à l'histoire de l'esclavage*, 2 vols. (Paris, 1931).

5. Lefebvre des Noëttes, *L'attelage*, 1:854.

6. Marc Bloch, for example ("Les inventions médiévales," *Annales d'histoire
économique et sociales* 7 [1935], 634ff.), is at such pains to determine whether the new
harnessing techniques preceded or followed the decline of slavery that he fails to
consider whether the new harness preceded or followed the horse!

7. Unfortunately the crudeness of the drawings makes definitive conclusions
impossible. A provocative twelfth-century illustration of oxen plowing (Paris,
Bibliothèque nationale de France, MS lat. 14,267), for example, seems to show an
appliance on one ox's hindquarters, but it might also be interpreted as a pen flourish or an ink blot. This is another instance in which technology is in the eye of the
beholder.

8. The total lack of other evidence for either animal or human chastity belts
made of leather is no reason to question the hypothesis proposed in this *inventio*.
The preservation of a physical artifact made of leather would be a nearly miraculous event, and we can, for now, pass in silence over the implications of the lack of
textual evidence in this matter.

9. The oldest extant relic of a chastity belt is an iron device formerly exhibited in the small Sala d'Armi of the ducal palace in Venice. A late seventeenth-cen-
tury writer (F. M. Mission, *Nouveau voyage d'Italie fait en l'année 1688*, 2 vols. [The
Hague, 1691]) asserted that it belonged to Francesco II, who had been put to
death in Venice in 1406. He included the iron device (described as "to lock up his
wife") among instruments of torture supposedly invented by the tyrant. There is no
proof for this assertion but considerable reason to believe that this particular
"Italian girdle" was fabricated later in the fifteenth century.

10. Another spurious but oft-repeated tale credits France's Henry II with
invention of the *serrure de jalousie* as an implement of torture and token of affection
for Catherine de Medici. Only later, when he discovered that some 300 keys for its
lock were in circulation, did his court coin the lament, "Love laughs at locksmiths."

THE END OF THE BAYEUX TAPESTRY

R. Dean Ware

Ten years ago, at a conference sponsored by the newly organized American Committee for Jutish Studies, I presented a paper that stated the case and laid out the evidence for the view that the Bayeux Tapestry, traditionally accepted among the source materials for the Norman Conquest of England, was, in fact, an artistic Jutish national epic, recording otherwise unattested events in early Jutish history. Moreover, I advanced the revolutionary thesis that the figures depicted on the tapestry were *life size!* Finally, I argued that the Jutes, shown as less than a foot tall, became progressively smaller in later years until they at last shrank into invisibility, thus explaining, literally, the historical disappearance of the Jutes.

Tonight I am much chagrined to have to recant this entire theory. While several other papers given at that conference, in contrast to mine, remain valuable contributions—such as Jo Ann McNamara's "Saint Wythelas, Mother of the Jutes," a brilliant addition to cult studies, or Vern Bullough's "What Happened to the Jutes: A Possible Sexual Explanation," which is required reading in most women's studies departments today—my paper, I must now admit, is but a historiographical curiosity. While the skepticism that my theory has met over these past years is, I confess, fully vindicated by the recent turn of events, I do think that the series of vicious attacks, which took on a totally unwarranted personal tone, that were published by Doktor Adolf Otfried Stumppf in various issues of the *Jahrbuch für mittelalterliche Gemütlichkeit und Wissenschaft mit Nachweis der wichtigsten Quellenforschungen und historiographische Schnitzel der Gesellschaft und Gesundheit bis Untergang der Bratwurst zum,* is inexcusable!

In any event, all this is now history, that is to say, *bad* history. I am acutely embarrassed by the whole business and can scarcely believe that I was once so deluded as to defend "the incredible shrinking Jute" theory, as it is now alluded to in the literature. Because just this spring I had the unexpected and great good fortune to discover the final panel of the Bayeux Tapestry, and I now know that it *is* concerned with the Norman Conquest! One unfortunate consequence of this development is that publication of my Jutish oeuvres, of which the essay "The Jutes and the Bayeux Tapestry" was the unifying piece, has been cancelled by Variorum.

Briefly to describe the circumstances of my recent discovery, I was at Hubbard's Auction Barn, in North Amherst, Massachusetts, on the eighth of March of this year and, not to go home empty-handed, I bought one of Hubbard's "grab bags." These are sacks of small miscellaneous items that Mr. Hubbard sometimes puts together and sells for some nominal price. I picked up one for $4.99, and at home, surveying the contents of this mystery package, I found that I had acquired: an Elsie Dinsmore story, with torn cover; a ceramic rattlesnake ashtray, chipped; a University of Massachusetts beer mug; and a small sampler, embroidered "Domus Dulcis Domus." As I examined this sampler closely, I noticed that the coarse linen fabric had innumerable tiny holes in it, as if earlier stitching had been removed. If I was right, it was palimpsest! I began to wonder what the original text might have been, and then I began to wonder about the age of the material. Fortunately, this latter question could be easily answered. Next day I went to our local Kmart and bought a carbon-14 do-it-yourself kit (I'd been intending to pick one up for some time anyway) and tested a snippet of material. You can only imagine my astonishment when I got a late medieval reading, plus or minus 750 years. I could barely contain my excitement. I think it was then that the possibility first occurred to me that against all odds . . .

I quickly measured the sampler. It was precisely 19 1/2 inches high! Was this simply an incredible coincidence or had I really found the missing final panel of the Bayeux Tapestry?

Next day I persuaded the physics lab people at the University of Massachusetts to permit me to examine the fabric using a Drexell binocular microscope, which employs a refracted polarized light that highlighted the segments of fiber where the molecular structure had been compacted by pressure of stitching. I counted 3,347 such holes exclusive of those made by the "Domus Dulcis Domus" stitching. What I had now, though, was a kind of connect-the-dots (or rather, -holes) puzzle lacking numbers. However, I learned that the Megalon DDC 1000 computer at the Graduate Research Center could be programmed to run through all possible permutations, that is, all combinations of hole connections. But while the process is simple, it is very time-consuming. Flexner's law states that the total number of combinations is 1 x 2 x 3 x 4 . . . 3,347, and that, in round numbers, is a gogoolplex squared! As any professional mathematician can tell you, even an unsquared gogoolplex is the number 1 followed by a very, very lot of zeros. But we had a bit of luck! On the third try the printout showed an enthroned figure, as hoped, but incredibly, instead of "Will-elmus Rex," the inscription read "Henricus Secundus coronatus est!" So the Bayeux Tapestry does not conclude with the coronation of William, as had been predicted by generations of scholars, but with that of his great-grandson. Therefore, among the many implications of this fact is that a great deal more of the tapestry is missing than was ever imagined. But how much more?

There are two logical ways to calculate the length of the segment that originally linked the extant part of the Bayeux Tapestry with the final panel now recovered. (1) The extant tapestry is 231 feet long, with about 100 feet occupied with background events, and 130 feet devoted to events of the year 1066 from 5 January through 14 October. Now that we know that the final panel depicts Henry II enthroned (1154), we see that some 88 years are missing. So if 1066 required 130 feet, then the subsequent missing part would be 130 x 88, or 11,448 feet, or something over two miles long. This is patently absurd! The fallacy of the strictly mathematical approach is the assumption that all years are treated at equal length, and I think we can safely assert that 1066 was an *exceptional* year. Therefore I reject this mode of calculating the length of the missing section and have adopted its alter-native, the literary approach. (2) In the *E* recension of the *Anglo-Saxon Chronicle*, the entry for 1066 occupies five inches of space in the Everyman edition, and the following entries up to 1154, when *E* terminates, measure 125 inches. Therefore, since five inches of printed history equals 130 feet of pictured history, that is to say, some 26 feet of tapestry per inch of type, then the missing portion must have measured 3,250 feet, or about three-fifths of a mile in length. This I consider a quite reasonable estimate, sup-ported, I might add, by the earliest reference to the tapestry in 1476, where it is cited in an inventory of the possessions of Bayeux cathedral and described as a "narrow very long hanging." I draw attention to the word "very"! Moreover, we know that the tapestry used to be displayed every year throughout the octave of the Feast of Relics (1 July). We can now appreci-ate the reason for this. Obviously only part of the tapestry could be shown each day, so it must have taken eight days to show it all. The Book of Kells at Trinity College, Dublin, is displayed the same way. Each day the care-taker unlocks the case and turns a page. The date at which the Bayeux Tapestry was mutilated cannot be ascertained. It was intact, as we have seen, in 1476; it was truncated when Montfaucon had it engraved and printed in 1728.

In conclusion, in light of this newly recovered final panel, I believe it is probable that the Bayeux Tapestry was commissioned by Henry II's mother, Matilda, following his coronation in late 1154. This surely explains the persistent French tradition that attributes the tapestry to Matilda, the wife of King William. They just have their Matildas mixed up. Further, I believe that the tapestry was made particularly to celebrate the recovery of the crown of England by a man in whom flowed English royal blood. Remember that Matilda was the daughter of Edith, the daughter of Saint Margaret of Scotland, the daughter of Edward "the Exile," the son of Edmund "Ironside," the son of Ethelred "the Unready," the great-great-grandson of Alfred, the descendant of Cerdic. As Edward "the Confessor" a century earlier was crowned on Easter, to symbolize the resurrection of the legitimate line after the Danish interlude, so Henry II represented (at least in his mom's eyes) the restoration of legitimate rule after the Norman interlude.

But, remembering the case of the incredible shrinking Jutes, I could be wrong![1]

NOTES

1. During the question period, a member of the audience stood up, announced "Ich bin Doktor Stumppf," and denounced the new Ware thesis as another fabrication, inasmuch as there was no proof that the supposedly newfound fragment existed. Whereupon Professor Ware, with only a slight smile of triumph, produced the fragment from his coat pocket.

LEONARDO'S LATEST INVENTION

Richard Kay

In the summer of 1985, I was delayed for some hours in Rome's Leonardo da Vinci Airport while our plane and luggage were being checked during a routine bomb scare. To pass the time, I was studying some photographs of a medieval manuscript that I happened to have in my briefcase. This sufficed for a Japanese gentleman to identify me as a paleographer who might help him with a manuscript he had just acquired in Barcelona.

It was a single leaf from the notebooks of Leonardo da Vinci himself, as you can readily see (figure 1). The owner kindly permitted me to photograph the manuscript, but he declined to identify himself. I gathered that he did something lucrative in offshore electronics and had acquired the leaf as a curio. In the absence of a more precise provenance, I must identify my find generically, so I have christened it the Codex Japponicus (siglum: JAP).

When I developed my slides, I discovered that Leonardo's notorious mirror writing could be defeated simply by reversing the slide (figure 2). But Leonardo was a good step ahead of me, as I discovered when I read the text in front of the horse: "Giacché questa / iscritta si può / leggere in un spechio. / faccia la si scrivere / su vetro sicché / lei può si leggere / del uno lato / e l'altro. [Since this writing can be read in a mirror, let it be read written on glass so it can be read from either side.]"

Leonardo's habit of "mirror writing" apparently had led him to envision a time when men would write, not with ink and paper, but with light and glass. Moreover, he evidently grasped the late-modern technique of "rear projection." Closely related to this insight is the observation written across the top of JAP's recto: "Come il sole fonte la gelata su una vetrina,

55

Figure 1.

Figure 2.

così un raggio de luce può / scrivere su vetro di Venezia s'il vetro sia traslu-
cente ma non trasparente, che si / può fare per abrasione con pomice.
[Just as the sun melts frost on a window pane, so a beam of light can be
made to write on Venetian glass if the glass be made translucent but not
transparent by abrading the surface with pumice.]" Here Leonardo has
anticipated the camera obscura. This is an excellent example of his keen
observation of natural phenomena as well as of his uncanny ability to
devise practical applications of such phenomena. His incessant modernity
is here especially apparent. Having solved the problem of creating a
translucent surface by the discovery of ground glass, the master ignored
the application of this principle to the view camera with its ground-glass
focusing screen, and instead he pressed forward to perceive how the principle could be applied to video screens, and particularly to the use of such
screens in word processing.

Here we can glimpse a master mind at work. Just beneath the horse's
front hoofs is a rare example of Leonardo's artistry in that literary genre
beloved by medieval scribes—the *probatio pennae: "doodle da vinci."* For the
significance of this genre to the Renaissance cult of the individual, see the
study by Hans-Fritz van Katzenjammer in *Vierteljahrschrift des deutsches Da-
Vinci-Verein* (102 [Frühjahr, 1976], 122–87), entitled "Das Individualitäts-
prinzip im italienischer Hochrenaissance mit besonder Rücksicht auf den
sogenannten *probationes pennae* des jugendlichen Leonardo da Vinci." But
even as the Master's hand was idly doodling, his mind was racing ahead to
glimpse the future: "La luce è più / veloce che la / mano la più veloce. /
Perciò se volete / scrivere più / veloce che / il scriba il più / veloce, la vos-
tra / macchina debba / scrivere con un raggio / di luce. [Light is faster
than the fastest finger. Therefore to write faster than the swiftest scribe, let
your machine write with a ray of light.]"

Proceeding from the general principles laid down in the foregoing
items, Leonardo has now definitely envisioned a machine that will write
with light. Therefore we can declare with complete confidence that he was
indeed the inventor of the word processor! Note that his incisive intellect
intuitively grasped the essential advantage of that useful device—namely
its superior speed. But, inevitably, there is more (figure 2, bottom right):
"I stampatori muovono soltanto una lettera / per volta. Ricordati siccome
la tua macchina / a scrivere debba muovere e rimuovere non soltanto / le
lettere ma anche le parole, le frasi, e / perfino i capoversi. [The printers
move only one letter at a time. Remember: your writing machine must
move and remove not only letters but also words, sentences, and even para-
graphs.]" Here Leonardo demonstrates his grasp of yet another advantage
of the word processor, namely its ability to transpose entries *en bloc.* This
note is precious for its explicit comparison to the art of printing, which was

then in its infancy. Incunabulists have long wondered why Leonardo's curiosity did not extend to printing; the reason is now apparent: for him it was already an obsolescent technology.

As readers of Leonardo's notebooks are well aware, his fertile and active mind rarely rested long on any one subject, so that notes concerning diverse projects will appear on the same folium. Here, above the horse's back in figure 2, is a case in point: a report on one of his better-known experiments: "Ancora il modelo della mia / sottomergibile rifuta levarsi / sebbene affondarsi / senza difficultà. [The model of my submarine refused to surface again, although it sinks without any hesitation.]" One can only admire the dispassionate objectivity of his reporting. But perhaps he was merely preoccupied with the invention of the word processor. At any rate, on the bottom half of JAP's recto he moved on to design the hardware for his writing machine. Thus, above the two hands in figure 3, we read: "Come i .10. digiti possono scrivere tutte le lettere e tutti i numeri. [How ten fingers can write all letters and numbers.]" Concerned as Leonardo was with human anatomy, he could not fail to confront the ergonomic problems posed by his hardware. Here he has taken the first step towards the modern typewriter keyboard by assigning two letters and a number to each finger. This tentative arrangement would, of course, be perfected in the now familiar QWERTY keyboard, which was not invented by Leonardo until he turned over this folium (figure 4).

As an industrial designer, Leonardo was by no means limited to anatomical ergonomics. To the left of the foot in figure 3, he enunciates the "user-friendly" principle that is only slowly coming to be recognized in the modern electronics industry: "Il vostro / disegno / debba essere / amichevole / a cuiunque / usa la / macchina / a scrivere. [Let your design be friendly to him who uses the writing machine.]"

Leonardo's notebooks contain a number of oracular statements that he called "prophecies." Below the hands in figure 3 is one concerning his writing machine: "Profetia del sucesso della macchina a scrivere. / Il bruno volpe veloce salta sopra il vecchio cane pigro. [Prophecy of the success of the writing machine: The quick brown fox jumped over the lazy old dog.]" The statement is meant to be obscure, of course, and I have not yet unraveled its subtle but elusive meaning. A Neoplatonic reference seems more probable to me, although an allusion to Machiavelli's *Prince* is also possible, as was suggested to me in a private communication by my distinguished colleague, Helmut Dingbat. I am, however, preparing a paper to refute the theory proposed last winter at the Sorbonne by Jean-Jacques Lefauve, who traces this enigma to Orphic sources.

In passing, we may remark that the Codex Japponicus provides explicit and unambiguous evidence that Leonardo invented the footnote (figure

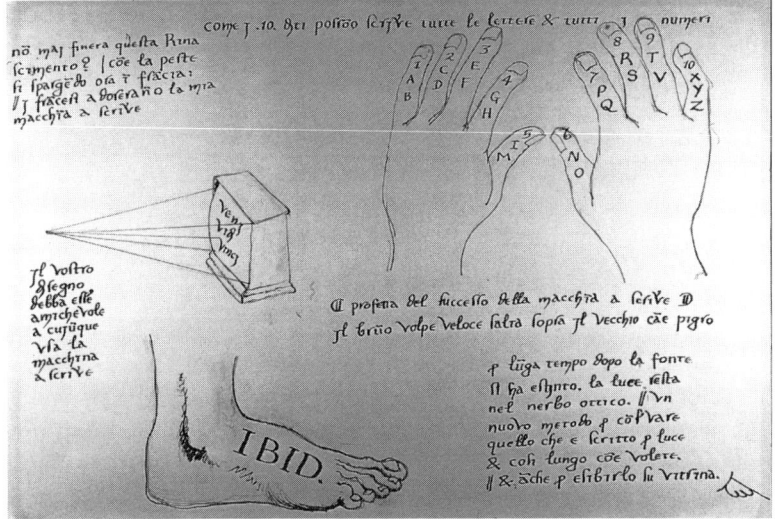

Figure 3.

Figure 4.

3, "ibid."). Another of Leonardo's *obiter dicta* (upper left) shows his intense awareness of the cultural currents of his day, as well as his shrewd appraisal of the emerging French national character: "Non mai finerà questa Rina/scimento? Come la peste / si spargendo ora in Francia. / I Francesi adoreranno la mia / macchina a scrivere. [Will this Renaissance never end? It is spreading now to France like the pox. The French are beguiled by every novelty. They will worship my writing machine.]" This concluding note of self-confidence is echoed in the sketch he drew immediately below. With a characteristic flash of intuitive vision, it would seem, he conceived the video monitor, or at least a television screen, that bears, as Leonardo's equivalent of the Archimedean *Eureka,* a triumphant tribute to Latin Humanism and, of course, to himself: "Veni. Vidi. Vinci." At the bottom of the recto of this leaf, Leonardo begins to confront the formidable technological problems posed by his ingenious conception: "Per lungo tempo dopo la fonte / si ha estinto, la luce resta nel nerbo ottico. Un / nuovo metodo per conservare / quello che è scritto per luce / et così lungo come volete. / E anche per esibirlo su vitrina. [Light lingers in the optic nerve long after the source has been removed. A new method for storing what is written by light as long as you wish and for displaying it on a sheet of glass.]" The subjoined index (or fist) indicates that we must turn the page to find his answer (figure 4). The greater part of the verso is devoted to Leonardo's struggle to discover the secret of electronic imaging. He begins, modestly enough, by inventing photography. Apparently he put a coin down on the sheet to demonstrate how sunlight can discolor paper. (Numismatic note: the circle, indicated by another fist, is 19mm in diameter.) Beside the resultant spot he wrote up the experiment: "Espozione alla luce scolora il papiro. / Quindi le lettere scritti per luce / possono trasferirsi a papiro, / a canovaccio, o perfino a un muro. [Exposure to bright light discolors paper. Thus letters written in light can be transferred to paper, canvas, or even to a wall.]" It remains to be seen whether this method was used to produce his own masterpieces. As you will see, JAP gives us reason to believe it was. Above this inscription is Leonardo's design for his writing machine, the prototype of all word processors (figure 4, center). Note that by now he has discovered the QWERTY fingering pattern that was later to be adapted to the typewriter by nineteenth-century imitators. His anticipation of the dot-matrix system of printing is also in evidence here with the inscription "LEONARDO / FU / IVI [Leonardo was there]," which may well be the original of the more familiar memento of the ubiquitous Kilroy. I do not lay much store by the initials "IBM" in the rondel, for the clumsy work shows signs of tampering and may well be an anachronistic addition by some more modern hand. As might be expected from a master architect, the design of the console itself is a work of exquisite simplicity in the classical mode.

Leonardo's genius for industrial design naturally excelled in matters of light and color, to which so much attention is devoted elsewhere in his notebooks. For example, he realized what colors were most restful to the human eye (upper right corner of figure 4): "L'occhio preferisce la lume arancia / più che la lume verde. [Orange light rests the eye more than green.]" We can surmise that Leonardo's genius had hardly come to grips with the problems of programming at the time these notes were taken. Nonetheless he has already grasped the fundamental principles, as the long note on the right of figure 4 attests.

> Trovare quello / che è scritto per / luce, e poi è collocata dentro / la macchina / a ricordare. / Per i vostri / commandi / lasciate / ogne nota / avere il suo / numero / e allora / il matematico / serà re. / Lasciate / le parole / di potere / al mago.

> [To find what has been written in light and committed to the memory machine: For your commands, let each note have its number, for then the mathematician will be king. Leave words of power to the magician.]

Since Leonardo was above all an artist, it is not surprising that he quickly realized the possibility of computer-generated graphics, which he discusses in the note at the top of figure 5: "Linea e colore tutti i due possono formarsi per luce, / sicchè l'un e l'altro possono cambiarsi come volete. / Quindi la macchina a scrivere può servire anche come / una macchina a disegnare. [Let both line and color be formed by light, so either can be altered at will. Thus the writing machine can also serve as a drawing machine.]" No doubt this sketch of the Mona Lisa is the gem of the Codex Japponicus. That the more famous Louvre version was in fact computer-generated now appears entirely plausible.

After this tour de force, Leonardo returns to the nagging problem of how to invent the science of electronics. A second prophecy clearly shows that his fertile genius had in fact perceived the proper line of investigation (figure 5, in box): "Altra profetia della / macchina <a> scrivere. / Uomini scriveranno / per lume e ricorderanno / per lampi. [Prophecy of the writing machine: Men will write with light and remember with lightning.]" Whether he pursued this inquiry to a viable conclusion unfortunately remains an open question. But the last entries on the Codex Japponicus strongly suggest that Leonardo did indeed hit upon the answer (across the bottom of figure 5): "Lo segreto della macchina a scrivere. / Definitione come la luce può ridursi al lampo. [The secret of the writing machine. A definition of how light can be linked to lightning.]" This tantalizing entry

Figure 5.

is followed by another (in parentheses) that can only fill the heart of every Leonardophile with despair: "Manco ancora del papiro. Impossibile con la macchina a scrivere. [I am out of paper again. This would never happen with the writing machine.]" Personally, I am of the opinion that henceforth he made his notes on his new writing machine, and it is to be hoped that some vigilant scholar will discover his tapes, discs, or whatever, and recognize them for what they are, so his full genius can be acclaimed to the Electronic Age he had anticipated.

INVENTIONES APUD AHA
(December 1989)

INVENTING OUR MOTTO:
INTRODUCTORY REMARKS AT THE AHA

R. Dean Ware

It is appropriate that the program of this year's meeting of the American Historical Association include a session presented by the Societas fontibus historiae medii aevi inveniendis, popularly called "the Pseudo Society." This organization operates under the patronage of Saint Isidore of Seville and is committed to revolutionizing the historical profession, or at least convulsing it. Our session fits in well with the theme of this year's convention because the French Revolution is actually a medieval subject. We have long thought so, and I am gratified to see that our position has now been adopted by no less an authority than Jacques Le Goff, who, in his new book, *The Medieval Imagination*, acknowledges that the Middle Ages endured until the middle of the nineteenth century, so that the French Revolution—along with the Reformation, the Industrial Revolution, the birth of modern science, and the Enlightenment—is but part of the last phase of an extended Middle Ages. Now that's *longue durée!* Scholars would be well advised to recognize that the earlier phases of medieval history are simply more ancient regimes, and that the search for the roots of the French Revolution are not to be found in the recent past of Louis XIV but in the earlier reign of Louis the Unnumbered, better known as Clovis.

Before I introduce our speakers, I want to say a few words about the origin, rationale, and modus operandi of the Pseudo Society. It is well known that the existing historical records have given rise to endless disagreement. The traditional scholarly community produces a steady flow of contradictory claims and conclusions touching every aspect of the past:

date, provenance, motive, consequence, relationship, significance, and so
forth. One has only to read James Kloppenborg's article, "Objectivity and
Historicism," in the October issue of the *American Historical Review,* or Jack
Censer's "Commencing the Third Century of Debate" in the current issue
of the same journal, to see that the historical profession is in chaotic dis-
array and that its work has proved an "unmitigated failure," to quote John
Higham's assessment in the revised edition of his *History: Professional
Scholarship in America.*

Therefore, because orthodox research has signally failed us, some academic practitioners have begun to explore variant, even aberrant, methodologies, a few of which will be illustrated during this evening's proceedings, and among which serendipity is not the least relied on. Serendipity
has been defined as "looking for a needle in a haystack and finding the
farmer's daughter." Recently, for example, while idling away an afternoon
among some manuscripts of an *eschatological* nature, I came upon several
scatological etymologies. Pure chance! I am now attempting to determine if
it is a case of simple misfiling, or if the genres were deliberately combined
because both deal with ends.

The Pseudo Society originated several years ago in Kalamazoo, Michigan, a hamlet just east of Benton Harbor, where a few dozen medievalists
hold a retreat each May, a sort of *sacre de printemps.* There a group of young
men and women, promising scholars all, avid to advance the frontiers of
knowledge, began "to boldly go where no man/woman/ person had gone
before." Sickened "by the skepticism of a skeptical age" (if in the afterglow
of Christmas I may be permitted to employ the words of Francis Pharcellus
Church's response to Virginia O'Hanlon's question, more famous even
than that of Pepin to Zacharius), disgusted by those who "do not believe
except what they see," who "think that nothing can be which is not com-
prehensible to their little minds," these adventurers turned their backs on
traditional history. Recognizing that the study of the *known* had led to
inconsistent and/or inconclusive pronouncements, because "familiarity
gives rise to its own peculiar blindness," the Pseudo Society deliberately
stands apart from the evidence and devotes itself to the *unknown,* thereby
creating opportunities for interpretation and explanation of "greater orig-
inality and insight." For there is another history, as it were, of which our
mundane experience is but a poor reflection. The task is to rise above the
distortions and imperfections resulting from flawed material and fallible
senses to create a past as it ought to be—"geschichte wie es eigentlich sein
sollte"—which, incidentally, is the society's motto. To help realize this
world "nearer the heart's desire," the Pseudo Society has devoted itself to

the *recherche des tomes perdus,* heartened by the knowledge that, as our motto declares, *Nulla nova—solum vetera inventa.*

Robert Kennedy, before he was assassinated, observed that most people survey the past that has been with its contradictions, puzzles, and evidentiary lacunae and are content to ask, "Why?" A few, however, imagine a history that could have been, with questions answered, problems solved, and ignorance dispelled, and they ask, "Why not?" These musings proved the inspiration for his brother Jack's well-known aphorism: "Ask not what history can do for you—ask what you can do for history!" The Pseudo Society has adopted these words as its motto.

We are indeed gratified to note that the efforts of the Pseudo Society have excited emulations of late, such as Eric Hobsbawm and Terence Ranger's *The Invention of Tradition,* Herbert Leibowitz's *Fabricating Lives,* Edmund Morgan's *Inventing the People,* V. Y. Mudimbe's *The Invention of Africa,* Werner Sollors's *The Invention of Ethnicity,* and, not to go on, K. M. Baker's forthcoming *Inventing the French Revolution.*

Let me bring my introduction to a close with this happy announcement: the governing board of the Pseudo Society has just named Peter Gay an honorary member for the brilliant review of Freud's *The Interpretation of Dreams* that he invented and published some time ago in *Harper's Magazine.* His critics, little people unable to acknowledge the superiority of poetic truth to literal truth, quite irresponsibly condemned him for "discovering" this document by one of Freud's contemporaries that provides important evidence as well as priceless insights. In defense of Peter Gay I need only quote the motto of the Pseudo Society: "It is better to find a single source than to curse the Dark Ages."

THE ENGENDERING OF THE FRANKS:
THE METHODOLOGY OF *URKONSTRUKTIONISMUS*

Jo Ann McNamara

Some years ago, addressing the American Historical Association in Chicago, Walter Goffart noted, with his usual stunning insight into the texts, that scholars studying the barbarians who invaded Europe in the fourth and fifth centuries A.D. tended to view them in aquatic terms, as waves, floods, and even occasionally trickles. Since then, hermeneutic techniques have emerged which confirm Goffart's suspicion that there was something liquid, shapeless, and flowing about those peoples as they emerged into the textual world. The barbarians floated out of the wavering, unboundaried, liminal soup of potentially acculturated humanity that lapped the frontiers of the constructed universe in the second century, just as Roman textators were sinking into that autumnal torpor which, according to Gibbon, rendered them incapable of responding to the threat of barbarians and Christians against the virile, sharply imagined structures they had maintained so long.

Gibbon's thesis, however, depends upon a mistaken assumption that the Germanic barbarians were virile and that the oriental Christians subverting the Empire from within were effeminate. By a careful application of the methodology of *Urkonstruktionismus* pioneered by the Societas fontibus historiae medii aevi inveniendis, it is now possible to locate the true root of the difficulty. Both Germans and Christians were the victims of Roman failure to concretize their gender characteristics in appropriate texts. My patient listeners will be justified in reacting sharply against this claim. Surely, you will respond, the Romans could not have been so sadly inattentive to both groups, one coming in from the north and the other gradually spreading among the orientals of the East. And surely, in ordinary circumstances, I would have to agree. But deconstruction of the classic texts and the urconstruction of texts which have previously been lacking to modern scholars will demonstrate conclusively that the sexual plasticity of both groups was extended long beyond the initial period of their entry into Latin texts by the malevolence of the shape-changing Celts, who themselves had long defied the Romans in defense of their Druid magic.

Now at last, urconstructionists can break the frightful *geas* that lay on Tacitus and tell the true tale of his unhappy experiences in Britain. Out of the haunted mists of their distant island, the Celts concocted the dreaded warrior women who fell upon the Romans and butchered them as awful sacrifices to their hungry deities. The screeching, black-clothed druidesses who filled the Roman legions with dread as they approached the holy isle of Mona were in fact engaged in completing the spells which would forever distort the vision of the young historian. As the first waves of the great barbarian flood began to lap against the imperial frontiers, it fell to Tacitus to undertake the task of giving them form and substance. Haunted by the phantom of Boudicca, Tacitus drew the arms-bearing Germanic woman from the imaged world where dragons, monsters, and Amazons stalked the nightmares of firmly gendered Roman men and placed her on the battlefield. Ammianus Marcellinus solidified the image in his portrait of the savage barbarian wives, red of face and brawny of arm, who rushed into the thick of battle, kicking, biting, and cursing, to defend their husbands.

The Celtic curse might well have dissolved without doing further harm, like the mist in the Mediterranean sun. But the Romans themselves, or at least the more unstable elements in their empire, were undergoing an internal corporological crisis that resulted, as Peter Brown has so brilliantly shown us, in the emergence of ascetic Christianity. It was, we must remind ourselves, to the Galatians that Paul preached the deconstructionist message of early Christianity: "neither Jew nor Greek, male nor female." Perhaps that stern upholder of the established gender system was himself the first victim of the Celtic curse—for the Galatians were Celts! Thus two centuries before Tacitus encountered their mystifying power, the enemies of Roman order had planted the seed of its destruction in the conquered East.

Christianity, the religion of women and slaves, began to work an evil spell within the sensible pagan world. By the third century it had crept into the ranks of the learned classes, who bore the responsibility for maintaining differentiated human categories. In Egypt, Clement of Alexandria dared to claim that the Christian goal was to make men more like women, while in fact its women were indisputably manly in their devotion to the faith. His successor, Origen, confirmed the trend by his auto-castration. (Origen's *Apologia* still awaits its urconstructionist.)

This crisis caused the philosophers on the cutting edge of Roman social perceptionality to let slip the firm boundaries their classical predecessors had constructed between the genders. The result was widespread enthusiasm of ascetic Christians for virile women, first apparent in the literature of martyrdom in the early third century. The hormonal difficulties that caused female Christians to turn into men in the arena were no cause for immediate alarm, but we have Tertullian's testimony to the effect that they were spreading to other women who suffered no more serious martyrdom than sexual abstinence. In his famous tract on the veiling of virgins, the irascible father passionately marshaled his considerable powers to refute the claim of the virgins of Africa that they were not women and therefore not subject to Paul's command that women be veiled. The subtle curse of the Galatians had found fertile ground among the burgeoning ascetics.

In swift response, biology began to accommodate itself to these new insights. Individuals learned how to live without eating, to fly through the air, and to root themselves as vegetables in the ground. By the middle of the fifth century, urconstructionists developed a series of new texts charting the biology of virgin birth. They popularized accounts of the transvestite saints who flourished in the deserts of Syria and Egypt. The traditional coldness of women established by Aristotelian biology was gradually overcome by the observation, finally canonized by Isidore of Seville, that women's libidinous drive is stronger than men's (*Etymologies* 11.2.24).

The key was hair. A prime function of menstrual blood in women who were properly cold was to purge them of substances they lacked the heat to concoct into milk or into beards or other hair produced by the heat of men. Galla, the path-breaking daughter of the conservative pagan senator Symmachus, transformed her sexual heat into androgenic glands that caused her to grow a beard. Clearly some Celtic Gaul had infiltrated the last bastions of Roman structure maintenance. Was it perhaps Saint Patrick himself, whose *Confession* modestly omits to outline his itinerary after his escape from Ireland to the Continent? Here indeed is fertile ground for a potential Ph.D. dissertation utilizing the new methodology. In any case, after Galla's experience, it was clearly too late for Paulinus of Nola's discourse on hair to stem the flood of uncontrolled hairy growth. In the East, desert monks and circus factions fought against their dissolving physiques

by cultivating long beards and moustaches, but even there they were subverted by the growing power of eunuchs in the palace of Justinian.

In the deserted places of the northern forests, bearded women began
to multiply. Their patron saint, Uncumber, presided over a cult specializ-
ing in the dissolution of marriage. It is in the context of this gender revolution that we must now place the engendering of the barbarian peoples
by Roman textualizers. Reversing the traditional hermeneutical approach,
going beyond the deconstructionist techniques of recent scholars, we can
now confidently approach the problem of barbarian ethnogenesis. Some
years ago, our first clumsy attempts at data enhancement grew out of our
research into the disappearance of the Jutes from English history. At that
time, I fell into a long and amicable dispute with our distinguished chair,
Professor R. Dean Ware. Based on my construction of the *Vita Wythelae,* a
hagiographical account of Saint Wythelas, the Mother of the Jutes, I attributed their difficulties to the unfortunate genetic confusion that caused the
Jutes to switch genders at crucial moments of cross-sexual contact.
Professor Ware, however, stubbornly attributed their destruction to the
growth-inhibiting factors illustrated by the so-called Bayeux Tapestry,
where they are depicted life-size. With growing methodological sophistica-
tion, however, I think we can at last compose our differences. The real
cause of the disappearance of the Jutes is the failure (dare I say refusal?)
of the Saxon urconstructor, Bede, to formalize them in his chronicle. As a
result, the process of textualization that we attempted inevitably produced
contradictory concretizations of the imaged subject. Excluded from Bede's
text, the Jutes were cast back into orality, which was dominated by the
Celts. Bede's singular determination to blot the Celts out of his world
order enabled him to control the shaping of the Saxons into unambigu-
ously masculine English gentlemen. But at what cost to the Jutes!

I now propose to apply this insight to the problem of the gender insta-
bility of the Germanic peoples, and particularly of the Franks, who ultimately became the chief focus for Roman textualizers. The Romans,
concerned about their inability to retain the firm gender system they had
constructed in their classical heyday, projected their uneasy fantasies upon
the unknown "other" and drew a monstrous, androgynous figure out of
the imperial *limines.* As their society further sank into corporological decadence, they imagined the dreaded Lombard women who marched into
battle with their hair tied under their chins.

The final product of this nightmare of creativity was the long-haired
Frankish king whose potency could not survive a haircut. Need I remind
this learned audience that it was Clothild, the agent of Gallic bishops, who

froze this image in the historical texts by her refusal to apply her scissors to her grandsons' hair. And it was another Gaul, Gregory of Tours, who commemorated the deed and the tradition. Once we have elucidated the origin of this cross-gendered, warlike figment of the sexually disturbed Roman imagination, however, we must still explain the Frankish success in evading the terrible fate that overtook the Jutes. The clue, I believe, lies in a close exegesis of the hirsutic preoccupation of Latin authors in the age of barbarian invasion. A semiotic analysis of the relationship between "barbarian" and *barbatus* will deconstruct this obsession so that, in the barbatology of Paulinus of Nola, Procopius, Gregory of Tours, and other chroniclers of the age, the discerning scholar will perceive their failure to engender the Merovingian dynasty stably enough to maintain the lineage.

The virility of the Merovingian queens grew in direct proportion to the decadence of their kings. The canny Gregory pursued the history of that transmogrification without comment on its inner meaning. But urconstruction may again be utilized to fill the gap between the last product of traditional Roman historiography and the new and more compatible area of hagiography. It is surely in the life of the Irish saint Columbanus, who refused with baleful curses to recognize the legitimacy of the warrior-queen Brunhild's grandsons, that the true underlying force that foiled the initial hopes of the Franks may be recognized. The Celtic curse still retained its power.

It was only the ruder provincial dynasty of the Carolingians, with the help of modern urconstructionists, who finally overcame the textual power of the decaying Latin tradition. Bernard Bachrach solidified the new dynasty at the crucial moment of its engendering with a spectacular feat of urconstruction: the famous Minnesota fragment. This priceless piece of data supports Charlemagne through the liminal period in which his dynasty was most vulnerable to the ancient curse. His aunt, Gertrude of Nivelles, had already partially given way when she refused marriage and submitted to a haircut at the hands of Irish monks. Charlemagne himself found his voice rising into the soprano range after his ill-fated marriage to a Lombard *(longobarda,* or "long-bearded") princess. Without the help of the Minnesota fragment, which exposes the malevolent efforts of the sister of the repudiated queen, he might have succumbed altogether. As it was, his daughters carried their Romanized lovers about on their shoulders. Had Charlemagne allowed them to marry, there might have been no saving the dynasty. Thereafter, but one crucial step remained. The shock of his sudden coronation in Rome on Christmas Day 800 A.D. threatened to throw Charlemagne back into the feminizing patterns of his youth. But his devoted textualizer, Einhard, was persuaded to supply him with a manful disavowal of Roman robes and a determined adherence to Frankish trousers which restabilized the classical tradition of two finally defined genders and thereby permitted the Carolingian Renaissance, and all subsequent Renaissances, to be invented by his grateful heirs.

But as late as the eleventh century, Adam of Breman still believed that bearded women inhabited the distant northern climes of Lapland. At the last meeting of this *societas,* William Cook revealed a newly constructed portrait of Saint Francis that conclusively proves him to have been an ungendered Irish bird. I feel certain that now that we have introduced our methods to a wider audience of historians, the links between the gender confusions of the barbarian world and the French Revolution will be clarified by modernists. Textualizers like Mozart/Ponti and Beaumarchais were busy imposing a similar gender crisis on the Old Régime with the creation of pants parts, the vogue for *castrati,* and other phenomena that threatened the Carolingian legacy. We need only remember the creative urconstructionists of the eighteenth century, who saw the effete aristocracy at Versailles as the descendants of the old Franks who conquered the ancient Gauls, to make the crucial connection that culminated in the women (or men dressed as women) whom contemporary textualizers blamed for the destruction of the French monarchy.

THE NAME GAME

Thomas F. X. Noble

A few months ago, while undertaking excavations in connection with the building of the "chunnel," workmen discovered, deep underground in western Normandy—or perhaps I should say "Neustria"—an amazing network of caves. Their curiosity was piqued by the fact that some of these caves showed signs of quite recent inhabitation. The French Ministry of Culture immediately sent a team—excuse me, an *équipe*—of archeological experts to investigate the site fully. Within just a few hours, they had made an astonishing discovery: an entire family of Franks was found to be living a few hundred feet under the soil of modern Normandy.

Word of this remarkable discovery leaked out immediately, and expressions of congratulation and interest poured in from all over the globe. President [George H. W.] Bush wrote to say that he thought he was pleased but had not yet made up his mind. Margaret Thatcher called to say that it was all very well, but she still was not joining the EMS on anything but her own terms. Similarly thoughtful remarks came in from all quarters, but let us not delay over them.

The family consisted of a man, his two brothers, his wife, and their three sons. They were immediately taken to Paris, where they could be looked after properly and where decisions could be taken as to how to proceed. They were given guest quarters in the German Historical Institute because they could not speak French and because in their own days, as in several days since, German speakers had more or less controlled France. In due course it was decided to hold a combination press conference and scholarly gathering. Interpreters were secured, rooms prepared, and everyone awaited the great day on which it would finally be possible to learn in detail about the Frankish world from some real Franks.

The conference was opened with a memorable address by a distinguished member of the Collège de France. For fifty spellbinding minutes, this *professeur extraordinaire* reflected on how marvelous it was that this miraculous discovery had been made in our time, which was not their time but that is indeed a slice of all time. The speaker hoped that the folk present would not overlook the *opportunité folklorique* that had presented itself to the international community of scholars, which is of course different from all earlier communities of scholars, not least in that we believe in neither the marvelous nor the miraculous but study both in time periods marked out precisely by Timexes or Rolexes, depending upon our own status, and so isn't it marvelous that after all these years we find that status is still measured by temporal pursuits, and wouldn't it be miraculous to find a student of status—at any rate one who was not a famous Parisian professor—wearing a Rolex. Your faithful reporter was taking notes but cannot swear that he got everything down verbatim. That is no problem, however, because the address in question has already been translated into four languages and published in six anthologies.

At this stage in the proceedings, the Frankish family was introduced to those assembled in the conference hall. The head of the household was named Cloddogrub, his brothers Burposlob and Smellobad, his wife was called Flabbobag, and their sons Laurentiolus, Moyses, and Crispus. It was immediately remarked that this was obviously a family of mixed Romano-Frankish antecedents. Two further interventions were then offered. First, a learned German professor asked how Flabbogbag had come to get her name, since the rules of *Namenkunde,* all worked out according to principles that are *streng wissenschaftlich,* demand that names be accurately given, whereas Flabbobag was thin as a rail. "Flabby," as the journalists had begun to call her, apologized profusely for disconcerting the honorable professor, while Cloddogrub said he would soon have something more to say about Frankish name giving. Meanwhile a professor from Munster announced that, as soon as the *Gruppensuch* computers could be reprogrammed to go *such*-ing for Cloddos, Burpos, Smellos, and Flabbos, there would be a weekend conference involving 111 papers, three public lectures, a tour of a castle, and published proceedings—all in the interest of learning more about significant noble families in the Frankish world.

At this point several of the professors of prosopography present expressed the hope that they would finally learn how Frankish naming patterns actually worked. They explained to Cloddogrub the reigning theory that Frankish names were made up of two or more "name radicals" and that, by tracing the appearance of these radicals in various extended families, it seemed possible to show filiation or, failing that, patronage and influence. Cloddogrub said he thought that was all very ingenious but, alas, wrong. He explained that Frankish children were named by relatives at the time of baptism. Now baptisms were happy and communal events, and on all such occasions the Franks were wont to consume large quantities of beer. Having thus induced the mirth that is born of inebriation, the assembled community then engaged in a contest to think up the silliest names possible. (One of the professors of Old High German asked whether this was a sort of flyting, and Cloddo said he didn't think so but that the principle was much the same.) So, after heated discussion, carried out according to strict principles of hilarity, a name was chosen and the child was made to live with it. From somewhere in the back of the room, an educationist asked if it weren't true that Frankish children were thus caused to lack positive self-images and to feel less than good about themselves. Cloddogrub explained that since just about all Franks had ridiculous names, it was actually a matter of status to have a name that was funnier than everyone else's. *Namenkunde, Namenforschung,* and *Gruppensuch* learned that the objects of their inquiries were merely jokes.

Now I decided to intervene. As you know, it has long been a matter of intense concern to Carolingian historians that we have the nicknames of only some of the members of the dynasty. You all have heard of Charles the Hammer and of Pepin the Short, of Charles the Great (or should it be the Big?), of Louis the Pious, and of Charles the Bald, for example. Doubtless you know of the learned controversies that have swirled around such serious questions as whether Pepin was actually short or whether Charles was really bald. I have no independent contribution to make to those important debates, but I have long been looking on my own for the lost nicknames of the Carolingians. The legitimation of my quest comes from a recently discovered capitulary text that I shall publish as soon as I can find an editor who will stop asking me where I found it. The crucial *capitulum* reads: "Omnes reges sive imperatores Francorum nomeniunculos se imposuere debent in die quando assumpserunt regnum." Naturally I was drawn to the word *nomeniunculos.* Can these "little bitty names" be the royal nicknames that have so long entertained our students? I think so. On the basis of my recent discovery, I asked Cloddogrub if he could shed any light on the matter for us.

As always, our Frankish guest was cooperative. He said that he vaguely remembered the law in question and that he thinks it was an attempt on the part of the ruling dynasty to assure the possibility of giving themselves their own nicknames rather than having to endure the names that the people gave them. Cloddo explained further that all kings did indeed have nicknames, but that some were self-chosen while others appeared by popular acclaim. He couldn't remember all the names but he did remember quite a few.

It seems that the four sons of Louis the Pious were called Groucho, Harpo, Chico, and Gummo. Cloddo couldn't remember who was who, but I think I have it figured out. Pepin must have been Harpo—have you ever heard of him saying anything? Lothair must have been Chico—at least I assume this because he was a considerable gambler and a notorious roué. Louis the German was, I suppose, Groucho, while Charles must have been Gummo. Lothair's son, Louis, was called "Louis the Schmuck" because of his general inability to do anything right. Arnulf was called "the Wimpy" because anyone with a name like that was always beaten up by the other kids on general principles. Zwentibold, it seems, had no nickname because everyone agreed that his name was already goofy enough. Carolus Grossus, it seems, got his name more on qualitative than on quantitative terms and was more usually known by his contemporaries as Carolulus Bumbulummus, "Charley the Gas Bag." Louis the Child, it turns out, was actually called "Louie the Kid." Henry the Fowler's name has been misunderstood. Actually he was Henricus Foetor, that is, "Hank the Stinky" or as we might say in more formal settings like this one, "Henry the Foul." Charles the Simple was really Carolus Sannio, more or less "Charles the Dingbat." I plan soon to publish a set of inscriptions concerning all these names. I found the inscriptions in the reredorters of several Carolingian monasteries, and the only reason that these crucial documents are not already before the community of scholars is that, once again, fastidious editors keep on asking questions about my footnotes.

I was able to put to Cloddogrub another question that interested me a good deal. As you know, some of the large and seemingly well attested Frankish families had the tendency, which is to this day the despair of orthographers and *Namenkundlers,* to give almost everyone in the family the same name. For example, there is that important family whose members all were called Hugo, Ugo, Odo, Otto, Udo, or something closely similar. I asked Cloddo about this. He explained that the reason for this was really quite simple. At the public assemblies of the Franks, the great clans usually pitched their tents together and gathered in a group for each day's deliberations. After the king and his officials had proposed a certain course of action, voting took place by means of a series of chants. That is, each member of each family group chanted in unison with his relatives his own name. A family like the Udonids were almost invincible and almost always got their own way. Cloddogrub's testimony, combined with some research of my own, permits a certain confirmation of this theory. You will doubtless know that every time the kings of the Franks met in a *placitum generale* with their nobility, the sources mention the presence of *adiutores*. Well, it seems perfectly obvious to me that this word needs to be emended—count your minims!—to *auditores*. Before the days when Ted Mack invented the applause meter, it was the king's *auditores* who listened to the chants and decided which noble faction had carried the measure. For a long time scholars have foolishly thought that political prominence was involved in concepts like *Königsnähe* and practices connected with property acquisition. Now you know the truth. Moreover, further research can now be profitably done in this promising field. We know that most noble families controlled monasteries and sometimes even cathedral churches. We also know that those religious communities were forever importing chant masters. I suggest, tentatively of course, that those chant masters were ringers imported to improve a particular family's chances in the semiannual shouting matches that decided policy in the Frankish Empire.

Those familiar with the history of the latter half of the ninth century will know that the Bosonids rose to great prominence at that time. I think I can now explain this phenomenon. Imagine, if you will, several dozen men and their many retainers chanting "Bozo! Bozo! Bozo!" in unison. I can also, however, develop other lines of interpretation from the evidence provided by the Bozos. As always in early medieval history, one must take several leads and follow them up to see if they lead to a common destination. First off, why were the Bozos initially found all over the peripheries of the Carolingian world? I think the answer must be connected with Thegan's testimony that Louis the Pious expelled the clowns and harpists from his court. I take it for granted, that is, that Bozos were clowns. Now, on perfectly acceptable principles of prosopography, it is normal to extend a family grouping whenever one can establish similarities in names, offices held, or geographical origins. This being true, I think we can easily suggest that Clarabelle and Emmet Kelly were Bozos. Now, I see no impediment to attaching Bonzo to the Bozos, and if Bonzo, then certainly Ronald Reagan. Calm down, I am not getting political here—there is no place for such a thing in serious scholarship. I am looking for serious evidence of filiations. Now, Ronald Reagan was descended from Brian Boru, Emmet Kelly was Irish, and Clarabelle had red hair. There can be no doubt that I have discovered the existence of another Irish colony in the Carolingian world, and that this time they are neither scholars nor metaphysicians but instead clowns, *joculatores*. And it is not for me to say whether or not it is a good thing that many centuries ago clowns began assuming high office.

The discovery of two family groups that rose to prominence because of the unusual resonating possibilities of their names brings me to reconsider another source that gives us lists of names that tend to repeat with alarming regularity. I refer, of course, to necrologies and confraternity books. The seriousness of research in this area is amply attested to by the fact that scholars have sometimes been able to publish several volumes, each running to several hundred pages, on the basis of a few scraps of parchment containing a few dozen names. I was only finally able to explain this curious phenomenon after doing some research in the archives that contain the papers of William of Baskerville. It seems that he was at one point doing some of his Sherlock Holmesian research on these very lists of names. The volume into which he had put his jottings was entitled *Virus paleographicus*. It seems that in a number of religious communities there could be found older monks who found the constant repetition of long lists of names of former members or benefactors to be exquisitely tedious and a potent distraction from more pleasing kinds of repetition, say, 150 psalms at a time. One of these monks, after a tour of Spain where he learned all sorts of strange and wonderful things, came home with a potion into which he dipped all the cut quills and feathers in the scriptorium. The scribes who handled these quills took in the potion through the skin and were led to a kind of dementia that caused them to go on repeating endlessly whatever they first wrote. William seems to have discovered the medieval equivalent of the computer virus. And of course the monks who introduced that virus were hoping that by their clever device they would bloat the lists so horribly that abbots and liturgists would agree to set them aside. I think there is here ample justification for caution in the use of these sources.

Bankers in London and Paris keep telling the world about the subsidiary benefits of the "chunnel," but I doubt they ever imagined the discovery of Cloddogrub and his family and the benefits that they would bring to the community of scholars. Cloddo surely has more to tell us, and it may be that he will one day attend another meeting, this time at Kalamazoo, and there reveal more about his world, and ours.

THE BADMAN OF BOSSY-SUR-INEPT:
MEMOIRS OF A MEDIEVAL PEASANT

Richard Kay

It is some time since Lord Acton announced that "the great historian now takes his meals in the kitchen."[1] But, as Eileen Power long ago observed, "It is no good taking your meals in the kitchen if you never talk to the servants."[2] The trouble with this admirable advice is, of course, that although today's medieval historian is positively eager to interview the workers and peasants, they rarely respond to his questions. Indeed, it is not in the kitchen but rather in the chambers of the Inquisition that they have spoken reluctantly to LeRoy Ladurie and Carlo Ginsberg.

The problem, of course, arises from the scarcity of literate peasants who can speak, or rather write, for themselves. But I am happy to announce tonight that this lacuna has been filled at last by my discovery of a peasant who was sufficiently literate to write his memoirs.

The document in question is a single quarto sheet of parchment that has been folded to make two octavo leaves, which bear the numbers 1 and 8, so the sheet must once have formed part of a quire, the three inner sheets of which have been lost, leaving a considerable gap in the text. I found this sheet in a box of fragments that had been salvaged from book-bindings in the course of rebinding. The Spencer Research Library at my university acquired the box in 1951 from the estate of an English provincial bookdealer, who in turn had purchased it from a bookbinder, probably in the 1930s.[3]

As such fragments go, this one is in pretty good shape. The text itself is not greatly damaged but nonetheless is a difficult one to read. Perhaps the pencilled note in a modern hand at the head of folio 1 recto com-

ments on the legibility, for it reads: "This hand is really a bastard." But
more probably the remark is to be understood paleographically, for the
script really is in the style known as *bâtarde*. Comparison with the dated fac-
similes published by the Bibliothèque nationale de France suggests that
the manuscript was written in the region of Paris during the last decade of
the fourteenth century.

Chemical analysis of several grease spots that stained the parchment
during or before the time of writing indicate that the writer worked by
candlelight, and hence during his spare time, and that he was working at
home, since as he worked he was eating some Brie cheese. This rather
untidy text has been corrected throughout in a neat, small, feminine hand,
which occasionally has also added brief marginal notes. It would appear,
therefore, that this fragment is the original autograph text.

The document needs no further introduction, since the author's own
prefatory explanation has survived. I will read you my translation and let
the Badman of Bossy speak for himself.

* * *

Jacques, called "The Badman" *(Malhomme)*, formerly of Bossy, now of
Paris, and second sergeant to the prefect of Paris, greetings to Bodo, his
only son, and a father's blessing on your youth and inexperience.

Praised be your remarkable mother for teaching you to read, for this
mystery will stand you in good stead, although up to now your knowledge
of letters has not gained you admission to the university, the clergy, or to
any useful profession. But, thanks to inscrutable Providence, as a man of
letters you can now become a respectable peasant.

Inasmuch as many will surely marvel that this can be and will require
you to explain how Lady Fortune came to smile on your unpromising
career, I must now tell you the whole story, of which at present you know
but part, so that you in turn can satisfy the curiosity of others. And lest
some necessary part of the matter slip from your city-bred brain, I am put-
ting it in writing "ad perpetuam rei memoriam," as a wise man once said.

I was born, as you know, in the village of Bossy-sur-Inept, in the dio-
cese of Chartres. And know that the true Latin name of this place is *Bos
Superinaptus*, which in the vernacular means "a real clumsy ox." Therefore
let no man tell you that the village is named after the River Inept, for truly
it is the other way around.

In my youth, our whole village was in the domain of the noble
Benedictine monastery of Saint-Silvestre the Lesser, better known as
Malmont, or in Latin "Mons-pessimus," from the inconsiderable outcrop-
ping on which it was built during the reign of Charles the Bald. From the
smallness of the place, this religious house can accommodate but six
monks and an abbot, so its inmates have always been the elite of the elite.

Bossy, I say, had belonged to these venerable monks from time immemorial, and we were all their serfs. But not for long.

In my youth our village was just recovering from the Black Death and had only thirty households. We were all expected to know each other, so that much of my youth was misspent in recognizing whomever I met, shaking their hands, bidding them "Bonjour," commenting unfavorably on the weather, and asking after the wife and kids. But then no one ever thought it was easy to be a peasant. And furthermore, know for certain, my son, that the hardest part of being a peasant is remembering things.

When you wake up before daybreak, you must remember whether it is a feast day or not before you can go back to sleep. And if it is a work day, you must remember whether you are working for yourself that day or for your lord. And when you finally set out for the field, you must know which of those little strips you are going to plow. More than once, I can assure you, I have spent half a day doing someone else's work. And you have to sing peculiar magic songs to the oxen, too, and that nonsense has to be word perfect.

The best way to keep things straight was to go to the village church first thing in the morning, because on the porch of Sainte-Sauvage are twelve little pictures of what to do every month. I can remember standing there shivering one December morning while we debated whether we had to wait until January to spend the day sitting by the fire, even though there were no more pigs left to butcher in December.

Then there were the manorial dues. If it was Saint Luke's day, you knew that the monks expected to receive something from us. But how embarrassing to show up with seven eggs when what they wanted was a basket of hazelnuts. And how tiresome to spend an hour rounding up your best pig, only to find it was supposed to be the best sheep instead.

I was always relieved to put these decisions behind me and get down to work. The happiest day of the week was the one on which we owed field service to the monks, for then my elder brother, who was head of the family, would send me with the family plow, while he stayed home to tend to his own work. Since we never got along, I was always glad to be rid of him for the day.

But my own work kept us apart even at home, for I had a way with the bees and tended the hives, which he did not dare approach.

I had already reached manhood and had committed to memory most of the daily, weekly, and monthly customs of Bossy and our family when disaster struck. The monks of Saint-Silvestre liberated their serfs. It was the fashion then, and perhaps somewhat to their advantage, even though they, of course, remained tied to their monastery by that stability of place which is the most captivating feature of Saint Benedict's *Rule*. But to me it meant that years of laborious rote learning were wasted. No need now to remember whether the monks wanted seven eggs in one basket or one measure of nuts in each of seven baskets. And no more happy days apart from my brother, for now that we were simply paid to plow the monks' land, your greedy uncle Jean could not get enough of that work for himself.

What was worse, he soon decided that he could do without my services altogether, and as I was no longer "tied to the soil," as they say, he could—and did—send me off to seek my fortune.

I had had enough of remembering village customs—and Saint Sauvage knows there were still enough of them to remember!—so I set off for Paris, where I fancied my knowledge of bees might provide my livelihood. But when I got there, or rather here, I found that my profession was wholly in the hands of women, who would admit no man to their guild. Thus I would have been reduced to begging had I not met your sweet mother, who was the clerk employed by that guild of waxworkers. We were soon married, and it was from her that I learned the art of letters that has stood me in such good stead. Reading and writing were a delight to me because I no longer had to rely on my memory. Instead, as soon as I could, I committed all that I had been carrying in my memory to paper, and it was a great relief not to have those customs running around again and again in my head, as they used to do

And a good thing it is for you, too, now that my brother Jean is dead and I am his only heir. For your mother does not want to live in Bossy, and it would not be seemly for a man of my dignity, girth, and years to return to the soil. But you, O my son, remain to preserve the family honor, and as you are otherwise unemployed, this inheritance is opportunity knocking. The only obstacle is your ignorance of country life, and in particular of the customs of Bossy and the rights of our family. But thanks to my foresight, everything you need to know has been written down long since and in good form. So here, my son, are the customs of Bossy, which you can peruse at leisure and never remember.

* * *

At this point, almost at the end of folio 1 verso, a large, clumsy letter *S* marks the beginning of the main body of the text, only a few lines of which have survived. Jacques apparently organized his material month by month, beginning with January, for his first entry reads as follows:

> Know *(Scavez)* that not all of January is spent at the fireside, for one must perforce gather wood to feed the fire, which is a good and sufficient reason to get out of the house. And know that in winter firewood is best gathered from dead trees that are still standing. Many such can be found on the slope above the spring of Saint Priapus, where at Midsummer . . .

There the text breaks off, depriving us no doubt of many intimate and precious details of peasant life.

Jacques had already completed his review of the annual cycle before he reached folio 8 recto, where the text resumes, and apparently the final pages of his little treatise form a kind of appendix to which he had relegated matters that did not fit into his synchronic framework.

The second fragment begins in the middle of a collection of proverbs, the first of which is: "If it rains on Easter, there will be seven weeks of bad weather."[4] Sometimes he adds a gloss for his city-bred son, as, for example, this one: "If a maid tell you that kissing is out of fashion when the gorse is out of bloom, know, my son, that there is no day of the year when the blossom is off the gorse."[5] But many are little more than recipes, such as, "Eat a raw turnip to cure bad breath,"[6] and most are already well known to students of peasant life. The last entry of the series, however, deserves to be given in full for its references to our author's home life.

> At Bossy [he writes] you may still hear an old song that my brother used to sing when he wished to tease me. It begins, "Frère Jacques, Frère Jacques [delete] yourself." [In our manuscript, the verb has been obliterated by the corrector, whom I take to be the author's wife.] The rest of the song [Jacques continues] sounds like nonsense, but my brother's gestures would make clear what was meant: "Tin-ta-na-ba-la-bum / Ding dong don."

These proverbial sayings are followed by a brief section on deportment, which suggests that Parisian manners of the period, or at least Bodo's, were less refined than what was acceptable at Bossy, since he had to be told, "Don't belch loudly."[7] And again, consider this admonishment: "When you stare, my son, don't point and laugh *at the same time.*"[8]

Modern scholarship has pondered conflicting statements concerning peasant hygiene, for although by some accounts "'even small villages had their public bath houses,' yet the French peasant's contemporaries incessantly complained of his filth and foul smell."[9] Jacques's advice to Bodo resolves this apparent contradiction, however, for he writes: "Do not marvel, my son, that you must bathe daily in Bossy, for working in the fields you will get dirty every day."

Modern scholars have also wondered why children are rarely mentioned in medieval sources, and Philippe Ariès has speculated that the reason is that they were considered to be nothing more than miniature adults. But Jacques's memoirs at last explain why medieval children are invisible in our sources. "My son," he writes, "you know that in Paris one never speaks of children, or if it is unavoidable, one speaks of them as if they were already grown up. This is also the custom in Bossy and everywhere, and for the same reason, that otherwise the fairies might hear you and steal them away." To which his wife comments in the margin: "I hope the fairies cannot read."

Jacques raises problems as well as solving them, however. He poses one for the demographers in the following passage: "You must take a wife, my son, and you may readily do so now in Bossy, though it was not so in my youth, when few were born and they were bastards, because no girl in our village could marry, inasmuch as the monks of Sainte-Silvestre rarely were able to agree among themselves which of them would exercise the lord's right to spend the first night with the bride."

Although time does not permit me to report every item in Jacques's collection, I cannot omit the legend of Saint Sauvage, the patron of his village church, with which he concludes his memoirs and which will accordingly be my finale as well.

> The patron of our village church is Saint Sauvage, who is little known outside our parish, at least by that name. She was a pagan and a very young virgin, who lived here in the days when the Gospel was first being preached in Roman Gaul, and her name in the Latin language was "Silvestris." Although still a pagan, Silvestris was infatuated with a handsome young missionary named Lupus, who was about to be martyred under the axe of the public executioner at Chartres. On the appointed day, Silvestris was preparing to go into town for the spectacle, when her mother insisted that instead she must deliver a basket of goodies *(bonbons)* to her sick grandmother, who lived on the other side of the forest. As the obedient but disappointed Silvestris pursued her lonely path through the woods, the holy Lupus appeared to her in a vision and asked where she was going. On being told, he replied, "I shall meet you there," and disappeared. Sure enough, when she reached her destination, she found Lupus in her grandmother's bed. He sweetly bade her to distribute her *bonbons* to the worthy poor in Chartres, and again disappeared. Repairing thence with all haste, she learned that Lupus had already been martyred, and indeed at the very hour when he had last appeared to her. She thereupon swooned into the arms of the executioner and, after certain formalities, her goodies were consumed by the gluttonous governor, while Silvestris herself was decapitated. The fresco in our church shows her wearing her blood-stained traveler's cloak and bearing a basket of goodies. She is also accompanied by a wolf, whom the artist has helpfully labeled "Lupus," but this is clearly a misunderstanding on the part of some careless or illiterate person.

Notes

1. Quoted by Eileen Power, *Medieval People* (rpt. New York, 1954), p. 16.

2. Ibid., p. 23.

3. University of Kansas (Lawrence), Spencer Research Library, Paleographical Collection. At the time of writing (December 1989), this box, which I examined in 1977, could not be located. Moreover, the cataloguing of its contents had never been undertaken due to their diverse and imperfect character. The box was acquired from the successors to Magnus Pickpenny, antiquarian bookseller, of Norwich.

4. This belief still persists: William E. Koch, *Folklore from Kansas* (Lawrence, 1980), p. 297, no. 3707.

5. Cf. *The Oxford Dictionary of English Proverbs,* 3rd ed., rev. by F. P. Wilson (Oxford, 1970), p. 329.

6. Cf. Koch, *Folklore from Kansas,* p. 95, no. 1120.

7. Still good advice.

8. Idem.

9. Barbara Tuchman, *A Distant Mirror* (New York, 1978), p. 173.

THE PSEUDO SOCIETY AT THE AHA:
COMMENTS

James A. Brundage

I think you will agree, ladies and gentlemen, that this was indeed a remarkable set of papers. Remarkable as much for their authors' audacity—not to say recklessness—as for their innovative reasoning and imaginative contributions to the lore and logic of pseudohistory, to whose elaboration our venerable society has been dedicated since its inception.

Whenever that was. For on that question our learned members have, for various reasons, not yet been able to reach total agreement. In a formal, legalistic sense, the society may be said to have originated on 10 May 1986, when we held our first public session at Kalamazoo, Michigan, in conjunction with the annual Congress of Medieval Studies at Western Michigan University. But many would argue that, although the society formally came into existence at that point, our group is in spirit, if not in form, actually a continuation of an earlier, short-lived body, the Society for Jutish Studies, to whose fevered, even convulsive, proceedings Professor McNamara has referred this evening.

Like the Society for Jutish Studies, the Pseudo Society is dedicated, as our stately Latin titulature proclaims, to creative scholarship, and specifically to the *inventio* of long-lost, or at least misplaced, medieval sources. It exists, therefore—so far as it can be said to exist at all—in order to provide a forum for the announcement of those *inventiones* that members of the society, or their invited guests, may have, as it were, become possessed of since the previous meeting of the society.

This evening's papers, as the more perceptive members of our audience will already have grasped, skillfully deploy a variety of the pseudohis-

89

torian's tools in novel and imaginative ways. Professor McNamara furnished us with a splendid example of the type of evidence enhancement that practitioners of pseudohistory refer to technically among themselves as *Vermutanalyse,* or "inspired analysis"—inspired by what? Well, perhaps this is not the place to pursue technical matters too deeply.

Using the rather specialized technique of *Urkonstruktion,* which is simply one derivative or subsidiary form of *Vermutanalyse,* Professor McNamara has argued, persuasively I think, that gender plasticity was the key element in accounting for the inability of Roman statesmen to rise to the potent challenge of those hairy, virile women who, not content with skulking along the frontiers of the Empire, actually crossed over to seize power from the flaccid grasp of the enfeebled successors of the Caesars.

I would like, however, to direct two comments to Professor McNamara concerning her very interesting paper this evening. First, would she care to consider the implications of her theory for the possibility that the generic term that both Greeks and Romans commonly used to describe the outsiders who eventually undid them (namely in Greek *barbaroi* and in Latin of course *barbari)* may actually have been a synecdoche for *barbae,* in other words, "the beards," or *barbati,* that is to say, "the bearded ones," rather than a derivative of the Sanskrit *barbara,* meaning, as we all know, "one who stammers"?

And secondly I wonder if she ought not integrate into her theory what I take to be the corroborative evidence of the twelfth-century *Apologia de barbis* attributed to Burchard de Bellevaux, also known as *Barbiloquus,* or "the talking beard"? I call her attention particularly to the passage in *Apologia* 3.1 where Burchard observes: "Contingit tamen, licet raro, et viros fieri sine barbis et feminas habere barbas."[1] He then goes on to speak a few lines later of situations in which men may lose their beards, as for example, "cum violenter vel medicinaliter genitalibus abscisis."[2] A page or two further on he devotes a whole chapter to the question of bearded women under the rubric: "De barbis feminarum contra naturam sicut Gallae,"[3] which is of course a reference to that bearded Galla, the daughter (or perhaps son?) of Symmachus, who figures in the fourth dialogue of Gregory the Great (or perhaps the Gross?).[4] It is understandable that she may have overlooked this rare source, since it was published by Goldschmidt in 1935 in an edition of only 350 copies on hand-laid paper.[5]

Turning now to Professor Noble's paper: it will not have escaped the notice of this learned audience that we have here a particularly daring specimen of what is technically known as *Zeugenschöpfung,* or "creative testimony," which is of course one specialized type of a basic technique of pseudohistory that we usually call "data enrichment." In other words, where evidence is lacking for certain features of a phenomenon or a sequence of events, one fills in the missing bits with what must have been there, even though contemporaries were not thoughtful enough to leave us a record of them. Now lest you leap to the hasty conclusion that there may be something a shade unsound, even perhaps a trifle fishy, about this mode of approach, let me remind you that practitioners of the hard sciences do this all the time. Paleontologists, for example, think nothing—or at least very little—about reconstructing a thirty-foot-tall dinosaur from a distal flange a centimeter long and a couple of dorsal scales. And the paleontologists are veritable methodological mossbacks compared to particle physicists, who invent virtual particles in order to make their equations come out right, even though no one has ever seen a trace of them or found any experimental evidence whatever that directly attests their existence.[6] Or, if you have difficulty relating to something as strange and colorful as pions or quarks, then I invite you to consider the computer mavens, who work quite routinely, and successfully, with virtual memories and even virtual disk drives that do not exist in hard reality.

Now, granted that Professor Noble is not a computer scientist, nevertheless the methodological premises that underlie his paper are not all that far removed from routine processes in the hard sciences. He does face in this paper, however, a peculiar difficulty that physicists and paleontologists can be thankful they do not have to cope with.

In this paper Professor Noble reports findings based on oral evidence, which medievalists only occasionally encounter,[7] although we run across its analogs commonly enough in written testimony. I must confess that upon first reading Professor Noble's paper, certain doubts arose in my mind as to the credibility of his evidence. Had he tested it with sufficient rigor? Should he not have sought some further assurance that their stories were reliable? As his witnesses claimed to be Franks, would it not have been in order to challenge them to the ordeal? But of course there are two practical difficulties with this: first, it is difficult nowadays to find a cooperative clergyman to make the thing work properly.[8] And second, Professor Noble might thereby have become liable under Salic Law to undergo the ordeal of boiling water himself, and I can quite understand if he hesitated to take that chance, even in the interests of pseudohistorical science.[9] Still, as an alternative, I do think he ought to have considered requiring his witnesses, Cloddogrub et alia, to purge themselves through oath helpers, for which Salic Law also provides when false testimony is suspected.[10]

I was partially reassured of the reliability of this oral evidence, however by the responses that Professor Noble reports to questions concerning *Namenkunde,* since these seem to be inherently plausible and consistent with independent documentary evidence. The responses of the witnesses concerning the sons and grandsons of Louis the Pious made me somewhat uneasy, however, since they might be construed to imply contamination of the witnesses' memories by later—much later—evidence from Marx Brothers movies and thus to call into question the integrity of the witnesses' remaining testimony. Perhaps Professor Noble might wish to respond to this observation, if time permits.

And in light of Professor Kay's paper, which centers on the village of Bossy-sur-Inept, perhaps Professor Noble might also wish to consider whether the first element of that place name could represent the hitherto unnoticed survival into the closing decades of the fourteenth century of Carolingian Bosonids?

Which brings me to the last paper on our panel this evening, the report by my colleague, Professor Kay, of another exciting feat of data enhancement, namely his serendipitous recovery from a box of binder's scraps of a previously unknown memoir of a fourteenth-century peasant. This is a specimen of that innovative technique familiarly known as *Urkundenfabrikation,* for which Professor Kay has previously shown such extraordinary talent, notably through his earlier discovery of a document that revealed that Leonardo da Vinci had invented the word processor.[11]

I have just one or two preliminary remarks and suggestions to put to Professor Kay this evening, pending closer examination of his newly retrieved document, once the Spencer Library reopens next week and provided the staff can find that missing box. One observation has to do with the village bathhouse. Professor Kay should, I think, keep in mind that "bathhouse" does not necessarily mean a place where people actually took baths. Indeed, the inventory of one fourteenth-century bathhouse at Avignon shows that it contained no facilities whatever for bathing, but did feature a large number of small cubicles furnished with beds.[12] Jacques Malhomme's advice to his son to visit the bath house daily, therefore, may be susceptible of more than one interpretation and may have little to do with either cleanliness or godliness. This may also suggest a possible reason for Jacques's cognomen, "Malhomme," particularly if the text of his memoir was revised, as Professor Kay suggests, by Jacques's wife.

Finally I should point out that by a happy coincidence Professor Kay's discovery exemplifies a third material state of the pseudohistorian's evidence. *Urkundenfabrikation,* as practiced by Professor Kay, differs from

Zeugenschöpfung, as demonstrated by Professor Noble, in that Kay's discovery consists of a written document, rather than the viva voce evidence of witnesses, and is produced out of a box, rather than a hole in the ground. It is therefore characterized by textuality, rather than orality, and is accordingly more static and less fluid than Professor Noble's discovery, while at the same time it is more solid, and hence less vaporous, than *Vermutanalyse,* exemplified for us this evening by Professor McNamara's investigation of gender plasticity in late antiquity. Now these material states of the evidence appear in fact to be functions of the density and excitation of their components. The material states can accordingly be thought of as lying within discrete segments of a curve defined by the values for density and excitement. We can therefore postulate that *Vermutanalyse* (represented this evening by Professor McNamara's presentation) produces papers high in excitement and correspondingly low in density of information content. Toward the other end of the curve, *Urkundenfabrikation* (here represented by Professor Kay's work) produces papers high in information density but low in excitement. While *Zeugenschöpfung,* as Professor Noble has demonstrated, produces papers of moderate information density and middling levels of excitability. We can therefore generalize by formulating an equation that expresses these relationships as a "Vacuosity Index" of pseudohistorical papers, such that:

$V_i = e^2 / d$
where V_i = Vacuosity Index;
d = density of information content; and
e = excitability

The vacuosity index thus permits us to measure with a precision hitherto unattainable, and perhaps even unimaginable, the relationship between the informational content of a pseudohistorical paper and the excitement of its findings. We accordingly conclude that the higher the level of excitement that a paper generates, the lower will be its density of information content—and, of course, by the assumption of commutativity, vice versa.

NOTES

1. Burchard of Bellevaux, *Apologia de barbis* 3.1, ed. E. Ph. Goldschmidt (Cambridge, 1935), p. 32.

2. Burchard, supra 3.3, ibid.

3. Burchard, supra 3.5 at 35–37.

4. Gregorius Magnus, *Dialogi* 4.3, in PL 77:340.

5. The *National Union Catalogue*, 84:480, however, does list seventeen other copies, besides my own, in U.S. libraries.

6. E.g., the Japanese physicist, Hideki Yukawa, who in 1934 invented the pion without a shred of experimental evidence that it existed, and Murray Gell-Mann, who invented the quark in 1963 because it made his equations neater; Sheldon W. Glashow, *Interactions: A Journey through the Mind of a Particle Physicist and the Matter of This World* (New York, 1988), at pp. 86–88 and 185–88.

7. One thinks here of the folkloric researches of scholars who deal with formulaic transmission of songs, ballads, and the like; see generally John Miles Foley, *Oral-Formulaic Theory and Research: An Introduction and Annotated Bibliography* (New York, 1985).

8. The clergy have been forbidden to participate in these tests since 4 Lateran c. 18 (1215), in *Conciliorum oecumenicorum decreta,* ed. Giuseppe Alberigo et al. (Basel, 1962) at p. 220. Whether this prohibition remains binding on Roman Catholic clergy might seem to be an open question, for although the prohibition has never been explicitly repealed, it also no longer figures in the current law of the *Codex iuris canonici auctoritate Ioannis Pauli PP. II promulgatus* (Vatican City, 1983).

9. *Lex Salicae* § 132, in *The Laws of the Salian and Ripuarian Franks,* trans. Theodore John Rivers (New York, 1986) at p. 144.

10. *Lex Salicae* § 48, supra at p. 95.

11. I should perhaps admit here a certain partiality for this variety of pseudohistory, since I have experimented with it myself in an earlier paper to this society entitled "Peccata papae," based upon my discovery of the personal diary of Pope Innocent III.

12. Jacques Rossiaud, *Medieval Prostitution* (Oxford, 1988) at pp. 5–6; James A. Brundage, *Law, Sex, and Christian Society in Medieval Europe* (Chicago, 1987) at p. 527.

ALIAE INVENTIONES PRAECLARIORES

(1987~93)

PECCATA PAPAE:
THE SECRET DIARIES OF POPE INNOCENT III

James A. Brundage

It is a distinct pleasure to report to this distinguished audience that I recently had the good fortune to salvage some fragments of a diary or journal kept by Pope Innocent III. Even before he became pope, Lothario dei Segni made a habit from time to time of jotting down his impressions of the people with whom he came in contact, and he continued this practice, as I discovered, even after his elevation to Saint Peter's Chair.

My discovery of this precarious document was, as often happens with notable *inventiones,* entirely serendipitous. I was not, in fact, looking for Innocent III's secret journal at all, and indeed had no idea that such a thing existed. When I chanced upon the diary, I was in fact looking for a brothel. Now it's not what you may think—the brothel I was looking for was medieval; it disappeared centuries ago, and, like a proper medievalist, I was in quest not of carnal consolations but of parchments—the skins medievalists love to touch.[1]

Let me describe the circumstances of my discovery, since they are peculiarly relevant to the evidence we are dealing with. I spent a few days last summer as a guest of a family friend, the contessa di Bella Figura, at her country house in the hills between Sovana and Pitigliano. One evening after dinner, as we sat talking over a dram of a powerful local *grappa,* my hostess embarked on a rather convoluted account of her family's history. I confess that I was listening only casually when suddenly a phrase jolted me to attention. The contessa had referred in passing to "questo bordello, che fu il fundamento della fortuna di nostra famiglia." "Bordello?" I exclaimed, "Che dici, cara? Ti prego di spiegare questo bordello." The *grappa,* as I said, was potent and had done wonders for my usually tongue-tied Italian.

And so she explained. One of her twelfth-century ancestors, Prurigino,[2] had come into a tidy sum of cash as the result of lucky speculation in the slave market, and consequently was looking for sound investment opportunities. A distant cousin, Cardinal Sorbilius, offered to sell him a major interest in the ownership of a massage parlor in the nearby port city of Orbatello. His Eminence needed to raise cash in a hurry to pay off a jealous husband and was willing to sell cheap. Prurigino plunged into the deal, as it were, with enthusiasm. He soon converted the massage parlor into a full-service brothel and profits increased twentyfold. Prurigino then convinced his partners to open franchise operations in nearby towns. They then began buying up boys to stock further establishments for those with, shall we say, Byzantine tastes. Prurigino invested some of his quickly mounting wealth in suburban real estate near Genoa, and made another fortune. By the time of his death in 1190, although often called "Stuprator Mundi" behind his back, Prurigino had become a pillar of Tuscan society. The wealth engendered by the bordello has by now supported nearly thirty generations of Belle Figure.

Naturally I was intrigued by this story, and as a historian of sexual mores, I was especially curious about the brothel. Were there any records? I asked. Did the family retain any documents concerning the bordello? The contessa thought for a moment as she sipped some more *grappa* and said that there might be—she vaguely recalled a box of old documents in the library. Would I care to look at them the next day? I said that I certainly would, and a few moments later I excused myself and tottered off to bed.

Next morning the contessa was as good as her word. After breakfast she led me into the library, to which I had paid one or two earlier visits without finding much of interest. With the aid of her chaplain (a strikingly handsome young cleric, who doubled intermittently as the contessa's librarian) she rummaged through some cabinets that I had never previously noticed. At length she came up with a large leather box. When opened, the box appeared to be crammed with miscellaneous papers and parchments in no obvious order. The contessa placed it on a library table and invited me to look through it; whereupon she and her chaplain departed, perhaps for devotions, leaving me alone in the library.

The contents of the mysterious box included nineteenth- and twentieth-century deeds, copies of wills, some eighteenth-century account books, together with a jumble of letters and miscellaneous documents of various dates in no apparent order and with no obvious relationship to one another. Scattered among this debris were a few medieval documents. These I set aside to examine with more care.

Once I had sifted through the contents of the box, I returned the modern materials to it and began to read the earlier documents. After an hour or so, I came upon a small packet of tattered parchments in Latin, many of them ripped and frayed about the edges and several stained with what appeared to be wine. They had obviously been written casually, for they were rather sloppily executed. Not, I thought, the hand of a notary or of a professional scribe at all, but nonetheless a practiced hand, written by someone to whom writing was no stranger. The script seemed typical of the late twelfth or perhaps the early thirteenth century. The text was heavily abbreviated and I guessed that the writer might have been a university student at some time. The individual leaves were reasonably uniform in size and fairly small—about twelve by twenty centimeters. I counted thirty-eight of them altogether.

At first reading, it soon became apparent that these documents constituted a narrative of sorts. The contents were not particularly coherent, because some passages were so damaged as to be illegible, and also because the leaves themselves were in disarray, a bundle of *disjecta membrana*. But some episodes seemed strangely familiar; then suddenly it dawned on me that I was reading disjointed fragments of an account of the life of Lothario dei Segni *and that it was written in the first person*.

When the butler came to call me to lunch, I was in a state of high excitement and at table I began to tell the contessa and her chaplain that I thought I had made a most extraordinary find. Neither of them seemed particularly enthralled; indeed, they both seemed rather languid. The contessa did say, however, that she recalled having heard that the grandson of Stuprator Mundi had been involved in some dealings with Innocent III, but she was uncertain of the details.

After lunch I excused myself and returned at once to the library, leaving the contessa and her chaplain to retire for their siesta—separately or together, I wasn't sure which. I had begun to wonder about their relationship, but that was a trivial curiosity compared to the parchments awaiting me in the library.

Now I began transcribing the document, or such of it as I could easily make out—a decision that proved fortunate indeed. I worked steadily through the afternoon and into the early evening, and by dinnertime I had filled thirty pages in my notebook. This amounted to nearly half of the Innocentian document. I had considered getting my camera and photographing the documents, but decided that both law and propriety demanded that I first secure the contessa's permission, which I determined to do at dinner. As I was still in the midst of my work, I simply left the box and the documents on the library table, closed my notebook, and (thank heavens) took it with me when I went to change.

We were a small company at dinner—the contessa and her well-favored chaplain (whom she called Don Giovanni, by the way), a local notary and his wife, a neighbor of the contessa's who seemed principally interested in horses, and his wife, whose fancy seemed to run mainly to fashions in leather goods. I was naturally full of my discovery, but the other guests clearly found it hard to conjure up more than a polite semblance of interest. Conversation after dinner was desultory and centered mainly on local events and personalities, to all of which I was of course a stranger. I therefore excused myself as soon as I decently could, pleading an exhausting day and the intention of making an early start on the remaining documents in the morning.

As I was leaving I drew the contessa aside and told her that I would like permission to photograph the documents the next day, and added that I thought that she should also have a professional photographer make a record of them as quickly as possible. She said she would think about it, then added as an afterthought that perhaps Don Giovanni could take on the job, as he was a keen photographer and very clever with a camera. I was not best pleased, I admit, at the thought of having an amateur, no matter how keen, make the photographic record of such important documents, but this seemed neither the time nor the place to protest, and the documents were, after all, the contessa's property. Leaving the matter at that, I withdrew and went at once to bed.

I was rudely awakened about two in the morning by a terrible commotion—people shouting, engines racing, no end of racket. When I put on a robe and slippers and ventured out to see what was going on, it became apparent that the disturbance was centered in the library, and the closer I hurried the more obvious it was that there had been a fire.

As I pushed my way into the library, through a mob of firemen, servants, and onlookers who seemed to have materialized out of every corner of the house, I caught sight of the contessa and Don Giovanni, and as I did so my worst fears were realized. Not only had there been a fire, but the documents I had been studying had been at the center of it. A clutter of smoke-smudged light stands, strobes, the charred remains of a Reflectasol umbrella, extension cords, a tripod, and a ruined case of camera equipment told the story immediately, and the contessa and her chaplain could only add circumstantial details to the tale that I guessed (as it were) in a flash.

After the other guests had left, the contessa had approached Don Giovanni about photographing the documents and he had leapt at the chance. So eagerly, in fact, that he and the contessa (doubtless more than a bit diddled by drink) had hauled his equipment down to the library so he could get started at once. Somehow, a cord had short-circuited, started to arc, and in the excitement one of the pair (each blamed the other), had knocked over the bottle of *grappa* they had brought with them. The bottle smashed, its contents sprayed over the documents, and the whole thing went up in a ball of flame.

It took only minutes to verify the worst. The contents of the box of documents, including Pope Innocent's diary, had been utterly destroyed. Nothing was left but ashes and some nasty-looking lumps of melted collagen. The rest of the library was a mess, but its contents could probably be salvaged—not that they were worth much anyway. The jewel of the collection, which I had discovered just a few hours earlier, had vanished beyond recall, save for my thirty pages of rough transcription.

Such, then, were the circumstances under which Pope Innocent's diary briefly appeared, only to be snatched away again forever. But the good news is that I was able to salvage some bits from the wreckage. My notebook preserves all that now remains of Innocent III's journal or diary. I can assure you, by the way, that it has been well photographed and that copies are deposited in six different places.

The portions of the manuscript that I transcribed were in no particular order and covered several periods of Innocent's life. In this preliminary report, however, I can deal only with a few excerpts.

One segment of the vanished document that I fortunately happened to copy clears up some questions that have arisen about the education of Lothario dei Segni. As you know, long-standing tradition pictures Innocent III as a trained lawyer and casts him as one of the great lawyer-popes who did so much to transform the medieval Church—into what is a question I will not attempt to deal with here. And as many of you also know, this traditional portrait has been challenged recently by an American scholar, who pointed out that the evidence for Innocent's legal training was late and who also contended that in fact Innocent wasn't much of lawyer.[3]

The diary conclusively supports this revisionist view. Lothario apparently wrote one of the fragments I copied after he had gone to Rome, perhaps about 1190, when he had just become a cardinal. In this passage, Lothario says:

<That> only proved what an idiot he was.[4] When I was studying law with Huguccio, I learned, before he kicked me out of class, that you can never, under any circumstances, have sex without sin. It was, in fact, precisely because I challenged him on this point that old *uentosus* threw me out on my ass *(in tergum meum me prouexit).* Of course he said he dumped me because I'd never learn to think like a lawyer, but that's just bullshit *(sed non est nisi defecationem tauri).* Anyway, it's just as well he did. I've made a much better thing out of theology. Here I am, a cardinal; and where is he? Still teaching first-year law students. Just shows you, theology's a better racket *(fraudem potiorem)* than law.[5]

This passage, I believe, definitively settles the matter. It tells us as clearly as can be that Innocent studied law with Huguccio, but only for a brief time. The reference in the passage to Huguccio's teaching on sexual pleasure indicates that Lothario was expelled early in his course, since the passage in question occurs in Huguccio's comments on Distinctio 13 of the first part of Gratian's *Decretum,* and thus the confrontation between teacher and pupil presumably occurred not long after Lothario began his legal studies.[6] This assumption is further reinforced by Lothario's reference to Huguccio as a teacher of first-year law students. This entry in the diary thus tells us that, far from having legal qualifications, Innocent III was instead a law school dropout, who found theology less rigorous but more lucrative than canon law.

Another passage of the diary not only refers to Innocent's student career at Bologna but also sheds light on his youthful sexual experiences. The passage was in verse, of a sort (I certainly could not dignify it as poetry) and was probably composed after Lothario had gone to Rome, but before he was elected pope.

> Olim in Bononia
> Prauem morem uiui,
> Pueros et puellas
> Omnes conscupisciui.
> 5   Quis in igne positus,
> Igne non uratur?
> Quis inibi demorans
> Castus habeatur?
> Quando Venus jussum dat
> 10 Iuuenes uenaui;
> Paucos me effugiunt
> Ceteros curaui.[7]
> . . . .

15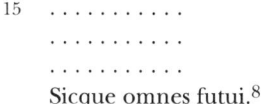

Sicque omnes futui.[8]

Brief as they are, these lines are extraordinarily candid and suggestive. They tell us of course that Lothario led rather a dissolute life while he was a student in Bologna, which certainly throws new light on his character. But far more startling, they tell us also that his sexual preferences inclined rather more to boys than to girls—at least I infer that from the fact that the direct objects of the verbs *uro, effugio,* and *curo* are all masculine. We must therefore readjust our picture of Innocent III to take account of the fact that he was a bisexual, with strong homoerotic preferences. This will, for example, markedly change the way in which we understand much of his moralizing in *De miseria humane conditionis;* it will require a careful reinterpretation of his marriage decretals and may demand a reappraisal of his relationships with members of the *curia Romana.*

Another fragment further amplifies this new insight into Innocent's personality. This is Innocent's account of his first encounter with Saint Francis of Assisi. Franciscan scholars have, during the past year, been forced to reevaluate their previous picture of Saint Francis in the light of Professor McGovern's revelation at last year's meeting of this society that, on the basis of his recently recovered account books, Saint Francis was a yuppie. This year they are in for another shock.

The fragment concerning Innocent's first encounter with Saint Francis commences, unfortunately, only towards the close of their interview.

<I told> him, of course, that this was utter idiocy and that I could not possibly contemplate approving any such way of life as he proposed. It would be nothing but an invitation to trouble, and God knows we have plenty of that already.

But You also know, O Lord, how it nearly broke my heart to discourage such a darling young man *(puerum tam suauissimum):* I couldn't simply let him go, just like that, without seeing him again, so I told him I would think things over and that he should come back next day. Since he had nowhere to stay in Rome, I told Cardinal Cataphagus[9] to find a room for him in the Lateran Palace—Lord knows we have plenty of empty beds in this dreary old rat hole *(in istam fuscam foueam)*—and to make sure to take very good care of him *(ut tractet eum cum sollicitudine peculiare).* I assumed the most eminent ass *(eminentissimum asinum)* would know what I meant. But no! Old fathead *(iste senex fatuus)* put him in one of the state guest chambers in the other wing of the palace, not next door to my room as I'd meant. I had a hard time getting to sleep *(mihi molestat insomnis)*, but when I finally did I had the most fantastic dream about that kid from Assisi [here, presumably in the grip of emotion, Innocent lapsed from Latin into Italian] *Che delicato! Che figura! Che culo! Che peccato!* [He then reverted to Latin once more:] But even better, I figured out a way to see a *lot* more of him. I told him he'd better write a rule and come back to consult with me about it. Just the ticket! *(Nihil perfectius!)* Of course the kid fell for it *(Sponte juvenis audiuit me dicentem)*. Now all I have to do is get me a new chamberlain, one who knows the score *(qui omnia noscit)*.[10]

Just here, alas, the fragment breaks off, but it seems reasonably plain that the traditional account of the approval of the Franciscan order will need to be radically revised.

At this point, I'm sorry to say, my time has run out and I cannot complete my survey of the incredible material in the *Diaries of Innocent III* this evening. But, to tantalize you further, let me add by way of conclusion that the other fragments that I salvaged include astonishing revelations about the relationship between the pope and young Frederick II, the hidden story behind Innocent's falling-out with Otto of Brunswick, hitherto-secret details of the divorce of Philip Augustus, a remarkably frank account of Innocent's dealings with King John, the inside story of the diversion of the Fourth Crusade, and hair-raising revelations about Innocent III's ties with the Mafia.

But a report on these matters must await a future meeting of this society and my definitive publication, forthcoming I should think in about thirty years, of my edition of the diaries, tentatively entitled *Was Pope Innocent?: Secret Diaries of a Peculiar Pontiff.*

NOTES

1. A line I stole / When mind was barren / From sometime colleague / Big John Perrin.

2. A rather uncommon name, presumably derived from the Latin *Pruriginosus*.

3. Kenneth J. Pennington, "The Legal Education of Pope Innocent III," *Bulletin of Medieval Canon Law* 4 (1974), 70–77.

4. "He" is unidentified but may refer to Huguccio.

5. Innocent III, *Diaries*, p. 7.

6. Huguccio, *Summa* to D. 13 pr. Many of Huguccio's contemporaries regarded his views on the sinfulness of sexual pleasure, even in marriage, as peculiar; thus e.g., *Glos. ord.* to D. 13 d.a.c. 1 ad v. *item adversus* and c. 2 ad v. *et quia*, as well as to

C. 27 q. 2 c. 10 ad v. *non poterat.* See also the Apparatus "Ecce vicit Leo" to C. 28 q. 2, in Salamanca, Universidad Civil, MS 2491, fol. 136rb–va. A few theologians, however, shared Huguccio's ideas on this matter; see Hans Zeimentz, *Ehe nach der Lehre der Frühscholastik* (Dusseldorf: Patmos-Verlag, 1974), p. 79.

7. At this point approximately four lines have been blotted out by a wine stain. The wine in question was definitely a *tinto,* but I was unable to identify the vineyard or year.

8. Innocent III, *Diaries,* p. 5. Lines 5–10 are strongly reminiscent of the Archpoet's "Confession of Golias," ed. and trans. George F. Whicher, *The Goliard Poets: Medieval Latin Songs and Satires* (New York, 1949; repr. 1965), p. 108. So reminiscent, in fact, that lines 5, 6, and 8 are actually identical with those of the Archpoet. Three explanations are possible: (1) Lothario copied these lines from the Archpoet; (2) Lothario and the Archpoet both appropriated these lines from a third source, now unknown; or (3) Lothario *was* the Archpoet. A fourth explanation, namely that the identity is purely accidental, cannot be ruled out, but seems unlikely.

9. Previously unknown. His Greek name is intriguing and hints at a new dimension in Byzantine-papal relations in the aftermath of the Fourth Crusade.

10. Innocent III, *Diaries,* pp. 23–24.

"OR/ORDURE":
FROM GOLD TO GARBAGE, OR
DECONSTRUCTING THE ANGLO-NORMAN
ROMANCE *TOPAS ET PLEINDAMOUR*

William Calin

In *The Canterbury Tales,* Chaucer the author assigns to himself, Chaucer the pilgrim, the "Tale of Sir Thopas." In that tale the narrating persona alludes to heroes of romance:

> Men speken of romances of prys,
> Of Horn child and of Ypotys,
>   Of Beves and Sir Gy,
> Of sir Lybeux and Pleyndamour—
> But sir Thopas, he bereth the flour
>   Of roial chivalry!   (7.897–902)

Kittredge and Lowes were unable to identify Old French or Middle English prototypes for Pleyndamour or, for that matter, Sir Thopas himself. Since Kittredge's day, the Anglo-Norman romance *Topas et Pleindamour* has been edited.[1] However, because modern Chaucer scholars are too busy serving on committees and sipping sherry to learn Old French, this crucial Chaucerian source has gone unnoticed. Of particular interest to Chaucerians is the fact that, in the Old French text, Pleindamour is not an epic hero but a courtly lady, Topas's beloved, a character in *his* romance; therefore Chaucer errs in associating her with Horn, Bevis, Guy, le Bel Inconnu, and Topas—all known, recognized male romance heroes—and thus intimating that she is male and a hero.

107

How and why should he have done this? One possibility, abhorrent to Anglicists but for that very reason a legitimate hypothesis, is that Chaucer got the story mixed up. After all, he is only an Englishman, and a medieval one at that. Even Anglo-Normans mix up their masculines and feminines: all the more so for a mere native. Actually, the English have had this problem ever since. In the nineteenth century it was known as *le mal anglais*. Furthermore, unlike Gower, Chaucer wasn't bright enough to write in Latin or French. As far as we can tell, resembling more than one professor today, he made his career out of a deft juxtaposition of personal charm, arch self-deprecation, and sexual harassment.

On the other hand, it is also possible that Chaucer (the author or his narrating alter ego the pilgrim) intentionally shifted Pleindamour's sex and gender, placing her ahead of Topas on the list, and thus made a comment, a gloss, a literary criticism of *Topas et Pleindamour*, using the Anglo-Norman text as an intertextual *mise en abyme* in his own "Tale of Sir Thopas."

An important episode occurs at the midpoint of *Topas et Pleindamour.* (From my friend Professor Karl D. Uitti of Princeton we know that, in the Middle Ages, midpoints without exception are placed approximately one-half way through texts.) Just after the famous negative spring-topos, an anti-topos-topos topos, deferred to the midpoint in order to shock the audience's perception and expand its horizon:

> Avril si est meis mult cruas,
> Qant de tere gaste lilas
> Genrent, ensembl' od els amur
> E suvendrur. Nel tems pascur
> Si muverent pluie e racines.   (2113–117)

This can be translated roughly as:

> April is the cruellest month, breeding
> Lilacs out of the dead land, mixing
> Memory and desire, stirring
> Dull roots with spring rain.

We discover Topas falling into a manure pile, upon which he utters a lyrical plaint bewailing his current state of *ordeet* and *ordeiement* (shiticity, garbagitude), redolent of Anglo-Norman heroism and culture in their entirety:

> Orz sui e orz serei,
> Orz devenrei;

Orz vol partir,
Orz deis pastir. . . . (2185–188)

No longer is he a knight in movement, but immobile, "figé dans le visqueux," a pitiful creature obliged to ground himself in Hegelian "Scheiss in Leben," Sartrean "l'état de merde en soi" (as distinguished from "la merde pour soi," which usually comes from the administration), and the Lacanian "dans un miroir textuel opaque le désir se réfléchissant s'avère quand-même bien merdique." We must also make the crucial metaphysical distinctions, at the heart of Heidegger's *das Scheissliche*, between *scheissend, dascheissend, geschissen, vorgeschissen,* and the neo-Nazi *Urvolksscheissend*—to be distinguished, of course, from the Aryan-Germanic *Urscheissvolk*, who, as we all know, populated the great American Midwest. Meanwhile, Topas's beloved, Pleindamour, abducted by the wicked Poindextre le Rouge, upon the point of being ravished, cries out: "Glotz! teis! Dex te maldie!" (2362) and skewers him with a kitchen knife with which she had been peeling *poireaux*. From this I deduce that Pleindamour, like Guinevere and Morgan, is not a woman but a fay, and not a fay but the representation of a pre-Christian, Celtic fertility goddess or warrior goddess, the last residue of our life-granting, pre-phallogocentric, matriarchal civilization, which has been interrupted by the death-dealing, sterile, patriarchal hiatus embodied in Homer, Virgil, Chrétien, Dante, Shakespeare, Cervantes, Goethe, Pushkin, and Proust.

I also submit that it is the contrast between Topas, wallowing in manure, his lance broken, and the armed, victorious Pleindamour, magnificently phallic, the Lacanian mother phallus, phallic because she lacks a phallus, a phallus because she isn't a phallus, which caused Chaucer, the canniest of the uncanny, in his androgynous deconstructive wisdom, to enroll her in the ranks of great male heroes.

Up to now, my paper has been all garbage. But the gold? Where is the gold? I have to admit, according to the Akehurst-Pickens edition, the Sargent-Baur glossary, and the E. Paige Wizotzka concordance, not once do the Old French terms for "gold" or any of their cognates appear in the text. Such a consideration might have caused our timorous forebears in philology, with their quaintly old-fashioned academic scruples, second thoughts. However, ours is an age in which mere literature has been superseded by criticism, and mere criticism by theory. Claudel and Proust, Yeats and Joyce, Rilke and Mann, dwarfs, cringe in the shadow of the figé giant of giants, Jacques Derrida. We modern critics, who re-create texts in our image, who use them as examples to buttress our theoretical structures, we, without whom texts would be inconceivable, are immune to such petty,

pedantic considerations. Only under the most extreme circumstances can
we permit mere textual evidence to inhibit our methodological freedom,
our free-floating critical potency.

Fortunately, such is not the problem today. Fortunately, two of my
graduate students, masquerading as adults, discovered at Mount Athos a
manuscript fragment of a fragment of a lyrical insert, on the margin of textuality, a one-line lyric that Pleindamour was humming to herself when
Poindextre le Rouge interrupted her *poireau*-peeling. (The discovery was
marred only by their provisional attribution of the line to a sonnet by
Petrarch.)

> Li jur sunt mult bel li reis gist od pucele AOI   (2336a)

My students are quite right in designating this lyrical-epic masterpiece
as "a *mise en abyme* of all courtly romance." Textually, the trouvère takes two
brief, assonancing ("bel/pucele") half-lines and fuses them as hemistiches
in one long Alexandrine. The textual process reflects, incorporates, and
embodies the physical joining of the King and the Girl. Man weds woman;
male, female; *animus, anima;* monarch, realm; spirit, flesh, in an androgynous fusion and synthesis. Therefore, the "AOI" at the end expresses vocal-
ly, textually procreative joy, the erotic ecstasy that the lower orders experience, or feign to experience, on such occasions. And, if we conceive the
bright light of day ("Li jur sunt mult bel") as symbolic of an alchemical cru-
cible, the wedding of the King and the Girl reflects the fusion of gold and
silver, sulphur and quicksilver, the cosmic masculine and feminine forces
of the universe. In this case, the "AOI" perhaps verbalizes their astonish-
ment upon stumbling on the resultant philosopher's stone *(lapis perennis).*
On still another level, *allegorice* and *Robertsonifer,* the King refers to Our
Lord, *Christus Rex,* and the "pucele" to the Blessed Virgin Mary, *ancilla Dei,*
in which case the "AOI" is a cry of joy, a *converso* acronym for "Alleluia!" or
"Alleluia gaudium!"

In quest of deep structures, I submit that in this lyric *fin' amor* occurs
not at night but in the golden light of day; that the suitor is a king not a
young chevalier; that the suitee is a maiden not an imperious lady; and
that, as my students observe, "it gets right to the point." "Li jur . . ." is not
only a *mise en abyme* for courtly romances; it is a counter-text and a counter-
romance in the style of *pastourelle* and fabliaux, in which the courtly, civilized, feminine code of *fin' amor* is subverted, decentered in favor of a phallic, martial, virile *Weltanschauung.* The "AOI" is borrowed from the Old
French *Rolandslied.* We must imagine a golden King, armed in the harsh

light of the sun (masculine reason, Bachelard's "Le soleil dur du bronz-age") wielding his phallic sword. Perhaps, then, "AOI" is a cry of pain, the pain women endure, according to public repute, when they are first impaled. Is this reading in contradiction to what I have said above? Splendid! It proves the dialogic imagination. Also *mouvance*. ("Mouvance" is a term medievalists employ when they pretend they are different from everyone else. It is otherwise devoid of meaning.) And, as always, sexuality equals textuality, and textuality equals itself.

On the other hand, the notion of a Greco-Hebraic, patriarchal, phal-logocentric Anglo-Norman poet is disturbing on ideological grounds. Therefore, we shall extirpate it.

Questing for all still deeper structures and more dialogic imagination, heteroglossia too, I observe that the first hemistich, concerned with day and having a masculine rhyme ("bel"), contains only five syllables. Admittedly, Anglo-Normans, who hadn't studied in Paris, didn't know how to count syllables. Still! Whereas the hemistich recounting the Girl, the androgynous hemistitch having a feminine rhyme ("pucele"), womanhood at and in the rhyme, contains six syllables, seven with the mute *e*, eight and a half with "AOI"! Note also that the days are beautiful, in the plural, therefore that the action of the King lying with the Girl, expressed in the present tense of the verbs, is continuous and habitual, therefore, uncom-pleted. Is it not possible that the golden King, like his hemistich, fails to measure up, to perform his martial, phallic act? That the act is continual-ly deferred, the Girl decentered, and the King present only in absence? That his lack is hers? Thus the trace of absence reveals the absence of trace, and the very structure of the text *(narratio interrupta)* undermines the event *(raptus flagrans)* and the ideology (patriarchal aggression) it purports to proclaim. Thus the text embodies its own signifying process. It is a metafragment, a metainsertion, a metaline, a metasomething. Further-more, is the Girl only a girl? In this heterodiegetic narrative with actorial not authorial focalization, the *récit* is filtered through the limited, benight-ed consciousness of the King, who thinks the Girl is a girl. And if he mis-reads her? Misprisions her? And if she were a Celtic warrior goddess? And if, at the moment of penetration, she deflowers her ravisher with the sacred sword of Kali? This would explain the loss of syllable in his hemistich. Also the "AOI" would be *his* speech utterance, *his* expression of annoyance yet also of comprehension and maturation upon being disem-boweled, his last and greatest *rite de passage*.

So often in medieval letters the male hero is also an implied author, a singer or maker of texts: the speaker in troubadour songs, Tristan, the

Machaut or Chaucer narrator. And so often the female hero is only an implied reader/listener to male texts—a narratee, singee, speakee. The patriarchally imposed structure, whereby male power and voice censor female power and voice, is deconstructed in *Topas et Pleindamour* where, as we have seen, Topas, his body occulted, narcissistically simpers to himself in his garbage, reduced to being his own narratee, singee, speakee, and thingy. In contrast, prior to disemboweling Poindextre, Pleindamour sings the song of the King and the Maiden then curses her ravisher (in octosyllables). She speaks and she slays, Poindextre reduced to being her reader, the subject of her text, and her text. For, Pleindamour, and perhaps also the Maiden in the song, in place of patriarchal black ink, causes red blood to flow, sacred female menstrual blood or trivial male blood redeemed in its new function. Poindextre *le Rouge* becomes red as his blood is spilled by Pleindamour (red with the charity of the Spirit, that is artistic creation), his useless white flesh redeemed as the parchment on which, *her* knife in *her* fist, she inscribes *her* text.

In conclusion, I wish to emphasize that I have constructed my reading of Sir Thopas and Chaucer not uniquely out of the garbage in *Topos et Pleindamour.* I have grounded it in the garbage of my own critical practice over two decades and a half [now four decades], but above all in the garbage of contemporary theory of literature, called theory (for short), the most seminal ordure of our time, which has had the greatest impact in raising sensory as well as intellectual awareness. In particular, I wish to acknowledge my debt to the three volumes by Yvonne Marysdaughter (formerly Yvette Johnson), author of *Les arcanes de la clitorisation,* followed by *Ecrites: Suite de la clitorisation* and *Aux barricades et aux presses universitaires: La clitorisation engagée.* Marysdaughter succeeded in composing fifteen hundred pages of Hegelian French without once committing a masculine noun or adjective. Actually, the nouns were the hard part; Marysdaughter discovered with amazement and delight that, once they were done, the adjectives all fell into place.

Nᴏᴛᴇs

1. *Topas et Pleindamour, roman du XIIe siècle,* ed. F. R. P. Akehurst and Rupert T. Pickens (Lexington, Ky.: French Forum Photocopy Service, 1981).

ISIDORE OF SEVILLE'S SAINTLY
INTERVENTIONS IN MEDIEVAL COMBAT:
THE *DE INTERVENTIBUS BELLICIS CALAMITOSIS*

James F. Powers

At the outset I should announce that this paper has been read at the Harbinger Hagiography Association, at which time it was awarded that association's Nimbus Prize. The trophy has regrettably short-circuited (at the cost of a badly singed suit), but I still possess the diploma (and the warranty).

The newly discovered hagiographical work which is the subject of this paper is entitled *De interventibus bellicis calamitosis,* a manuscript found at the monastery of San Lorenzo *el Luchadorlimo* (Saint Lawrence the Mudwrestler) in a little-used part of that establishment—its library. San Lorenzo had formerly been the headquarters of a small twelfth-century military order known as San Lorenzo *Levantadorpolvo* (Saint Lawrence the Dustraiser) from the hard-riding style typical of the knights of that minute commandry, but its location on the south flanks of the Cantabrian Mountains increasingly far from the zone of Reconquest combat, along with an unforeseen pluvious climatic change in the region, apparently led to the later name and the curious form of devotional asceticism to which it alludes. The very strict *regula* only allowed a thorough cleaning of the monastery on a tricentennial basis, and the most recent one (delayed a couple of centuries through an unintended bureaucratic mistake) turned up the *De interventibus* manuscript, which had slipped behind a comparatively little used bookshelf filled with manuscripts on the evils of eroticism.[1] It has been written in a late twelfth-century hand in a type of Vandal cursive which has taken some years to transcribe, due in part to the rarity of this strangely surviving script, and also to the excited state of the scribe, who was taking dictation directly from the miraculous apparition that manifested itself in the monk's cell. The numerous spatial gaps in the work were subsequently filled with illustrations at various times in the following century, until the mudwrestling regimen seems to have led to the closing of the scriptorium. The manuscript seems on occasion to have influenced the decorative program of the San Lorenzo monastery as well (figure 1).

Figure 1. Mudwrestler corbel, apse penthouse, San Lorenzo Luchadorlimo. [In actuality, a corbel from the church of Saints Mary and David, Kilpeck, Herefordshire, England, showing an embracing couple. Photograph by James F. Powers.]

De interventibus bellicis calamitosis purports to be a direct dictation from Saint Isidore of Seville, the patron saint of the Pseudo Society, to a monk named Juan el Crédulo (John the Gullible), when he appeared in El Crédulo's room late one evening. Both monk and saint appear to have been in an agitated state, the former due to the obvious paranormal circumstances and the latter due to his dictation of events, which constituted both a failed long-term endeavor and its concurrent agonizing reappraisal, rendered in a kind of hypermanic supernatural state. The apparition appeared at the end of a long day, including an extended visit which El Crédulo had made to the church of Saint Isidore in Leon. The narthex of this church had already been sealed off and converted into a pantheon-mausoleum where the remains of the kings of Leon kept company with the bones of Saint Isidore, whom King Fernando I had interred there a little more than a century before. Its vaults had already acquired their marvelous fresco paintings of the life of Christ and the coming Apocalypse. Possibly El Crédulo had been under the watchful eye of Christ Pantocrator for too long (figure 2) or had seen the excessive slaughtering of innocents and animals that confronts the viewer in those candlelit chambers. His mind keyed to a high spiritual degree, El Crédulo returned to the agitated dust of San Lorenzo's commandry, trying to secure a few post-Compline winks, when the resident spirit of the Leonese church appeared within the aura of a glowing backdrop, that terminated at the saint's hips—the kind of compromise between a nimbus and a mandorla then fashionable in the styles of saintly manifestations.

The tale Saint Isidore had to tell bore tragic connotations, which the monk wrote down as quickly as the saint spoke—an endeavor which required the entire night and the missing of two meals the ensuing day. *De interventibus bellicis calamitosis* was the result. In it, Saint Isidore reveals a grand design, heretofore unsuspected, for the influencing of western history. The saint came by his mission during his lifetime, an interest manifest in his *Historia Gothorum,* a history of the Visigothic peoples and their march to the Iberian Peninsula and their domination of the native Hispano-Romans. Saint Isidore perceived the Visigoths to be an important and valuable force in the history of early medieval Hispania, and he played a vital role in educating them and their kings to their destined task of making Germans dominant in the peninsulas of the western Mediterranean, while absorbing the best the former Roman Empire had to offer. By Isidore's death in 636, the Visigothic kingdom was unified, orthodox Christian, and ostensibly on its way to its wonted historic destiny. Infighting among the Visigothic aristocratic families vying for the crown, together with the untimely arrival of the Muslims in 711, seriously threatened this grand design and led Saint Isidore to his first dramatic appearance on the battlefield. Given the saint's tendency to get things somewhat tangled (his *Etymologiae* was well known in Heaven), the Deity's permission for Isidore's intervention at the battle of the Rio Guadalete came grudgingly, but it nonetheless came.

Figure 2. The Pantocrator's unflinching gaze, *De interventibus bellicis calamitosis*, Biblioteca San Lorenzo Luchardorlimo, MS 69, fol. 3r. [In actuality, the apse fresco from Tahull, Spain, now in the Catalan Museum of Art in Barcelona. Photograph by James F. Powers.]

Aware that the Muslim Berber chieftain Tarik was proceeding with an army from his landing place at Gibraltar, and that King Rodrigo was bringing his Visigothic army south from Toledo, Isidore rightly divined the locale of their meeting south of Seville at the Guadalete River on 19 July. El Crédulo's manuscript here gives us a dramatic reinterpretation of the famous conflict. Historians have traditionally ascribed the defeat of King Rodrigo to the desertion of two Visigothic nobles, Sisbert and Oppa, together with their retinues, during the battle, both magnates being members of the family that Rodrigo had ousted from the throne a year or two earlier. We now know the true story. Saint Isidore originally appeared aglow in sunlike rays before Sisbert's wing of battle, intending to encourage him onward with greater vigor. Sisbert and his men became thoroughly frightened by the apparition and veered off the battlefield to the right. Trying desperately to redirect them, Isidore suddenly reappeared on the opposite side of the field in order to bring Sisbert back on line. Here Oppa and his men observed the apparition, and his wing reacted much as Sisbert's had, but pulling off to the left. At this point Tarik's Berbers fell on King Rodrigo's center, driving it backward. In a last effort to save the king, Isidore inspired Rodrigo to flee and regroup to the north. Blinded by the saint's guiding light,[2] Rodrigo rode straight into a swamp, catapulting off his mount into quicksand, leaving behind only his white horse mired to its knees and his gold saddle encrusted with jewels, which thoroughly mystified the Berbers who found them. *Sic transit gloria mundi.*

Isidore was not pleasant company in Heaven for decades after these events, as he admitted to El Crédulo. The Muslims overran most of Hispania; the Visigothic nobility who survived fled to the northern mountains not far from the monastery where the saint was reciting his tale. The only conflict from which Isidore might have taken solace occurred at Covadonga in 722, but this Christian victory was a mere skirmish and had been achieved by the Asturians under Pelayo, not by the Germans. The battle of Tours in 732 possessed no attraction, having occurred in Gaul. However, later in the century, Isidore again secured permission from the ever-patient Deity to intervene in the course of historic events. In 788 Isidore inspired a group of Muslim dissidents in the city of Zaragoza to invite the still sufficiently Germanic Franks (in Isidore's view, at least) under Charlemagne to invade Spain and to have Zaragoza handed over to them by the dissenters. Isidore then inspired Charlemagne to accept the offer and sat back to enjoy the fireworks.

Again the unforeseen created a crisis. The dissenters having lost control of the situation, the city refused Charlemagne entry. This was particularly embarrassing in that the Frankish king had packed quickly and left his siege equipment back in Aachen. When Charlemagne turned to leave Spain without combat, Isidore suffered a near-fatal attack of chagrin, which only his prior death kept from being terminal. Once more saintly whisperings penetrated royal ears, and Charlemagne found himself marching through Basque country, devastating the huts and cottages that then constituted downtown Pamplona. But the Muslims were now far behind, and the Basques became the stand-in by setting an ambush in the pass above the smoldering embers of Pamplona.

Isidore thus obtained his conflict in the Roncesvalles Pass of the Pyrenees, but as matters worked out, it only involved the rear guard of the Frankish army, commanded by the obscure Prefect of the March against Brittany. The saint intended to have this hapless commander, Roland by name, lure Charlemagne back to Spain for some serious fighting. Isidore thus strove to persuade Roland to blow the signal horn that would bring back the main core of Charlemagne's army for a large-scale conflict. However, Isidore's Latin inspirations appear to have been confused in translation by Roland's Frankish German, and the leader thought he was receiving commands to break his sword on a rock, much to the consternation of his soldiers, to say nothing of Isidore. The end product bore frightful similarity to the Guadalete conflict, leading Isidore to offer the now-famous epigram about Roland having had too many Basques in one exit.

At least the scale of combat had been smaller. Some have argued that Isidore may have fabricated the cover story, known as the *Song of Roland,* which was formulated to put these events in a better light, but in his relation to El Crédulo Saint Isidore disclaimed any such dissimulation, blaming the distortions of the conflict instead on the Capetians (whose millennium historians have recently celebrated) and their nascent propaganda office with its lackey troubadours.

The Roncesvalles ambush seemed to have smothered Saint Isidore's interest in battlefield intervention for a very considerable time after that. Franks could not be trusted to follow saintly inspiration properly, and as time wore on, the Carolingians became so softened by their Gallic habitat that Isidore no longer accepted them as German. Nor did the curious mix of Asturians, Cantabrians, Gallegans, and Basques, leavened by only a few Visigothic leaders, who initiated the Hispanic Reconquest appeal to Isidore as the makers of the Germanic dominance in the Mediterranean peninsulas that the saint had sought to advance. He also had little taste for the cowboy mentality that the Hispanic kings seemed to have developed as the result of their growing frontier experience. Yet temptations abounded.

The Virgin Mary gained considerable earthly fame by her appearance at Covadonga, creating an almost legislative blast of wind to send the Muslim arrows swirling back on the Muslim archers who fired them. Saint Michael made regular appearances, sword in hand, at various geographic promontories in Europe (minimum elevation, two hundred feet). Saint James began to appear over the battlefields of the Reconquest, slaying Moors and occasional slow-footed camp followers,[3] encounters which Isidore had spurned. But another frustration could not be borne. The saint described to El Crédulo the care and patience with which he bided his time. Isidore's interest shifted to Italy, possibly drawn by the twelfth-century *Play of the Antichrist* (recently revived in Chicago), which recounts how the Germans under Frederick Barbarossa won an impressive string of victories. The play also portrays the Germans as becoming victims of false miracles, but this possibly escaped Isidore's notice. He was impressed by the vigor of Barbarossa in his Italian campaigns and was encouraged by the 1160 siege of Carcano, where the Italians had Frederick in a bad way but fumbled away the siege. This, plus the Italian fondness for retreat, seemed to offer a more promising theater of operations for Germanic triumph and consolidation in the Mediterranean. Isidore chose 1176 as the critical year to work his grand design.

The saint first attempted to assure a full levy of Frederick's potential force by encouraging his vassals to complete cooperation, but his holy appearance late at night in Henry the Lion's bedchamber so frightened that powerful German noble that Henry took the apparition as an omen of disaster and refused to permit his Bavarian and Saxon contingents to participate in the campaign. Isidore felt obliged to conclude his recruitment campaign at that point. The saint then inspired Frederick to assemble his forces in Italy around the emperor's base in Pavia. This process included joining Frederick's contingents with those from western Germany that had just crossed the Alps, and then marching the whole back to Pavia. All of this was to be accomplished while trying to swing widely enough around Milan to avoid a conflict until the emperor could gather additional forces located in northeastern Italy. Saintly inspiration and the Italian road map did not mix well, and the route selected proved within reach of Milanese interception. The Milanese and their Lombard allies interposed themselves in the path of Frederick's army at Legnano on 29 May 1176. Here again, Isidore's account taken down by El Crédulo offers us a dramatic reinterpretation of the ensuing conflict.

As the Lombard force marched along the road, the Milanese *carroccio* (the ox-cart bearing town standards) developed a flat tire (not easy for a wooden-wheeled vehicle). Some of the mounted knights were dispatched forward to find a spare, and they ran into an equally surprised advance guard of German knights. The German knights routed the Italian knights, sent them into headlong retreat, and pursued rapidly. Saint Isidore perceived this to be the onset of combat and generated his bright-glowing visible manifestation over the Italians to give Frederick's cavalry a clear target. However, the blinding light caused Frederick's knights to crash headlong into the Italian infantry without previously knowing they were in the path. The Milanese infantry defended the *carroccio* furiously, knowing the ill-mannered individuals one has to contend with on Italian roads.

Meanwhile, the fleeing Italian cavalry encountered the Brescian cavalry coming up the road to reinforce the Milanese after finishing a late breakfast. During the following conversation, both had occasion to notice the bright Isidorian glow up the road and turned to investigate without knowing its source. Riding quickly around the snarled and tangled infantry, the Italian knights collided with the German flank. The result took on the appearance of a Roman piazza in the rush hour. The still-blinded Germans, surrounded by cursing foot and horse (the horses were particularly profane), panicked and retreated down the road toward Como. Emperor Frederick was unhorsed in the conflict, shed his armor, and fled disguised as a pizza vendor among the audience the conflict had caused to gather there.[4] His disguise misled Isidore, who did not recognize him and was not able to render Frederick the same terminal assistance in departing the battlefield that he had given to King Rodrigo of the Visigoths four and a half centuries earlier at the Rio Guadalete. Every dark cloud has a silver lining.

El Crédulo's manuscript becomes somewhat less coherent at this point in the text, Isidore's dictation having descended into a kind of stream-of-consciousness narrative about viewing collapsed policies and moods of deep dejection.[5] The saint mumbled on regarding future plans, among them the hopes he had for enlisting women in this military cause, although he feared their aggressiveness, willingness to fight without armor, and use of unconventional equipment (figure 3). We know there may have also been some efforts directed to giving animals combat training.[6] The experiment seems to have gone astray, leading to the development of curious hybrids of sheep which drastically cut the monastery's wool production in favor of feathers (figure 4). Moreover, the local Asturian chain of monastic refectories serving fried chicken to pilgrims suffered economic reversals from which it never fully recovered. San Lorenzo's decorative program, for a time inspired by El Crédulo's remembrances of Isidore's visitation, soon disintegrated into utilizing more earthbound iconographic subjects (figure 5).

Figure 3. Women in combat, *De interventibus bellicis calamitosis,* Biblioteca San Lorenzo Luchardorlimo, MS 69, fol. 9v. [In actuality, an illustration showing female warriors from a Prudentius *Psychomachia,* in Paris, Bibliothèque nationale de France, MS lat. 8318, fol. 53r. Reproduced by permission.]

Figure 4. A Rhode Island Red Merino sheep, from *De interventibus bellicis calamitosis,* Biblioteca San Lorenzo Luchardorlimo, MS 69, fol. 11r. [In actuality, an illustration from the Luttrell Psalter showing a sheep with a chicken's head, in London, British Library, MS Add. 42130, fol. 240v. Reproduced by permission.]

Figure 5. Two rainspouts from the crossing tower of the church of San Lorenzo Luchadorlimo. [In actuality, two corbels from the parish church at Cervados, in Palencia province, Spain. Photograph by James F. Powers.]

De interventibus bellicis calmitosis thus offers us significant insights into a serious saintly effort both to formulate and to put into action a historic policy of great potential impact on European history, as well as a detailed explanation of the combat engagements that were the result of that endeavor. Saint Isidore does not seem to have attempted any further interventions into history in general or military engagements in particular. However, some have thought that Isidore did attempt to pursue his old goals in a new way, which may serve to explain why a saintly glow reputedly appears in the sky over Germans' automobiles which ply the *autopistas* and *autostradas* of the Mediterranean in more recent times—a glow that is commonly visible only over roadside wrecks. In this more constrained manner,[7] Saint Isidore thus seeks to advance even in our own day the cause of German culture and leadership in the peninsulas in which he lavished so much effort during the centuries of the medieval period.

NOTES

1. The rediscovered manuscript was put on permanent reserve and consequently lost.

2. Illustrated in *De interventibus bellicis calamitosis* (Biblioteca San Lorenzo Luchadorlimo, MS 69, fol. 5v). This entire folio was given over to El Crédulo's depiction of the Isidorian manifestation. To the naked eye, however, the folio appears to be completely blank. Some scholars who have seen the manuscript have argued that the illustration is borrowed from the contemporary manuscript of Saint Suiciosdedos, *The Proof of God Illustrated,* from the same scriptorium.

3. Not reproduced here is an illustration in which Numor Montazuma Gonzalez deals with his Moorish adversaries, aided by his Christian mascot Phydeux, while Santiago looks on approvingly, from an altar panel at San Lorenzo Luchadorlimo. [In actuality, a sandstone relief of Prince Arikankharer slaying his enemies, Worcester Art Museum, 1922.145.]

4. Not reproduced here is an illustration showing how, to rescue the situation, Frederick apparently attempted a radical new approach to mounted lance combat by riding upside down, from *De interventibus bellicis calamitosis* (Biblioteca San Lorenzo Luchadorlimo, MS 69, fol. 7r). The same subject appears in a fresco in the abbot's lavatory at San Lorenzo. [In actuality, a mural from Claverly parish church, England, showing a confrontation of mounted knights, one apparently unhorsed.]

5. Not reproduced here is an illustration in which Saint Isidore views the collapse of his policies, from *De interventibus bellicis calamitosis* (Biblioteca San Lorenzo Luchadorlimo, MS 69, fol. 8r). [In actuality, an illustration showing Lot's wife turned to salt while Sodom collapses, from the Shah Abbas Bible, in New York, Pierpont Morgan Library, MS 638, fol. 4r.]

6. Not reproduced here is an illustration showing hares with catapult and bows beseiging a castle, from *De interventibus bellicis calamitosis* (Biblioteca San Lorenzo Luchadorlimo, MS 69, fol. 5v). [In actuality, a marginalium from the Metz Pontifical, in Cambridge, England, Fitzwilliam Museum, MS 298, fol. 4r.]

7. Not reproduced here is the author's photograph of Saint Isidore's modern handiwork: a wrecked German automobile, smashed with the assistance of an unsympathetic Italian driver.

JOINVILLE'S SECRET HISTORY

Charles T. Wood

Of all the medieval kings of France, Louis IX—Saint Louis—is undoubtedly the most revered. Even to his English contemporary Matthew Paris he was "the king of mortal kings," while others were quick to dub him "Brother Louis," "Louis the Just," or simply "le bon roi Saint Louis." Why, then, did it take so long to have his sanctity formally recognized, and why, in the end, was the process so difficult? Louis died a crusader in 1270, after all, but in spite of an intense French campaign aimed at his immediate canonization, the papal proclamation came only in 1297. Indeed, insofar as Boniface VIII appears to have acted less in response to the merits of Louis's case than to the brutal attacks to which he was then being subjected by Philip the Fair, Louis's grandson, one can surely argue that a voluntary papal declaration of Louis's sanctity might never have been forthcoming.

For years now, I have asked myself why this should have been the case. After all, Louis's extreme piety and its implications were widely assumed even in his own lifetime. Consider, in proof, the familiar story from Joinville's *Life of Saint Louis* of an incident that occurred on Louis's first crusade, ca. 1250 or 1251:

> Journeying day by day we came to the sands of Acre, where the king and the host encamped. At that place a great troop of people from Great Armenia, who were going on pilgrimage to Jerusalem, having paid a great tribute to the Saracens, by whom they were being conducted, came to me. Through an interpreter, who knew their language and ours, they besought me to show them the sainted king. I went in to the king, who was sitting in a tent, leaning against its lodgepole, and he was sitting on the sand, without a carpet or anything else under him. I said to him: "Sire,

outside there is a great troop of people from Great Armenia, going to Jerusalem, and they pray me, sire, to cause the sainted king to be shown to them. But I have no desire as yet to kiss your bones." He laughed aloud, and told me to go and fetch them, and so I did.

Other stories could just as easily be cited, but this one strikes me as the most compelling. That is, if a group of pilgrims as geographically removed from the scene as these Armenians assumed that Louis was a saint twenty years before his death, even a Church that was increasingly slow in its bureaucracy should have found it possible to move more rapidly—and under much less pressure—than, in fact, it did.

There is, however, an explanation, though to get to it I shall first have to insert a brief aside. As many of you know, in 1973, just as Watergate was getting under way, I published a modest contribution to the debate called "Magna Carta: Seventh Crisis of John Plantagenet." At some point soon thereafter, I sent a copy to C. Warren Hollister, thinking that he, too, might have something to say. Professor Hollister responded on 9 April 1974, pointing out that John wasn't really his field. He added, though, that he was becoming increasingly troubled by the way in which Henry II's dying words—usually rendered as "Shame, shame on a conquered king"—have been translated. What Henry had spoken in Old French, chroniclers had recorded only in Latin, so, as Hollister put it: "Making careful allowance for the double translation problem, I have concluded that what he actually said was, 'You won't have old Henry Plantagenet to kick around anymore.'"

Now, all of this would be irrelevant to the present paper except for the fact that Professor Hollister then went on to add:

More directly in your own field, I recently blundered on a quite exciting discovery—a hitherto unknown poem in Old French about the life of Saint Louis, which I have ascribed tentatively to Joinville. I hope to have a complete translation soon. The opening lines run as follows:

Though you've come a long way, old Saint Louis,
And brought your barons to heel,
I credit another, your shrew of a mother,
That smothering Blanche of Castile.

As you can well imagine, excited as I was by Hollister's discovery, I remained unpersuaded by his tentative attribution. Although Blanche is far from being admired in Joinville's *Life of Saint Louis,* the opprobrium here so starkly expressed seemed a trifle excessive, even granting the seneschal's blunt disposition. More disturbing, perhaps, was the fact that everything in the *Life* suggests an author who, though often baffled by the outlook of his biographee, nevertheless remained in awe of his accomplishments, not their doubter, as in the poem. Most telling of all, though— or so I thought at the time—none of Joinville's previously known works exactly prepares its readers for the idea of "Joinville the poet." After all, any man who prefers to commit thirty mortal sins to becoming a leper would appear to lack the poetic outlook.

Still, strong as the anti-Hollister position once appeared to be, I find myself in the embarrassing position of having to confess I was wrong. In 1987 I was in France, and since I had recently put the finishing touches on a book devoted at least partially to Joan of Arc, I thought it would be fun to pursue her career, starting at Domremy and ending at Rouen. Because, however, Joan's own triumphal journey to Reims had taken her close to Joinville itself, I decided to make a brief detour to see what there remained. The castle of the sires de Joinville is long gone, of course—a victim of Revolutionary and Napoleonic fervor—but I found that in the attic of the small *musée municipale* there remained a few forgotten and uncatalogued odds and ends—all that had survived the Jacobin sack of 1793. And among those fragments there was a book—a small register, really—that seemed on first viewing to be a condensed manuscript version of *The Life of Saint Louis*. Its principal interest, one that I recognized immediately from previous work on Joinville manuscripts at the Archives nationales, was that it was unquestionably in Joinville's own hand. Perhaps needless to say, that led me to inspect it more closely. That's how I came to discover that it was not *The Life of Saint Louis*, at least not as we know it now. Rather, it was what I have here called Joinville's Secret History, and it ends, still in his own hand, with the poem that Professor Hollister discovered long years ago.

* * *

The difference starts with the History's opening pages. For example, the *Life* begins with a dedication to Louis X and a report that that king's mother had asked Joinville "to have a book written of the holy sayings and good deeds of our king Saint Louis." The author then goes on to say: "What I have written besides this, I have written to do additional honor to that true saint, for it is through them that a man can best see that from the beginning of his reign to the end of his life no layman of our time spent his whole life in so saintly a manner."[1]

The Secret History on the other hand, while often similar in its phrasing, betrays a different emphasis. Its dedication is to Philip III and reports that *his* mother, Louis's wife, had been the one to ask for a book about her late husband's good deeds and holy sayings—evidence needed for the canonization campaign. The text then continues: "What I have written, however, I have written to tell the truth about that man whom some would honor as a true saint; for it is only in this way that we can begin to see that from the beginning of his reign to the end of his life no layman of our time spent his whole life in so foolhardy a manner."

Now, contrary though such a position may have been to Marguerite of Provence's seeming wishes, I doubt that it would have either surprised or displeased Philip III. For everything suggests that while Louis IX loved and favored his eldest son, also named Louis, after that son's premature death he showed much less confidence in the abilities of his new heir, Philip. In *The Life of Saint Louis,* for example, a crucial passage reads as follows: "The great love that [the king] had for his people was shown by what he said, when he lay very sick at Fontainebleau, to his eldest son, my lord Louis. 'Dear son,' he said, 'I pray you to win the love of the people of your kingdom. In truth, I would rather that a Scotsman came from Scotland and governed them, so long as his rule was good and fair, than that you should be seen by the world to govern it ill.'"

In the Secret History, however, the corresponding passage reads: "When the king lay very sick before Tunis, he said to his son Philip: 'Son, because you are incapable of winning the love of the people of your kingdom, I pray that a Scotsman will come from Scotland to govern them fairly and well, which is better by far than having you govern it ill.'"

Still, however harsh Louis's judgment of Philip, in large measure it accords well with what we know of the latter's reign, and the same point could be made about much of the other new evidence to be found in the Secret History. What we have in it is not so much a Louis who is factually very different from the one to be found in the *Life;* rather, what emerges is a fuller and more honest admission on Joinville's part of the extent to which he resented—indeed, passionately disliked—the ways Louis found to pick on him and hold him up to ridicule. As Joinville freely admits in the *Life,* Louis "did all that lay within his power, whenever he spoke to me, to instil in me a firm faith in the Christian religion which God has given us." On the other hand, the Secret History reveals explicitly just how humiliated Joinville often felt as a result of Louis's constant attentions:

> When the king took the Cross for the second time, much was I pressed to join him, but I, who could never tell him a lie, firmly replied: "Sire, great-

ly though I long for the liberation of the holy places, sick unto death am I of your pestering questions. When I confess that I never wash the feet of the poor on Maundy Thursday, much less my own, you respond in the presence of others with demeaning homilies about my need to do so. When I admit that I'd prefer to commit thirty mortal sins than to be a leper, you laugh up your sleeve with your Mendicant friends, all the while professing that you admire the subtlety of my mind. And when you ask me whether I want to be respected in this world and enjoy Paradise after my death, instead of accepting my answer, you insist that the best way to attain these goals is by imitating the pompous pretensions of your wind-bag friend, Robert de Sorbon. When Bishop Peter of Châlons excommu-nicated me, you refused to give me justice in your court, all the while pre-tending that your inaction was designed to chastise the bishop, whereas it was I, not he, who was the excommunicate. I stay home, then, not to defend my lands against the depredations of your officials and not to express a silent opposition to crusades, but only, sire, to gain freedom from your constant campaigns aimed at my moral improvement."

Given the extent of this angry resentment, it seems scarcely surprising to find that Joinville's initial assessment of Louis's supposed virtues was not as high as he later made it appear. He did not doubt Louis's admiration of all the qualities—wisdom, prudence, and courage, and so forth—that were summed up in the term *preudome,* and even in the Secret History he reports Louis's admission that "I would dearly love to have the name of being a *preudome,* so long as I deserved it, . . . for a *preudome* is so grand and good a thing that even to pronounce the word fills the mouth pleasantly." On the other hand, he then uses that remark to point up the extent to which, in his judgment at least, Louis was far from deserving that title:

I do not understand [Joinville laments] how any sensible military com-mander could land his troops on the Nile delta two weeks before the annual flood. And what a landing it was! When we arrived off Damietta, all his council advised him to stay in his ship until he saw how his knights had fared in *their* landing. After all, if he were to land with them and was to be killed, the whole enterprise would be lost. But he would have none of it. Instead—and having no idea how deep the water was—he was the first to leap overboard: in full armor, his shield round his neck, and spear in hand. He sank like a rock, of course, but luckily the water was shallow enough that he was able to make it to shore.

Similarly, if Louis's military impetuosity here seemed in Joinville's mind to betray a certain lack of prudence, you can imagine even without a direct quotation just how Joinville reacted when he learned that Louis, after being freed from Egyptian captivity, had insisted that these infidels actually be paid the additional ten thousand pounds that they were owed—but that the king's financial advisers had craftily held back through the simple expedient of double counting when they were paying the ransom. Joinville claims in the *Life* that his horror of bad language was fully as great as Louis's, but that assertion would be difficult to sustain on the basis of *that* passage from the Secret History. Even Godefroy's *Dictionnaire de l'ancienne langue française* failed me in trying to translate it, though the general drift was pungently clear.

That fact suggests, surely, that Joinville may have been unusually sensitive to matters of finance, and other parts of the Secret History confirm this hypothesis. Consider, for example, the following tale of what happened on Cyprus even before the crusade made it to Egypt:

> While we were waiting at Cyprus, the empress of Constantinople sent me a message that she had landed at Paphos. The purpose of the empress's visit was to ask the king's help for her husband, who had stayed at Constantinople; and she did her work so well that she took back with her more than a hundred letters in duplicate from me and from other friends—letters in which we were bound by oath, should the king after his return from overseas, decide to send three hundred knights to Constantinople, to fulfil our undertaking and make the journey.
>
> In fulfillment of my oath, when we were actually leaving on our way home, I told the king in the presence of the count of Eu, whose letter I have, that if he wished to send the three hundred knights, I was ready to keep my word and go. As usual, though, the king answered that he had not the means to do so, for his hopeless mismanagement of financial affairs had left his treasury what he called "ill supplied." Indeed, he confessed that he had drained it to the dregs.

As for where the money went, Joinville can only marvel incredulously:

> The king was so generous in almsgiving that wherever he went he gave gifts to poor churches, to lazar houses, almshouses, and hospitals, to poor gentlemen and gentlewomen or, in short, to every outstretched hand that came his way. Every day he fed a crowd of the poor, added more gifts to girls, to fallen women, to poor widows and women in childbed, and not content with that, he went on to build churches, many religious houses (among them Royaumont), and several hospitals, all of which, perhaps needless to say, he endowed richly.
>
> Some of his household naturally grumbled at his giving such generous alms and spending so much on them, but he answered blindly: "I would rather my extravagance should be in almsgiving than in the pomp and vainglory of this world." And to think that this is a man who dearly

wanted the name of being a *preudome*—this king so profligate with his money that he lacked the wherewithal even to clothe himself decently, let alone as a king ought to do! Small wonder, then, that he should have been forced to give justice out under a tree at the forest of Vincennes—he had no money left with which to do otherwise.

Doubtless such judgments seem harsh, especially for a modern historian who knows much better than the protagonists themselves just how difficult the medieval politics of scarcity could be. At the same time the Secret History forces us to recognize that Joinville's wrath arises not so much out of his outrage over the reckless expenditure of funds within a society that had few resources, but more out of the plainspoken seneschal's recognition that Louis's own practices were often far different from what he preached to others. Here, for example, was a man who could drain his treasury to the dregs, but who could also turn a blind eye to his own deficiencies when preaching to his children:

> Before going to bed, he used to have his children brought to him and tell them stories of good kings and good emperors, telling them that they should take such men as examples. He told them stories, too, of wicked men of high estate who, through their reckless prodigality, had lost their kingdoms. "I remind you of these kings," he said, "so that you may be careful to avoid their example and not to incur the anger of God," but in so saying [adds Joinville] never once did he think to himself about the extent to which his own prodigality threatened an equal doom.

More could be added, of course, since the Secret History is very rich, but I suspect that the passages already cited should be sufficient for you to grasp the significance of this hitherto-unknown manuscript. Besides, the rest follows almost ineluctably from what I've reported: for example, Joinville's horror over Louis's Treaty of Paris with England, his outrage over the eagerness with which Louis's field administration was prepared to accept bribes, or the extent to which no sensible policy decisions could be reached in a world where, in Joinville's phrase, "the king surrounded the city of Paris with men of religion" and where mendicants—the Secret History, like the *Life,* mentions the Brothers of Carmel, those of the Sack, and the Order of the White Mantles in addition to swarms of the more familiar Augustinians, Dominicans, and Franciscans—where such men, to repeat, not only impoverished the crown but led Louis down paths that were, in Joinville's view, far from those of practical kingship. As the Secret History puts the case in one of its more temperate passages:

Because the king loved all who wore the religious habit, none such as came to see him (as, God knows, they all did) failed to find what he needed for his support. It always started with little things—vestments, chalices, and the like—but it was sure then to go on to houses, farms, a nice little place on the Seine near Charenton, a townhouse with some outbuildings round it near the old Temple Gate, and who knows what else?, seemingly world without end. As for Louis's judgment in these matters, the only thing I need to point out is that the Brothers of the Sack were soon suppressed, just as, after Louis's death, the White Mantles were likewise suppressed at the Council of Lyons, held by Gregory X. All *I* can say is that if Louis always went too far, like most popes, Gregory X didn't go far enough.

I could go on, but unlike Gregory X, I think I have gone quite far enough, at least for the purposes of this paper. It's clear, I think, that if the French failed to get Louis canonized in the 1270s, the chief reason was Joinville's Secret History, a tract clearly written at that time and an impediment that it was going to take Philip the Fair's strong-arm tactics against Boniface VIII to overcome. For if Joinville had "no desire as yet to kiss [Louis's] bones," it was not to be expected that a pope as distrustful of mendicants as Boniface was—and especially of those Franciscans whom Louis so dearly loved—would have wanted to kiss them either.

That observation made, it leads to one last point, just why the Joinville of *The Life of Saint Louis* should have been so much more respectful of his late sovereign than was the one who wrote the Secret History. I have no definitive answer and doubt that one will ever be forthcoming, but some points seem clear. The *Life* as we have it is dated 1309, at which point Louis had been dead for forty years; his Egyptian crusade lay sixty years in the past; and Joinville himself was well past eighty, indeed nearing ninety. Moreover, whether he had initially approved of it or not, Louis was now officially a saint. Given these facts, it seems to be not improbable that Joinville experienced that change of heart so typical of war veterans in their golden years—one that we can see even today as elderly veterans of Montgomery's Eighth Army meet amicably and annually with their counterparts from Rommel's Afrika Korps; indeed there may still be a few Anciens Combattants de Verdun yet alive and prepared to swap stories with Falkenheyn's men whom, in 1916, they would not let pass. Joinville, I submit, was that kind of man, and his Secret History should stand, therefore, not just as evidence of Saint Louis's *worldly* shortcomings, but more as a monument to the enduring truth that time is indeed the healer of all things, even of passions engendered by wars and their leaders.

Notes

1. This and subsequent quotations are from John of Joinville, *The Life of St. Louis,* trans. and ed. René Hague (New York, 1955), unless taken explicitly from the unpaginated manuscript of Joinville's Secret History, in which case the translations are at least partly my own.

BOETHIUS ON KING ARTHUR:
A NEWLY DISCOVERED TEXT

Maureen Fries†

The opera of Anicius Manlius Severinus Boethius have long been thought complete. Besides his translations of and commentaries on logical works and the *quadrivium,* and his treatises on theology, his fame in the Middle Ages and since has rested largely in his ultimate work, the *Philosophiae consolatio.* Now a fortuitous circumstance has allowed me to discover, and to reveal tonight for the first time to an audience, the existence of a previously unknown work of Boethius, to which I have given the title *Artorii consolatio,* since its central figure is the hitherto only conjecturally historical King Arthur.

The finding of this Boethian manuscript on Arthur, or Artorius as the philosopher calls him, was in itself an extraordinary circumstance. I had been spending the summer at the British Library, working in the Manuscript Room. One muggy July day, unusually warm for London, I had just returned from my usual lunch at the Museum Tavern—shepherd's pie washed down by a pint of the best bitter. At my usual desk I found, among the material on which I had been working, an ancient-looking and tattered manuscript tied up with a piece of dusty twine. Since I had not ordered anything new and the strange bundle had no identifying marks of any kind, my first impulse was to send it back. But curiosity and a working lifetime's accumulation of scholarly interest prompted me to take a quick look at the manuscript before I did so. That look turned into days of fascinated (and somewhat furtive, since I had not made a formal request for it) perusal of a text I soon recognized as the product of Boethius, both from internal and external evidence—to which I shall turn after a brief description of the contents of the book. (All translations from the Latin original which follow are my own.)

As in his much longer and better-known treatise on the consolation of philosophy, Boethius here assumes a persona. But this time it is not a representation of the historical author in the text but of Artorius, who so names himself early in the manuscript. The king speaks from Avalon ("insula malorum" or "insula pomorum," as Boethius variously styles it—interestingly not the curious *insula avallonis* of Geoffrey of Monmouth's later coinage). Wounded *letaliter,* as he tells us, he has been borne to this fortunate island by an unknown agency. In some detail he describes the charm of his surroundings: only soft winds blow; no rain, hail, or snow ever fall; and the sun shines softly in a perpetual spring. Grain and vines replenish themselves without any tending, and the ageless inhabitants cohabit in peace and plenty.

But in the midst of this paradise Arthur chafes, not only at his grievous wound, but at the loss of his mundane glory as the mighty leader of a fearless male fellowship and the ruler of a powerful kingdom. Bemoaning his former possessions, he is comforted at his bedside by his former advisor, whom Boethius calls "Myrddinus"—a use of a transliterated Welsh form which was replaced later in Arthurian tradition by "Merlinus" because of its unfortunate possible association of Celtic influence upon Boethius's text (an influence to which I shall later return). Myrddinus tells Artorius not to fret, but to relax and enjoy the pleasures of Avalon—indeed, he himself is a little distracted from the woes of his former pupil by the attentions of a lovely and nubile fairy woman who caresses him ceaselessly.

Suddenly there appears before them a quite different lady, a female who greets Artorius by name as if she knows him. Her appearance is mystifying. At one moment she seems the comeliest of women, the fairest of skin and of body Arthur has ever seen—more beautiful than Guinevere (whom the king mentions here for the only time in the work)—with a pink and white complexion and provocatively full breasts. But at the next moment she seems the oldest and ugliest crone he has ever encountered, her cheeks rough and wrinkled, her chins triple and speckled with black hair, her body short and thick with broad buttocks. Her clothing, too, changes with her appearance. As the young and lovely woman she wears the ancient Roman bride's dress, with its *tunica recta* and its *cingulum herculeum,* its vestal-inspired tresses with their crimson net topped by the *flammeum,* its wreath of myrtle and orange blossoms. But as the crone she exhibits the universal and all-enveloping nutgall-black cloak, or *palla,* of death. In both guises, she carries a crystal globe in her left hand and a *virga ligni* in her right.

Seeing Myrddinus, the wonderful woman stamps her foot. "Who let in this bastard?" she cries. (Here, and in the rest of this passage, Boethius follows the nice classical distinction between two words for "illegitimate," choosing *spurius,* or "son of an unknown father," to describe Merlin, while reserving *nothus,* or "son of a known father by a concubine," for Arthur.)

"Who let in this *malum medicum,* this interloper in Avalon?" she cries again. "He cannot offer any hope for what ails you, Artorius."

Turning directly to Myrddinus, she continues: "Did thou not work all sorts of evil on him heretofore? Was it not through thy machinations, *intraplipem,* that he was born *nothus* of Uther? Did thou not guide him from a young age to form an exclusively male fellowship *(consociatus maris)* to which women were not considered fit to aspire *(non sociabilis)? O homuncio!* Did thou not encourage him to become a man of war rather than of peace? Did thou not abandon him to his enemies when he could have most used thy aid? Thou hast led this man to a wrong way of life from which I must rescue him. Now begone, o male chauvinist pig!" (I trust I may be forgiven this modern idiomatic phrase as a translation for Boethius's "acerbissimo procinoque marum.")

To this angry speech the *senex* Myrddinus replies only, "Virago!" as he sinks away with his *prostibulum* into the mists of Avalon.

Artorius lies astounded in his bed as the lady turns to him once again. "Alas, brother, how your mind is wounded as well as your body. Do you not know me? Although you were once powerful and proud in a society operating from man to man *(viritim),* it was I—a woman—who bore you here to Avalon for healing. Pray, do you really not recognize me? Please try—it will help bring you to the cure which is necessary."

Arthur tells us that, in a sudden flash of recognition, he perceives the identity of his interlocutor. "O sister Morgana," he cries, as she takes his hand and squeezes it, "Rightly called *fata!* What do you here in this strange although beautiful place? Are you a prisoner here, as I seem to be?"

Morgana laughs. "No, brother, and this is not a prison but a place to discover true freedom. I have borne you here on my boat to be healed not only of your physical wounds but of your spiritual faults as well:

> That man can only fall
> Who has men by his side,
> But that man can conquer all
> Who has woman as his guide.

What, do you not understand me, Artorius? Speak, then, to me of your problems, so that I can help you to overcome them."

"Most of what I will tell you," Arthur replies, "you already know. But I can see you think that recounting my misfortunes is necessary for my healing. As you are aware, I spent my youth under Myrddinus's tutelage, learning to be a great ruler."

"Myrddinus!" Morgana interrupts angrily. "Do not speak of that wretched mountebank *(pharmacopolam circumforaneum)*. His teaching helped to precipitate your misfortunes."

"But I must give you a true account of my deeds," Arthur answers, "and Myrddinus is part of it." As Morgana nods sulkily, he goes on. "I came to the high kingship of the Britons, as you know, in the aftermath of the Roman departure from the land. As a Roman citizen and a British aristocrat, I commanded the allegiance first of a chosen few and then of many who were tired of the anarchy and bloodshed around them. With skillful strategy and force of arms, I conquered those who threatened the establishment of a British nation, the Saxons first and then my domestic enemies. Attracting to my side the most famous warriors of western Europe, I formed them into a mighty striking force. At last we were ready to take on Rome itself. But on leaving for the Continent, I made the mistake of leaving Britain in charge of my nephew Modred—who, as you know, most feloniously seized it in my absence. Upon hearing this news I had to return, from the very brink of victory. In my encounter with Modred and my other enemies, whom he had rallied around him, Fortune was against me. Although I killed him, I was myself wounded mortally and—as I now remember—you yourself bore me here to Avalon. Since I awoke in this beautiful but strangely inactive land, I have been tormented by the thought of the loss of my men and my kingdom. This in brief is my story."

Morgana looks on Arthur in a friendly but unmoved fashion. Then she says: "I knew when I brought you here that you would feel yourself an exile from men and affairs; but you yourself and not the things you have lost are responsible for that feeling. You are ignorant of the true wellspring of human affairs when you blame the goddess Fortune for your fate. Instead it is that monster Merlin *(monstrum hominis Myrddinus)* who has caused you to be cast down. Let me remind you of his nature and habits. He pretends to aid men but then leaves them desolate, for it is his nature to be changeable and to turn his seeming favorites from the top to the bottom of his wheel. Let me show you his methods."

With a wave of her *virga ligni*, Morgana conjures up a vision of Myrddinus. He wears a pointed hat and a long, dark, wide-hemmed gown embroidered all over with astronomical symbols, and he is turning a wheel all bedecked with precious jewels and gold, upon which ride the figures of eight kings. "Now listen to what this wicked rogue *(scelus)* has to say," she goes on.

Then the magician speaks: "When you emerged naked from the womb of Ygerna, whence you had been conceived by the agency of Uther, I took you and arranged for your nurture and education into kingship. Favoring you, I endowed you with all the goods you desired. Now you have lost those goods, as do all who trust in this wheel. Behold, look on eight others who, along with you, Artorius, will become known in future time as the Nine Worthies. Here are Hector, Alexander, and Julius Caesar; here, Joshua, David, and Judas Maccabee, all of whom preceded you. And here are Charles the Great and Godfrey of Bouillon, who will follow you (as I have divined from my magic arts). All of these either have fallen, like you, or will fall."

Laughing, Myrddinus gives his wheel a spin, as the figures of the kings try desperately to cling to their perches, and Arthur views in alarm his own empty chair spinning by. Then, with a wave of Morgana's wand, Myrddinus and his wheel are gone.

Shaken, Artorius asks Morgana how he can be saved from the grievous effects of Merlin's wheel.

"You must understand," she replies, "that, in terms of true happiness, all of your previous values and actions have only been monster producing *(monstrifera)*. Among the false goods you have pursued are arms, worldly glory, power, and particularly the neglect of, or even oppression of, female values. What you thought was good proved to be only transitory and even harmful to your character. When I appeared to you at the beginning of our encounter, my ugly figure was an emblem of what your male dominance had been, and my beautiful guise of what your attitude should have been. True happiness does not consist in the achievement of masculine pursuits, which are incapable of producing any real satisfaction, but in surrendering yourself to the will of the supreme good. This resides only in the Mother Goddess herself, and is negated by the idolatrous goals you previously set for yourself.

> The Mother is the end
> Toward which all things tend
> As lover and as nurse
> She unites the universe."

But Arthur wonders, if the Mother is all good, why there is apparent success for evil in the world, as in the case of Modred's treachery. "Evil,"

Morgana says, "is triumphant only under the false cover of the male perception of things. Those who avoid such error and follow the female principle are rewarded by her presence in their goodness, while those who per-
sist in male dominance only seem successful on the sublunary plane—in
the eyes of her Eternity they are known for what they truly are. Even in
earthly terms, the success of the masculine way is transitory: witness the
kings who seemed to fall from Merlin's wheel. You do not see, you will not
see, any women riding that wheel, nor any man who has given his cruder
self over to the feminine. Indeed, your own recent fall from that empty seat
you saw can even be good if it allows you to see the difference between the
seemingly and the really valuable."

But Arthur objects that men must be men, and women, women, and
that he cannot see how the masculine can be compatible with a divine
principle which is female.

"All human action is relative," Morgana replies, "and men more free
when they engage in the contemplation of the eternal feminine, less free
when they are joined by male bonds as in your former fellowship, and still
less free when they are bound by masculine ideas of what is right. They are
in utter slavery when they lose their putative consciousness of the feminine
and give themselves wholly to such masculine pursuits as war and domination over others. The Mother, nevertheless, who beholds all things from
eternity, foresees and disposes even of masculine mistakes according to
their merits."

Here Artorius further objects: "But if the Mother foresees what is to
come of masculine-inspired acts, then how can men be said to choose
freely as you have implied?"

"O brother!" Morgana cries, "Your process of male reasoning cannot
comprehend fully the mystery of divine femininity. To understand this,
realize that the higher power of knowing includes the lower, but the lower
can in no way rise to the higher. To grasp this truth, your masculine reason
must not look down to merely virile things, but upward, to the sublime
femaleness. The Mother alone is perfect, the whole and simultaneous pos-
sessor of all life; she is in full possession of herself, always present to herself, and holds the infinity of time before herself. But her eternal present
means that her knowledge transcends all movement in time; her vision
does not change the possibility for male-inspired error in the world, it simply sees it for what it is in the eyes of the feminine. This is the difference
between female and male necessity. The Mother anticipates but does not
cause every future action, although she does convert it to her own present
knowledge. Such divine female power constitutes the true measure of all

things. Yet all your actions, even your mistaken ones, have been committed in the sight of a judge who, in her wisdom and power, is capable of forgiving all."

And Morgana matches her actions to her final words by sweeping Arthur from his couch and crushing him lovingly to her copious breasts, as *The Consolation of Arthur* ends.

That the *Artorii consolatio* is the product of Boethius is unquestionable. Its philosophical pattern of the achievement of knowledge in the gradual movement from ignorance to wisdom by a human male figure under the guidance of a supernatural female one is recognizable from the same author's previously known *Philosophiae consolatio*. Its subject, the inquiry into human happiness and the possibility of achieving it in the midst of earthly confusion, is also similar. What I have only occasionally indicated in the summary above is that the two works are also structured in alternating passages of *prosae* and *metra,* which I hope to approximate in the *en face* English translation to accompany the work in my planned edition. Even more revealing are the echoes and sometimes actually identical phrasings between the one work and the other. Both also present, inter alia, a human necessity. To readers well acquainted with Boethius, there is no doubt that we are hearing, here, his own unmistakable voice.

Important as my discovery is to philosophers, however, it is even more significant for students of Arthurian literature. Any of the latter in my audience will already have noticed striking similarities between the *Artorii consolatio* and certain subsequent and famous Arthurian works. To name just a few examples, the description of Avalon and the figure of Merlin later emerge in much the same manner in the works of Geoffrey of Monmouth; the doubled figure of Morgana in various French verse and prose romances and in the Middle English *Sir Gawain and the Green Knight;* the wheel of falling kings in the *Alliterative Morte Arthure* and elsewhere. We can now conjecture that later medieval authors knew the matter of the *Artorii consolatio* or some subsequent version of its contents—perhaps it was even ancestor of the famous "Welsh book" Geoffrey cites as the source for what has heretofore (and, it turns out, mistakenly) been assumed to be his original contribution to Arthurian legend.

How Boethius himself became familiar with the Welsh Arthur and his history is more difficult to determine. Early allusions in the Welsh poetry cycle *The Gododdin* (composed around 500, and so contemporary with Boethius) indicate an available source, but they are fragmentary and do not present the more complete story Boethius has. Tales of Arthur's prowess have long been supposed to have traveled from Wales to

Brittany—and from northern France the legend seems to have made its way to Rome, perhaps through the agency of itinerant traders or story-tellers proper. The finding of this manuscript, in any case, represents one more link in search for a historical Arthur, now almost certainly a real person born in the late fifth century, and probably dying in the early sixth, perhaps (given the similarities with the *Philosophiae consolatio*) shortly before Boethius himself.

Time does not permit the consideration of other ramifications of this important find: for instance, how would Boethius's feminism as it emerges here have affected the course of medieval misogyny had it been known? Such topics will probably have to be postponed until I find a publisher for my proposed edition of the *Artorii consolatio*. For all those who have long deplored the sloppy system for distributing materials in the British Library, at least this discovery shows that it can, on occasion, yield forgotten riches to the reader of discerning vision.

LIBRI PONTIFICALES EXTRAVAGANTES

Thomas F. X. Noble

Those of you who attended a few years ago the inaugural session of this learned society had the pleasure of hearing the estimable Professor Bullough discourse in a properly pseudolearned fashion about a number of provocative *Kama Sutra* manuscripts that he had discovered in rarely consulted Central European repositories. Shortly after returning home, inspired by Bullough's paper, I called my travel agent to book passage to Europe to consult those manuscripts for myself. To my considerable surprise, I found that it was not possible to get a seat on any plane for the next six months. It seems that others among Bullough's audience had been similarly inspired.

Well, in due course, I got to the manuscripts and began work on them. You understand of course that my interest was solely in the texts. Indeed, I read these codices from cover to cover and never even noticed the pictures. In fact, I was far too excited to be distracted by lurid pictures of countless men and women doing peculiar things to one another—did you know that it is possible? Well no, I suppose you didn't, but that is another story. You see I discovered in one of these manuscripts a text that I quickly determined to be a heretofore unknown version of the *Liber pontificalis*. Most scholars have assumed that, with the exception of the Tortosa manuscript uncovered in 1925, Duchesne had seen and dealt with all surviving versions in the preparation of his massive edition—an edition which, as you will soon see, is flawed by severe omissions.

What, you may ask, could possibly have escaped the encyclopedic knowledge of Duchesne? Just this: I discovered the *Liber pontificalis* for the Officium locationis papalis—that's right!, for the "rent-a-pope agency." Implausible, you say: that is exactly what I thought too. At first I was so shocked by my discovery that after painstakingly transcribing the whole of my text, I sent a copy to Rome for verification by the highest church authorities. I waited for months and months and then got an intemperate letter, in Latin of course, from His Excellency Joseph Cardinal Ratzinger, insisting that my text was a forgery attributable either to feminist nuns or to Charley Curran.

Once it had become clear to me that I would have no help from the current papal administration, I decided that I would have to press on alone with my researches into the strange doings of earlier papal governments. It finally became clear to me just what I had found. Perhaps you will recall that during the Byzantine period of papal history—say the period from 500 to 750—the imperial regime played a significant role in the selection and installation of popes. When a reigning pope died, notice of that fact was communicated to the emperor or to his representative, usually the exarch of Ravenna. Permission was then granted to proceed to a new election, and after the election had taken place, news of its outcome had to be communicated, once again, either to the emperor or his agent, who would then grant or withhold approval. If approval was granted, the new pope would be installed promptly, but if it was withheld, the whole business might have to be repeated. The result of all this electoral confusion was long vacancies in the papacy, often six or eight weeks or more. Because popes could not be persuaded to die on any sort of routine or schedule, situations often arose where major celebrations were due to come up just when a pope inconveniently departed to meet the man whose vicar he had been. Here, then, is where the rent-a-popes came in: the archdeacon of the church got the *primicerius* of the notaries to issue a special *cautio*—I actually found several of these—to the Officium locationis papalis to send over a suitable pope *magna cum celeritate*. My *Liber* reports on the lives and activities of these popes, and of this you shall hear more presently.

First, however, I must bring up one or two methodological concerns. I was very concerned that my *Liber* was an insufficiently grand text to bring before this learned society, and so I made arrangements to take my manuscript to the laboratory of the infamous Dr. Brundage. There, through the miracles of modern technology, I was able to have my evidence enriched and my data enhanced. Now, before all of you go rushing off to Milwaukee, or to Lawrence for that matter, I should tell you that Dr. Brundage is currently trying to work himself out of two problems: first, he fell into his own machine and had his career enriched and enhanced, which is all very well, but he came out wearing a funny little blue-and-red bird suit; second, Dr. Brundage has his attorneys investigating the possible pirating of his processes: enriched evidence and enhanced data seem to have turned up recently in the Utah fusion laboratory, in the front offices of a couple of dozen major-league baseball teams, and in George Bush's budget office. Here then is what my improved manuscripts have to say.

Of course there is not time to tell you about all the rent-a-popes, so I shall select just a few. You might be interested in Pope Fanullone (that is, "Pope Do-Nothing"). He was hired when the emperor laid rough hands on Martin I and hauled him off to Constantinople. Fanullone was so terrified, and so anxious to live to spend his pay, that when he was hired, he entered the papal *cubiculum,* locked the door behind himself, and refused to come out. Then there was Pope Ganzo (that is, "Pope Pimp"), who not only had his name on the available list at the agency but who also ran some questionable rackets in Trastevere. In his pontificate a new officer appears in the records, the *primicerius lenonum,* the "chief officer of the procurers," who had his office decorated with salacious murals. This was the great chamber later redecorated by Leo III, whose artwork has been interpreted ideologically by scholars who have not realized that he was merely covering up scenes that would have made Etruscan tomb painters blush. I suspect that you have never heard much about Pope Scimunito, good old "Pope Dumbbell." He got hired after the death of Gregory II in 731, and no sooner had he checked into his new lodgings than he rifled the papal treasury and invested the proceeds in an icon factory in Constantinople. Last, I might mention Pope Guapo, that is "Pope Boss." Guapo seems to have had one signal failing. He gambled a great deal and he always lost. Because he ran Rome's protection rackets, no one would really challenge him; but as there is honor among thieves he decided to use his pontificate to pay off his debts. How he did this is rather interesting. You may recall that Hadrian I had to reroof some of Rome's churches. The reason why, quite simply, is that Guapo sold the lead and tin to pay debts. Plus, you know those manuscripts that wound up at the Frankish court? Right! Guapo sold them. And I could go on all night telling you about the relics he sold. These rent-a-popes, then, were pretty colorful characters.

My new *Liber* reveals other things, too, about the papal administration in the eighth century. It is well known that the other *Liber pontificalis* contains precious information about many subjects but especially about the papal government. You will, however, look in vain through that book for any mention of the *primicerius* of the apostolic bingo-callers. This critical officer was one of the most important financial officials of the papal government, and he served under regular popes and rent-a-popes alike. My discovery of this officer makes it possible for me, for the very first time, here tonight before this distinguished assembly, to explain a central anomaly of early medieval papal history. How, scholars have long wondered, did Zachary I, Hadrian I, Leo III, and Gregory IV finance their massive building campaigns? The answer is that they did it the way the Catholic church has always done it: with the profits from Friday-night bingo. While I am truly thrilled at having solved this vexing problem, I must report that I now confront a different and more serious one. That is this: how did the Catholic church run bingo before the foundation of the Knights of Columbus? This problem is so significant that an international team of scholars must set to work to solve it right away.

As is often the case in serious scholarship, when one problem is solved, other solutions follow in turn. For years scholars have been debating the precise significance of small bronze and copper objects, marked with both Greek and Latin lettering and found in some quantities all over Rome. Some have thought them small-denomination coins, while others say they are pilgrims' offerings. I can now report to you that they are actually bingo tokens. The fact that these tokens have both Greek and Latin lettering is another fact of immense significance. You see, I find it a shocking example of the failings of German scholarship that neither Bernhard Bischoff nor Walter Berschin has commented on the cultural and intellectual implications of bilingual bingo in early medieval Rome.

One last point emerges from my new Scholars have long talked about a Greek party in early medieval Rome, that is, about persons who did not wish to see the popes liberate themselves from the Byzantine Empire and strike out on their own as independent heads of state. In my text I have found out exactly who the members of this Greek party were: they were the shareholders in the rent-a-pope agency, who realized that no Greeks meant no vacancies, which meant no jobs.

I guess the moral of my story is that the next time you have a chance to listen to Vern Bullough talk about dirty books, pay attention: you might learn something.

THE SAN GIMIGNANO DOSSAL AND A NOTE ON A NEW DISCOVERY ABOUT THE PESCIA DOSSAL

William Cook

For more than a decade, I have been trying to complete a catalogue of early Italian paintings of Saint Francis of Assisi. In addition to visiting countless churches and museums in Italy, I have spent many days looking at museum catalogues, sales catalogues, and photographic archives. In my research, I've turned up paintings of Francis from Mallorca to Moscow and from Cracow to Pasadena. There have, of course, been moments that belong in the theater of the absurd. When photographing a painting at Villa La Pietra, where Sir Harold Acton lives, I set off his alarm system that included a loud horn on his roof and an alarm in the police station. Oddly enough, only the octogenarian, half-deaf Lord Acton noticed.

Part of my search for a complete list of paintings of Francis consists in seeking information about paintings that no longer exist. One in Kiev was taken by the Nazis; one in Amalfi was stolen; several were sold as part of estates without sufficient records. One of the most fruitful sources for paintings that have disappeared during the past three centuries is a book written by Fra Niccolò Catalino in 1652. In the middle of the seventeenth century, there was a tremendous controversy between the various branches of the Franciscan order about the proper habit, in particular the proper shape for the capuche. The industrious Fra Niccolò had the clever idea of making drawings of old paintings of Saint Francis for the purpose of arguing that the capuche of his branch of the Order was identical to that of Saint Francis. In his book, *Fiume del terrestre paradiso,* Fra Niccolò published quite a few drawings. Some are of paintings that survive today, and in general he gets high marks for accuracy, although occasionally he did not understand the particular story depicted in one of the early dossals, because those stories' sources were the various accounts of the life of Saint Francis by Thomas of Celano, which the Franciscans had suppressed in 1266. It is only thanks to Fra Niccolò that we know of the existence of a dossal at San Miniato al Tedesco, several panels by Margarito of Arezzo, and the portraits of Francis and Anthony of 1270 by Meliore once in Barberino Valdelsa.

I had examined Fra Niccolò's tome while in Siena several years ago. I recall wondering at the time if the good brother's original drawings survived, but I had no luck in my attempt to answer that question. However, I was able to learn that Fra Niccolò was Sienese, and that he probably died in the friary in Siena. There was a fire in the Franciscan convent in Siena about the time he died, and I was not able to find any trace of Fra Niccolò's work when I was allowed to prowl around the old buildings there, one of which now belongs to the Carabinieri. It was not easy to explain to Italy's crack policemen why I wanted to look in the nooks and crannies of their office. I felt a lot like Jessica Fletcher and was treated accordingly.

Several summers ago, I had the opportunity to purchase a small apartment in Siena only a few meters from the Campo. As I sat in the notary's office waiting for the closing (a ceremony that everyone interested in ritual should be required to observe), I was given the opportunity to look at the recent—by Italian standards—history of my apartment. It was clear from a close observation that the building was medieval in origin, probably thirteenth century. I discovered that the apartment had been sold in 1702 by the heirs of a Signora Francesca Bianciardi. Since the property had been part of her dowry, her family name is recorded: Catalino. Could it be that my apartment belonged to a relative of Fra Catalino, and might she not be of special importance to my artistic friar since she was named for the saint of whose order Fra Niccolò was a member? An intriguing possibility, to say the least. I realized that redecorating might be fun after all, since I convinced myself that perhaps, just perhaps, Signora Bianciardi, *nata* Catalino, might just be a favorite relative to whom her cousin, or uncle, or whatever he was, might have left his paltry earthly possessions, including his drawings. One evening, while struggling with a recalcitrant stove, I discovered an indentation in the kitchen wall. Indeed, what I so wanted to find was there—the drawings of Fra Niccolò Catalino. There was also a much disintegrated Franciscan habit with a note attached suggesting that this was the one and only habit of the faithful follower of Saint Francis, the Blessed Niccolò Catalino. I soon dismissed the idea that I had an important relic when I realized that in all probability the title "Blessed" had been conferred on Niccolò by his relative, Signora Bianciardi, rather than by the Church.

The drawings were everything I had expected. There were a few details that the engravers of the published plates had ignored or misunderstood, and thus I was able to draw more accurate conclusions about the narrative parts of the lost dossal of San Miniato al Tedesco, just to cite one example. Of more value were Fra Niccolò's notes on the back of his drawings, which describe the specific locations of paintings, their general condition, and so forth. For example, it seems that by the middle of the seventeenth century, virtually all the early paintings of Francis had been removed to side altars or sacristies. The fact that they had been moved to relatively unimportant places in the churches provides some explanation for why so many have since disappeared.

Although I was quite taken by this discovery—more so because I naively supposed that these drawings belonged to me as the owner of the apartment on the Via delle Donzelle—it appeared, as I glanced through the drawings in those first exciting minutes, that they did not add any major pieces of information to what I knew about them from the published version. One question that occurred to me was whether there were any drawings by Fra Niccolò that had not been published in 1652. It did not appear so at first perusal. However, toward the bottom of the stack of drawings was an envelope with a crumbling wax seal and a command in bold letters that the envelope be burned by whoever came into possession of it after Fra Niccolò's death. These words were clearly not in Fra Niccolò's hand. Calling upon my modest knowledge of sigillography, I realized that this was not a personal or family seal but rather some sort of official seal of a guardian or convent of Franciscans, probably Sienese. On the opposite side of the envelope were many lines written in a weak hand that I concluded, by comparison with the notes on the drawings, was probably that of Fra Niccolò toward the end of his life. As I read, it became clear that what was inside was an extraordinarily interesting drawing of a peculiar painting he had seen; even Fra Niccolò's tale, however, did not prepare me for what I found inside.

Here in brief is what Fra Niccolò had written, probably on his deathbed as he prepared to hand over his drawings to Signora Bianciardi on the Via delle Donzelle. Fra Niccolò had been shown a painting of Saint Francis that was hidden in the sacristy of San Francesco in San Gimignano. How long the painting had been there he did not know, but he stated that it is clear from the style of the painting that it was contemporary with others he had been studying. It had been cut down from its original size, and

the narrative stories that once existed on either side of the main figure of
Francis were gone except for borders where the cutting had been a bit
uneven. He said that he could make out some letters of an inscription on
the back which he guessed once said "Vera imago Sancti Francisci." Fra
Niccolò's notes continued. This painting had been ordered destroyed by
the minister general Crescentius of Jesi because it had become an object
of ridicule and because the image was being used in the sermons of some
secular clergy to denounce the Franciscans. However, in all probability a
friar had hidden the painting behind an altar, and it had come to light just
a few years before Fra Niccolò saw it, when the church was thoroughly gut-
ted inside and remodeled in the baroque style. The guardian who showed
the painting to Fra Niccolò, a certain Fra Silvano da Siena, hoped to be
instructed about this odd image by his friend and fellow Sienese.

Fra Niccolò did not know what to make of this painting and made the
mistake of showing his drawing of it to his own guardian in Siena, Fra
Modesto Bianciardi, who may have been related to him by marriage, since
Bianciardi was the married name of the relative to whom Fra Niccolò
entrusted these drawings. Fra Modesto forbade Fra Niccolò to publish or
write about this recently discovered work from San Gimignano. Perhaps
out of affection for Fra Niccolò, he did not destroy the drawing (and of
course he had no jurisdiction over the convent in San Gimignano,
although obviously the painting was ultimately destroyed); instead, he forbade Fra Niccolò by his vow of obedience ever to show it to anyone or to
discuss it. He must have placed it in an envelope with his seal on it and with
instructions to destroy it, and later the dying Fra Niccolò added the explanation of this oddity among his drawings. One wonders whether Fra
Niccolò's narrative was written so that the envelope would be destroyed or
so that the curiosity aroused would encourage someone to open it and preserve its contents.

I assumed that the cause of all this controversy was that Francis was
shown without the stigmata. After all, we know from several papal bulls and
from stories in Thomas of Celano's treatise on miracles that there were
early paintings of Francis without the stigmata and even that the bishop of
Genoa had ordered them removed from a painting in that city. I did not
want to open the envelope without consulting someone at the Archivio di
Stato, which fortunately, is literally only a stone's throw from the apartment on the Via delle Donzelle. The next morning I consulted Professor
Armando Santini, who agreed to perform the "surgery" for me of opening
the envelope without damaging the document inside or the seal. He first
x-rayed the contents to be sure he understood where the folds were and

whether there were other things in the envelope. Professor Santini and his assistant, known only as Cianchino, knew little about Saint Francis. In passing they mentioned that the drawing contained in the envelope showed Francis with unusually prominent stigmata. With that revelation, I was thoroughly confused, since I no longer had any intelligent guess about what this strange image consisted of. Unfortunately, we had to postpone the opening of the envelope for several days because of the Palio. Professor Santini assured me that since his *contrada,* the Bruco, had not won for thirty-three years and that since it had drawn an excellent horse, he would be much too unsteady to take on this delicate task. Fortunately the Bruco was not victorious, for I fear that I should still not know the contents had Professor Santini been able to celebrate the first victory of his *contrada* since he was nine years old. Two days after the victory of the *contrada* of Nicchio, Professor Santini and his assistant removed the drawing from the envelope (figure 1).

How could I have anticipated this! I wish that I could tell you precisely what this tells us about Francis of Assisi and that all the questions this drawing raises have been sufficiently answered. However, I can do no more tonight than to make public for the first time this discovery and to suggest some of the most important questions it raises. Before beginning, let me state that I have no secure explanation of the strange inscription "BROCK" next to Francis's left foot. Since one would expect to find a date there, it may be a faulty transcription caused by the painting's damaged condition at the time Fra Niccolò saw it. Could this be the Roman numerals MCCIL, thus dating the painting to 1249?

In the light of recent scholarship and a film from France about the cult of Saint Guinefort, who was a dog, it is perhaps appropriate to ask whether this painting seriously raises the possibility that Saint Francis was not a human but rather a bird. Due to the fact that this drawing shows Francis as having both human and birdlike features, we can probably dismiss the idea of Francis being a bird of some sort and the stories of his life as attempts to make the cult of an animal acceptable to the authorities.

Since the head and wings seem to have a different shading, is it possible that Francis is presented here in some sort of disguise. One thinks of the story in 2 *Celano* when the youthful Francis swapped clothes with a beggar so he could experience poverty. Did Francis seek not only a "poor like me" experience but also an "avian like me" one? The fact that the figure is standing on a precipice might suggest preparation for a test flight, but the fact that he wears a habit that is clearly not for the purpose of covering his private parts weakens this interpretative scheme.

Figure 1.

If this interpretation is adopted, it leads also to the somewhat embarrassing question of what happened to Francis's genitals. Richard Trexler
suggests in a recent book that when Francis whips Brother Ass with a cord,
he is really striking his penis. Could this drawing suggest that Francis in

fact destroyed his genitalia? Francis also appears to be missing a fifth toe on his right foot.

Bonaventure speaks of Francis being transformed into the likeness of the seraphic vision, which was after all Christ under the species of a seraph. Might this work suggest that what Francis experienced at La Verna was some sort of mystical experience that was not complete and that somehow Francis's transformation became interrupted, thus leaving a composite stigmatized figure? The stigmata make clear that this drawing represents Francis after the experience at La Verna. Bonaventure mentions a falcon that cared for Saint Francis at La Verna, and both Giotto and Pietro Lorenzetti place the falcon at the stigmatization. Was there somehow a kind of mystical vision *manqué* in which the appearance of Christ as a seraph was interrupted by the appearance of the falcon and that as Francis was being transformed into Christ, the falcon inadvertently was caught up in the metamorphosis so that Francis was transformed partly into Christ and partly into a bird? If this occurred, it would help to explain Bonaventure's error in stating that the falcon appeared to Francis in the night, for Edward Armstrong in his book *St. Francis: Nature Mystic* demonstrates that the type of falcon which would have inhabited La Verna never appears at night. In fact, this bird would have appeared at dawn, which was the time of the stigmatization. Perhaps, Bonaventure deliberately erred in his natural history so that if there were in any rumors of Francis's strange transformation into both Christ and a bird, they would be effectively countered by Bonaventure stating different times for the falcon's appearances to Francis and his vision of the seraph.

If what I have hypothesized is indeed what happened at La Verna, the leaders of the order could hardly allow this to become known. Imagine what the Dominicans would have done had they learned of it! This might explain why after the stigmatization Francis preferred solitude and that when he spoke of returning to minister to lepers, he was kept from this service. There are several stories in the Franciscan body of sources that might be read to support the interpretation that Francis was transformed at least partly into a bird. In 2 *Celano*, Francis tells of a vision of a hen with many chicks. He goes on to say, "The hen is I." Could this be a pious reworking of Francis speaking after this mysterious vision but before his death? We are told in the *Mirror of Perfection* that Francis especially liked the hooded lark because it looked like a member of a religious order. But could we not read the following passage about a lark in light of the discovery of Fra Niccolò's drawing to be a description of the post-stigmatization Francis?

She walks along the road to find grain, and even if she finds it among rub-
bish, she pecks it out and eats it. As she flies, she praises God very sweet-
ly, like good religious who despise earthly things, whose minds are set on
the things of heaven and whose constant purpose is to praise God. Her
plumage resembles the earth, and she sets an example to religious not to
wear fine and gaudy clothing, but cloth of a humble price and color, just
as earth is inferior to other elements.

The last part of the text, which seems to be about a habit more than about
feathers, really makes more sense in light of the lost painting from San
Gimignano than as a cute allegory about a lark.

The "interrupted mystical experience" theory may also help to explain
a couple of the greatest oddities about events in the years immediately following Francis's death. First, why did Pope Gregory IX, who later claimed
to see the stigmata personally, not mention them in his canonization bull
of 1228? Did he fear that such a proclamation would lead to an exhuma-
tion of the body? And why was Francis's body transferred secretly from San
Giorgio to the basilica by Elias in 1230? Was there a fear that any public
procession risked the possibility that the casket would be opened? It is
hard to imagine the impact on the Franciscan order of people seeing this
feathered saint if his body were preserved, or the bones and beak of the
saint if they had decomposed!

At this point, it would be imprudent to suggest that the possibility of
some sort of falconization interference with the stigmatization is more
than a hypothesis. Scholars are going to have to reexamine the entire body
of a hagiographical literature as well as the papal bulls about Francis in
light of Fra Niccolò's drawing in order to reach any sort of historical cer-
tainty.

If this is not enough of a problem for Franciscan scholars, I have
another revelation, this one about the earliest painting of Francis—the
dossal in Pescia dated 1235 and painted by Bonaventure Berlinghieri. No
one has ever challenged the authenticity of the inscription on this painting that gives both the date and the artist. Recently the Soprintendenza
delle Belle Arti of the province of Pistoia has ordered a cleaning of the dossal because infrared photographs made clear that each time the original
face of Francis appears, it had been scraped from the wood and over-
painted, probably only a few years after Berlinghieri executed the work.
Computer enhancements have allowed the restorers to know precisely
what the original face looked like, and they have begun to replace the later
paint with what modern technology tells us is virtually identical to what
Berlinghieri painted in 1235. It will be years before the restoration work is
completed and revealed to the public. Fortunately, I have a friend working

on the restoration. He must remain anonymous for obvious reasons. Just last week, he sent me a photograph of the first restored face of Francis in the scene of Francis preaching to the birds.

I can tell you, this painting now takes its place with the San Gimignano painting drawn by Fra Niccolò as a source of controversy, and both cry out for us to reinterpret all we know of Francis in light of their existence. For now I shall ignore the problem of having Francis stigmatized but not yet tonsured. What is obvious is that the face of Francis bears an uncanny resemblance to that of the Irish actor Mickey Rourke. Despite the dark hair, his features seem unmistakably Celtic. Was Francis indeed an Irishman? If so, we could explain a lot of the animal lore associated with him, since Edward Armstrong has clearly demonstrated the many affinities between Franciscan nature stories and the tales associated with the early Irish monks. If this is the case, did Berlinghieri give Francis dark hair (the so-called "black Irish" didn't exist in the thirteenth century) to make him more acceptable to his Italian audience? Did Francis dye his hair?

There is a more likely explanation, however. We need to search the archives carefully to discover whether any commerce existed between Umbria and Celtic areas of the British Isles. One can certainly imagine that a cloth merchant like Pietro Bernardone would buy wool from the British Isles. If so, did he perhaps sire a child by a Celtic lass and bring him to Assisi to raise? It is important to recall that Pietro Bernardone was childless at the time of Francis's birth. We recall examples in the next century, such as the wife of Francesco di Marco Datini, who agreed to raise her husband's bastard as her own since she was childless. This might also help to explain the child's name change. Maybe Lady Pica agreed to raise the child only if he were given a name associated with her—namely "Francis," since she came from a French-speaking territory. Since the child's name was originally "John," does that mean that Francis was originally given the Celtic version of this name, "Sean"?

Historians are often perplexed by how to use visual evidence in a useful and judicious way. What I have tried to do this evening is to take some extraordinary new evidence, examine it carefully, and suggest ways of using it to learn some new things about Francis of Assisi. I may have discovered two great cover-ups in Franciscan history that make us reevaluate every word written about the alleged human, supposedly Italian, saint. I now urge the sociologists and cultural anthropologists to observe Franciscan studies carefully in the next few years in order to study the relationship between learned religion and popular piety. How long will it take for the first back-yard statues to appear that show the "real" Francis: part Italian, part Celt, and part bird?

NEWLY DISCOVERED DANTEANA FROM THE BIBLIOTECA BENGODIANA

CHRISTOPHER KLEINHENZ

We live, alas, in a trendy age, one given more to reveling in the fluff of life, to embracing the latest fashion, and to finding facile solutions for difficult problems, more to these ephemeral pursuits than to the undertaking of the serious, hard, but rewarding work of true research, scholarship, and intellectual engagement. Philistines crowd the academic arena, descendants of the Huns and Vandals besiege the gates of our ivory-towered city, and purveyors of critical jargon sow insidious seeds of corruption in what were once fertile and verdant fields. When, O when will these intemperate assaults on scholarship cease? When, I ask, using a Dantesque expression, when will we be rid of the stench that pollutes the pure air of scholarly research?

Even the great, centuries-old bastion of Dante studies has been assailed by the idle prick of the critically careless pen and by the mind-numbing fog of wrongheaded notions pronounced by philologically illiterate pseudocritics. How long must we endure the excesses of numerologically oriented scholars, who would reduce the magnificent edifice of the *Divine Comedy* to a sort of computerized game? How long must we suffer their "discoveries" of intricate and "meaningful" verbal correspondences which seemingly lurk everywhere among the poem's 14,233 lines? How long must we tolerate the barbarous plays on words and revisionist readings of verses that would make Dante do flip-flops in his tomb in Ravenna? Consider, for example, the serious proposal, recently advanced, that the line in *Purgatorio* 30 "Guardaci ben! Ben son, ben son Beatrice [Look here! For I am Beatrice, I am]"[1] should be interpreted as the disclosure of Beatrice's name: "Guardaci ben! Ben son Benson Beatrice [Look here! I am indeed Beatrice Benson]." Alas, the good Florentine name "Portinari," which we have accepted as true with good archival cause for six and one-half centuries, has now yielded to Benson!

Consider as well the depravity of the critic who would seriously entertain the thought that the last verse of the *Inferno*—"E quindi uscimmo a riveder le stelle [It was from there that we emerged, to see—once more—the stars]"—should be construed as Dante's warm and punning, yet strangely polite and formal, greeting to the stars: "arrivederLe, stelle! [See you around, stars!]." To all these critics we would like to say in the immortal words of Dante's twentieth-century namesake, Jimmy Durante, "Good night, Mrs. Calabash, wherever you are!"

One particular branch of scholarship, much maligned in recent times, is textual criticism. However, as James Willis in his book *Latin Textual Criticism* put it: "There are many useful jobs which can be done by men who do not like to think. They can dig ditches, clean automobiles, and compile concordances. They cannot, however, become good textual critics."[2] Yes, textual criticism is, to use a time-honored expression from my native Indiana, "a long row to hoe," and while in recent years it may have taken the eight count, this academic pugilist would not call it down and out. Indeed, my own experience would argue otherwise. As we all know, philology, textual criticism, and literary criticism are based on the discovery and interpretation of texts, and in this paper I would like to recount my own long and arduous search for, and ultimately felicitous discovery of, the holograph of Dante's *Divine Comedy*.

In the academic year 1970–71, during an extended stay in Italy, I fell prey to the obscure but insidious malady *morbus Dantis,* whose symptoms include, among others, sleeplessness, mental agitation, recurrent ocular fatigue, and prolonged periods of almost cataleptic meditation. The existence of this dread malady has been known to historians of medicine and to literary scholars for over six hundred and fifty years; indeed, statisticians have argued on good evidence that over the past six centuries it has probably afflicted even more people than did the Black Death of 1348. However, unlike the plague, *morbus Dantis* is rarely fatal, and unfortunately so, for the pathetic, zombielike plight of some victims has been described as a sort of academic version of *Night of the Living Dead*. Experts trace its cause to a virus that infiltrates the mind and body of young adults, usually of college age, but cases have been reported at all points on the age spectrum. There ensconced, the virus usually remains dormant until its fury is unleashed by some external stimulus.

The onset of this grim disease—which had doubtless been with me ever since my undergraduate days—was triggered by my residence in the great medieval university city of Bologna, which Dante visited and where, we presume, he studied for a period of time in the 1280s. The fury of this transsecular virus was released in me one morning in November as I was walking from my office near the present site of the University of Bologna to the Ristorante Pappagallo, where I was going to treat myself to a fine lunch. Detouring slightly, I passed by the two towers—the Asinelli and the Garisenda—in the Piazza di Porta Ravegnana and was struck by their impressive size and dominance over the urban setting (figure 1). In my contemplation of these mute reminders of Bologna's medieval past, I forgot momentarily about the *lasagne verdi al forno*, the *tortellini alla panna*, and the *cotoletta alla bolognese* that awaited me. My thoughts turned to Dante, who more than seven centuries earlier on that very site was so engrossed in looking at the towers that he failed to see a very gracious woman who was passing along the street. He memorialized this moment in a sonnet, which is preserved for us in several late medieval codices and, without attribution, in a register of Bolognese notarial documents of the year 1287—the *Memoriali bolognesi*. As I gazed at the towers, Dante's verses coursed through my head with their mocking reproach of his eyes that failed to see the lady: "Non mi poriano già mai fare ammenda / del loro gran fallo gli occhi miei, sed elli / non s'accecasser [My eyes could never make amends for their great failure, even if they were to be blinded]."[3] Then, slowly, in deep thought and with bent head, I continued my journey toward the Ristorante Pappagallo, which lies almost in the shadow of the two towers (figure 1).

After consuming gargantuan portions of Bolognese specialties and lingering over the usual postprandial espresso and the necessary *digestivo*, I began to peruse the local newspaper—*Il resto del Carlino*—and my eyes were drawn to an article on the *terza pagina* concerning Dante's autograph manuscripts.[4] An Austrian scholar, it was reported, had, in collaboration with a team of scientists, perfected a sonar device that could detect the presence of foreign objects inside apparently solid structures, such as walls, floors, and so forth. He wished to test his machine on the Pomposa Abbey (figure 2)—which lies roughly halfway between Ravenna and Venice—in the belief that Dante had hidden his manuscripts there, within those ancient and hallowed walls. Let us review the facts. In late July or early August 1321, Dante, returning from Venice where he had been sent on an ambassadorial mission by the Da Polenta family and ill with fever, stayed overnight at the famous Benedictine abbey of Pomposa. From there he returned to the final refuge of his long period of exile—Ravenna—where he died on 13 or 14 September 1321, leaving his wife Gemma and his cat Biancaneve even more desolate in the old family homestead in Florence

Figure 1.

Figure 2.

[deleted figure showed the complex of buildings in Florence known as the "case di Dante" located at the corner of via S. Margherita and via Dante Alighieri]. Today, Dante's much-contested remains still rest in Ravenna [deleted figure showed Dante's tomb].

Here, now, is the Austrian hypothesis. On his return from Venice, Dante realized that he was mortally ill. He was, of course, carrying the autograph manuscript of the *Divine Comedy* with him, as he always did: he never left home without it! Therefore, wishing to prevent his great poem from falling into the hands of unworthy men and to protect it from the ravages and depredations of his querulous times, Dante hid the autograph manuscript inside one of the walls of Pomposa Abbey in the dead of night—*a lume spento.*

The offer of the Austrian scholar to "scan" the walls of the Pomposa with his high-tech sonar machine was viewed with some alarm by ecclesiastical authorities, who considered such devices to be the tools of the devil. The *coup de grâce* was administered by an officious Roman functionary whose latent xenophobia manifested itself when he volunteered that if anyone were to find Dante's manuscripts, that someone had better be Italian, by God! At that point delirium took hold of the Roman functionary, producing in him a paroxysm of babbled phrases—"Viva l'Italia!" "Mamma mia," "Pasta e fagioli!" And the Austrian was sent packing to Vienna with machine and theory untested.

The combination of external and internal stimuli which assailed me that long-ago fall morning in Bologna aroused in me that ancient longing to pursue what has been for countless scholars a will-o'-the-wisp, the elusive pot of gold at the end of the rainbow, yea, even the Holy Grail. In short, I dedicated myself immediately and irrevocably to that last great crusade—the quest for the autograph manuscript of Dante's *Divine Comedy*. In truth, we possess no manuscripts in Dante's hand, no authorized version of any of his works, not even a grocery list, unlike the well-known cases of Petrarch and Boccaccio. And so began the search, the new grail quest, which was to consume my time, energy, and financial resources for the better part of the past two decades. But not without results.

Indeed, I have the great pleasure in this essay to announce for the first time in print my discovery, in the summer of 1990, of the autograph manuscript of Dante's *Divine Comedy*. Given the magnitude and international implications of this discovery, the Italian authorities have agreed to delay the announcement until after publication of this essay. These officials include, among others, the prime minister, the *onorevole* Giulio Andreotti, and the members of the venerable Accademia della Crusca, which is housed in the Villa Medicea del Castello. Press releases are scheduled to appear simultaneously in the *Corriere della sera,* the *Times* (London), the *Chicago Tribune,* and the *Wisconsin State Journal.* Guest spots have been scheduled on "Good Morning America," the Johnny Carson show, "Jeopardy," and "Wheel of Fortune." In this essay, then, I would like to present a coherent account of the several stages of this quest and to furnish some idea of the extraordinary benefits that this discovery will have on the scholarly profession. The first of these, I should add, will be a salutary terror, a point to which I shall return below.

* * *

Some twenty years ago I began my own obsessive pursuit of the elusive holograph. Taking the lead from the disappointed, and deported, Austrian scholar, I went first to Pomposa, where I was able to determine—after much careful tapping of walls and floors with blunt instruments and after examining every single scrap of parchment in the capitular library—that Dante had most certainly not hidden or left his manuscripts there. Other places beckoned me—those cities, towns, and castles throughout central and northern Italy in which the exiled Florentine poet sought and received hospitality. All these places I examined in a similarly thorough fashion: the charming hills of the Casentino with the picturesque but dilapidated castles of the Counts of Romena [deleted figure showed a castle] and the pleasant town of Poppi, and the great university city of Bologna. I followed Dante's trail to Assisi [deleted figure showed a typical medieval street in Assisi], Verona, Lucca, Pisa [deleted figure showed the twelfth-century Duomo and Campanile (the famous "Leaning Tower") of Pisa], and Siena. I traveled to Padua—indeed, to the very palazzo where Dante stayed in 1306—and to the great basilica of Sant' Apollinare in Classe outside Ravenna. I journeyed to Paris and the hallowed *Salle des manuscrits* in the Bibliothèque nationale de France, to the British Museum in London, to Venice [deleted figure showed the Rialto Bridge spanning the Grand Canal], and the island of Torcello in the Venetian lagoon, and many other places. With no results.

If the manuscript cannot be found by searching the places where Dante had been, then, I reasoned, we must look for clues in the text itself. Dante's delight in speaking obscurely challenges us to match wits with him. Using a concordance of the *Comedy,* I searched for key words in the proper semantic field.[5] While the words *manoscritto, codice,* and *pergamena* do not occur in the poem, I was encouraged by the presence of words such as *carta* (eight occurrences), *scrittura* (ten), *volume* (nine), *scrivere* (thirty-two), *libro* (two), *libello* (one), and even the title of the work itself *comedìa* (two).

I even experimented with numerous word combinations. But all these high hopes and great possibilities led nowhere. In fact, after so many useless peregrinations and unproductive "bright ideas," I had almost given up hope. But then, in the waning post-Kalamazoo days of spring, the moment of revelation came, not as it did for the notorious mass-murderer Son of Sam through the neighbor's dog, but in a decidedly Augustinian context of the "Take up and read" sort.[6]

After dining in a restaurant in Chinatown [deleted figure showed the Shanghai Low restaurant on Grant Street in San Francisco, the site of the beginning of the great discovery], I broke open my fortune cookie and took up the slip of paper and read out loud: "May neither sacrifice nor great distance disturb your hope for happy ending and divine peace." I was momentarily mystified. My wife thought that the awkward syntax and strange vocabulary suggested major problems in translation. On further reflection, it dawned on me that this was undoubtedly the sign that I had been seeking. All of the elements were present in the fortune-cookie message—the notion of divine, the prospected happy end to the quest, and a comedy, as we know, always ends on a happy note. Moreover, the three key words in the Chinese conundrum all had Dantean overtones: "great distance" is synonymous with "exile" (essilio), which was Dante's circumstance when he wrote the poem and its efficient cause; "peace" (pace) signified the condition for which the poet so ardently yearned; and "sacrifice" connotes "martyrdom" (martiro), which was the constant psychological and often physical state of the exiled wanderer.

Clutching the slender strip of paper, I rushed home to the Dante concordance and found that these three words occur together only once in the *Comedy*, in *Paradiso* 10, in the passage describing the blessed state of Boethius:

> Per vedere ogne ben dentro vi gode
> l'anima santa che 'l mondo fallace
> fa manifesto a chi di lei ben ode.
> Lo corpo ond' ella fu cacciata giace
> giuso in Cieldauro; ed essa da *martiro*
> e da *essilio* venne a questa *pace*
> (124–29, emphasis mine)
> [There within, through seeing every good, the sainted soul rejoices who makes the fallacious world manifest to any who listen well to him. The body from which it was driven lies down below in Cieldauro; and he came from martyrdom and exile to this peace.]

In this passage a place is given: Cieldauro, the church of San Pietro in Cielo d'Oro (Saint Peter's of the Golden Ceiling) in Pavia (figure 3).

Dante refers here specifically to the magnificent tenth-century tomb of Boethius erected by Emperor Otto III (990). The tomb is located in the crypt, under the high altar, and bears a Latin inscription by Pope Sylvester II that reads, in part: "Hic iacet corpus suum liberatum ab omni doloribus mundi fallacis. . . . Anima sancta in pace requiescat et vita aeterna gaudeat [Here lies his body free from all the troublesome things of the fallacious world. . . . May the holy soul rest in peace and enjoy eternal life]." Dante consciously echoes these phrases in his description of Boethius in *Paradiso* 10.

With these pieces of the puzzle now in place, I assumed that it would be a simple task to look in the ecclesiastical library of San Pietro in Cielo d'Oro and find, covered with the dust of centuries, the long-lost holograph of the *Comedy.* But my patient examination of all the codices in that repository proved that such was not the case. Could I have misread the evidence so badly? Was the fortune cookie so cruelly deceitful?

Figure 3.

I decided to take a closer look at my text, and my examination of the first verse in the passage from *Paradiso* 10—"Per vedere ogne *ben* dentro vi *gode*"—provided the necessary clue. For not far from Pavia, on the old medieval road that leads eventually to the church of San Pietro in Cielo d'Oro, is the community of Bengodi (figure 4) whose origin lies shrouded in the mists of the Late Empire. Despite its humble beginnings and current nondescript state, except for the lovely flocks of sheep that graze nearby (figure 5), Bengodi has had one, or perhaps two, days in the sun. Once, in the year 1164, Otto of Freising reports in his chronicle that Frederick Barbarossa spent the night there, prevented by a freak thunderstorm from reaching Pavia. A few centuries later, Bengodi played a decisive role in the battle of Pavia. It was in Bengodi that on the evening of 23 February 1525, Francis I, having left the comforts of Fontainebleau and France far behind, and blissfully ignorant of the impending attack of the imperial troops of Charles V, sought the solace of Bacchus at the medieval tavern—the Osteria del Sole—and was roused the next day from his sodden slumber to find himself a prisoner. Poor Francis!

One other event has a direct bearing on the subject of this essay. In 1360 Galeazzo Visconti sent a missive to his administrative overseer in Bengodi, directing him to gather all secular manuscripts from church libraries in the district in order to form what would become the local civic repository. In issuing these orders, Visconti was probably following the example set by his great friend and mentor—Francesco Petrarca—in the

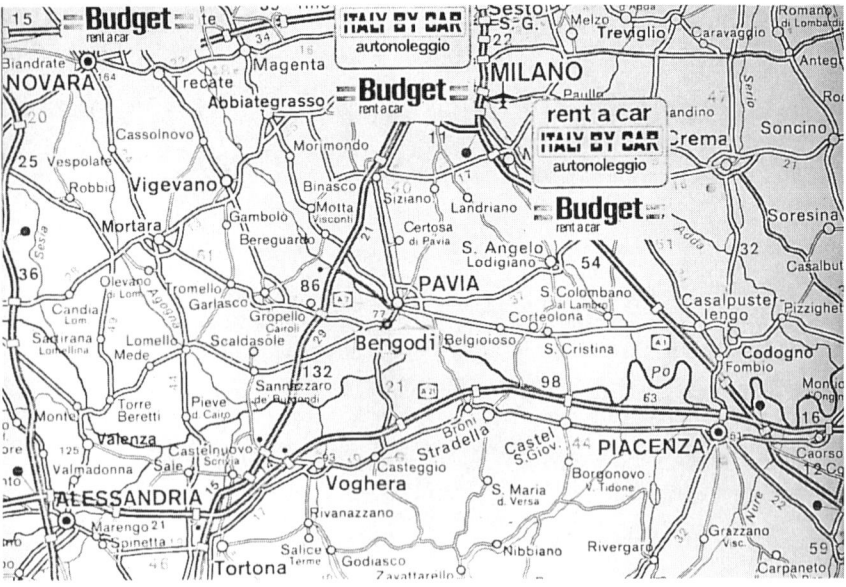

Figure 4.

Figure 5.

search for codices. Petrarca was then residing in Milan and no doubt filling Visconti's head full of humanistic garbage.

I visited Bengodi late last summer, almost twenty years since the onset of *morbus Dantis* during my Bolognese residence. The Biblioteca comunale of Bengodi occupies two rooms in the dank north wing of the sixteenth-century Palazzo Schiaccianoci. Despite its auspicious founding by edict of Galeazzo Visconti, the library has been closed for lack of funds, personnel, and local interest for over a hundred years, so I enlisted the assistance of the local *tabaccaio* and wine connoisseur, the octogenarian Giuseppe Pappardelle, whose grandfather was mayor of Bengodi in the 1880s and whose younger brother still herds sheep in the vicinity. With their help I gained access to the library.

Thick layers of dust, mildew, and grime encrusted all of the books and furniture in those cheerless two rooms. I carefully opened the shutters to admit the first ray of sunlight in a century. The stale air that escaped from that closed chamber was no doubt similar to that which greeted British

Egyptologist Howard Carter upon entering the tomb of King Tutankh-
amen. To adapt a memorable phrase used in Francis Ford Coppola's epic
film *Apocalypse Now* to describe the smell of burning napalm, I could truly
say that those rooms "smelled like victory." While a bookish odor of sanctity hung in the air like an oppressive cloud, this was, for me, the delightful uplifting scent of triumph which promised to fulfil the dreams of
countless scholars.

After much searching among shelves laden with many an ancient volume, I came to a special cabinet identified by a card written in a late eighteenth-century hand as containing "manoscritti e incunaboli," and there,
on the top shelf, lodged far in back, much higher up than would be possible to see without the aid of a small step stool, was a medium-sized, uncatalogued parchment codex, bound in leather and fastened with a heavy
metal clasp. On the first folio in an early fourteenth-century hand two
words appear in large script: "DIVINA COMEDIA." All 178 folios, which measure some 36 cm. by 24 cm., are ruled, and the text in a single hand is written in a single column, beginning on the second folio with the famous
exordium "Nel mezzo del cammin di nostra vita." There are no illustrations or historiated initials, but much marginal commentary in the same
hand as the text. With trembling hands I rapidly paged through the codex
to the final leaf, hoping against hope that there would be a colophon.
There was. It is composed of ten verses in *terza rima* followed by two lines
in prose, all in Italian, which read as follows:

> Pensa, lettor, che tu sei a la fine
> di tutte le vergate mie carte,
> le quai son pien di parole divine.
> O tu ch'onori scïenza ed arte
> considera il viaggio che inseme
> fatto avemo per vie lungh' e arte
> e mira le dottrine sì supreme
> sotto 'l velame de l'allegoria
> la qual a mo' d'i teologi si spreme
> in questa mia Divina Comedía.

> Io Dante Alighieri fiorentino di nascita ma non di costume ciò scrissi di
> mia propia mano e lo terminai 'l dì nove d'aprile ne l'anno MCCCXXI a
> Ravenna e lo fidai a la grandissima cura di messer Severino di Pavia.

> [Think, reader, that you are at the end / of all my ruled pages / which are
> full of divine words. / O you who honor learning and art, / consider the
> journey that together / we have taken through long and narrow ways /
> and admire the very lofty doctrines / under the veil of allegory / which

in the manner of the theologians is expressed / in this my Divine
Comedy.

I, Dante Alighieri, Florentine by birth but not by custom, wrote this in my
own hand and completed it on the ninth day of April in the year 1321 in
Ravenna and I have entrusted it to the great care of Master Severino of
Pavia.]

The first words that came to my mind were those uttered by the great
philologist Michele Barbi when he certified the Hamilton codex (Berlin,
Staatsbibliothek, preussischer Kulturbesitz, MS 90) to be Boccaccio's holograph of the *Decameron:*[7] "è lui!" Centuries of searching had come to a successful conclusion in those once dank, sunless, cheerless, and airless rooms
in Bengodi, which had now for this occasion become radiant and odorif-
erous once again! In their simplicity the ten verses of the colophon are
remarkably like many of the addresses to the reader scattered throughout
the poem. The concluding autobiographical statement removes any possibility of doubt as to its authenticity. It discloses, moreover, the reason why
the manuscript was in the environs of Pavia—it was entrusted to Messer
Severino di Pavia—and why the clues for its discovery are found in the tercets in the *Paradiso* given to *Severinus* Boethius. Indeed, these ten short
verses sweep away much of the critical debris accumulated over the centuries. No longer will we have to debate endlessly over the kind of allegory—allegory of poets or allegory of theologians?—employed in the
Comedy. Moreover, we now know both from the colophon and from the
first folio that Dante himself intended for his poem to be called the *"Divina" Comedía;* and thus, the printer who first attached that adjective to the
title in 1555 was unconsciously but felicitously carrying out the will of
Dante himself. And speaking of the will of Dante, I should note that, as dis-
coverer of the autograph manuscript, I have obtained from the comune of
Bengodi exclusive rights to act for the next seventeen years as Dante's literary executor. In this office it will be my sad duty to execute not a few of
Dante's more reckless critics. However, since the pen is always mightier
than the sword, these will be bloodless, critical massacres.

Let us now turn our attention to some troublesome passages in the
poem to see how our discovery of the holograph and its extensive margin-
alia can aid us in their resolution. For many Dante critics the ill-fated day
of reckoning has come. How many academic careers and scholarly reputa-
tions made in the prediscovery, halcyon days will survive unscathed? Guai
a voi, critici pravi—woe to you, depraved critics, who made scholarly hay
while the false sun of unauthorized and corrupt texts shone.

For the purposes of this essay, the review of these passages will be rapid. As we might suspect, Dante's precious glosses treat a wide variety of topics and present us with a wealth of information about his reading. Some critics may decry the often very pedestrian quality of the poet's annotations, but this is the way it is. Dante takes great care, for example, to note the precise source for many references, often providing the parallel text and brief commentary. The first spoken words in the *Inferno*—the Pilgrim's "*miserere* di me [have mercy on me]" addressed to Virgil *(Inf.* 1.65)—bear the brief gloss: "richiama 'l salmo penitenziale [recalls the penitential psalm]" referring to the fiftieth psalm in the Vulgate. The name "Semiramis" in *Inferno* 5 is glossed with a reference to specific chapters in Paulus Orosius's *Historia adversos paganos,* and the long-uncertain identity of Ciacco, the glutton in *Inferno* 6, is finally clarified by the marginal annotation: "*id est,* Ciacco de l'Anguillaia rimatore fiorentino [that is, Ciacco dell'Anguillaia, the Florentine rhymer]." The perennial controversy over the identity of "colui che fece per viltade il gran rifiuto [the one who through cowardice made the great refusal]" may now be laid to rest, for Dante's marginal gloss states unequivocally: "*id est,* Ponzio Pilato, colui che vilmente rinunziò a giudicare Cristo [that is, Pontius Pilate, the one who through cowardice refused to judge Christ]." So much for the oceans of ink spilled on behalf of Pope Celestine V and others who seemed to fit the description of this emblematic figure, the only one singled out among the souls of the cowards in *Inferno* 3.

Perhaps the most *vexata quaestio* concerns the identity of the DXV—the "cinquecento diece e cinque [five hundred, ten, and five]"—of whom Beatrice speaks in *Purgatorio* 33 as the redeemer, the one who will reestablish order in the temporal sphere. To preserve some of the mystery of this prophecy, Dante first refers us back to his account of the apocalyptic encounter between the Veltro (greyhound) and the Lupa (she-wolf), by saying "sì come dissi de la lupa nel primo canto de l'Inferno," and then notes "*id est,* DXV ossia DVX, ma per giugnere a la sposizione giusta cercate 'l verse si nomato [just as I said of the she-wolf in the first canto of the Inferno, that is, DXV, or DVX (= Lat. *dux* 'leader'), but to arrive at the correct explanation search for the verse so named]." What did the poet mean by this new puzzle—to arrive at the proper interpretation we must search for the verse so named? After some meditation it occurred to me to look at the five hundred and fifteenth line in the poem, and lo and behold it reads "ch'e' sì mi fecer de la loro schiera" *(Inf.* 4.101: "they made me one of their company"). In this verse Dante is welcomed as the sixth member of the group of poets in Limbo—Homer, Virgil, Ovid, Lucan, and Horace.

Dante is, thus, the DVX; he is the poet who will set the world aright; he is
the Veltro (the "greyhound"), as one group of prominent scholars has
maintained. But, wait a minute, the Veltro is a misnomer, for the holograph does not have "Veltro" in *Inferno* 1.

Let us recall the context: Dante the Pilgrim's ascent of the mountain
has been impeded by the three beasts and especially by the *lupa*, the she-
wolf. Virgil elaborates on this animal's awesome powers and concludes
with the veiled prophecy of the one who will drive the *lupa* back into Hell.
From the autograph manuscript we now know that Dante wrote these crucial tercets as follows (the new readings are stressed):

> Molti son li animali a cui s'ammoglia,
> e più saranno ancora, infin che 'l *verro*
> verrà, che la farà morir con doglia.
> Questi non ciberà terra né *ferro*,
> ma sapïenza, amore e virtute,
> e sue nazion sarà tra Feltro e *Cerro*.
>
> *(Inf.* 1.100–105)

> [Many are the beasts with whom she mates, and there will yet be more,
> until the *boar* shall come who will deal her a painful death. He will not
> feed on earth or *iron*, but on wisdom, love, and virtue, and his birth shall
> be between Feltro and *Cerro*.]

The immediate reaction of most readers of Dante's *Comedy* to the substitu-
tion of "boar" *(verro)* for "greyhound" *(veltro)* would understandably be one
of dismay, disbelief, and perhaps even derision, so conditioned have we
been by this reference to the sleek hunting dogs of the aristocracy.
Nevertheless, we must now determine the meaning of the passage in the
light of this new—and correct—reading. And since the new reading is in
rhyme position, we have two other new readings as well. Let us begin with
the *verro*, the boar. In the first place, unlike the word "veltro," *verro* is a
hapax in Dante's works, a fact of no small importance, given that it occurs
in a prophecy. In the second place, Dante himself, perhaps anticipating
some hesitancy of future readers to, as it were, embrace the *verro*, notes in
the margin—"sì come disse Plinio ne l'ottavo de le Istorie naturali [just as
Pliny said in the eighth book of the Natural Histories]." The passage in
Pliny speaks of the characteristics of the boar, namely its tenacity, its feroc-
ity toward other animals that encroach upon its territory, and its particular
aversion to the lupine and vulpine species. Isidore of Seville repeats these
notions. The interpretation of the *verro* in medieval bestiaries lends support to Dante's choice, for they unanimously comment on the boar's

Christlike nature. Indeed, the boar is often linked to the griffin, a fabulous animal well known for its Christlike double nature, as we may observe in illuminations from bestiary manuscripts, which often present the griffin and the boar moving simultaneously upward to Paradise. The boar consumes neither earth *(terra)* nor iron *(ferro)*, two food groups that, conversely, comprise the principal diet of the she-wolf. The she-wolf feeds on earth—that is, on all that is corruptible and holds man captive to ephemeral, earthly pleasures—and she pigs out on iron—that is, on all that belongs, properly speaking, to the age of iron, that last and most degenerate of the four Ovidian ages. The identification of the *verro*'s place of birth—between Feltro and Cerro (figure 6)—is readily apparent, for the town of Cerro—so named because of the fine oak trees that once abounded there—lies some 150 km. due west of Feltro toward the Tyrrhenian Sea, and at the halfway point on a line drawn between these two locations we find—what else?!?!—Florence, the birthplace of Dante [deleted figure showed the birthplace of Dante as seen from the Forte di Belvedere]. Finally, the paronomastic play on *verro* ("boar") and *verrò* (future tense of *venire* 'I shall come') confirms Dante in his self-assigned role as the DXV.

While paleographic arguments could be adduced to explain the corruption of *verro* into *veltro,* this is not possible for the other received readings *ferro* > *peltro* and *cerro* > *Feltro*. I would suggest that the first scribes, either through ignorance or through a conscious desire to obscure the identity of Italy's redeemer, transformed these readings and thus gave countless critics a formidable exercise in decipherment for over six and one-half centuries.

And so, to conclude these brief remarks on what may be the most important literary discovery of our century, I should note that on many matters Dante scholarship must now arise from its deconstructed state and be completely reconstructed. For the textual premises on which so many seemingly erudite commentaries have been based are now proven to be incorrect, for example, the false Veltro (Hound) that has yielded to the true Verro (Boar) in *Inferno* 1. The great global upheaval and renewal in Dante studies will not come to pass without the shedding of blood or sweat or tears or ink, but the rooting out of the old rot should not, if you will pardon the pun, be "boring."

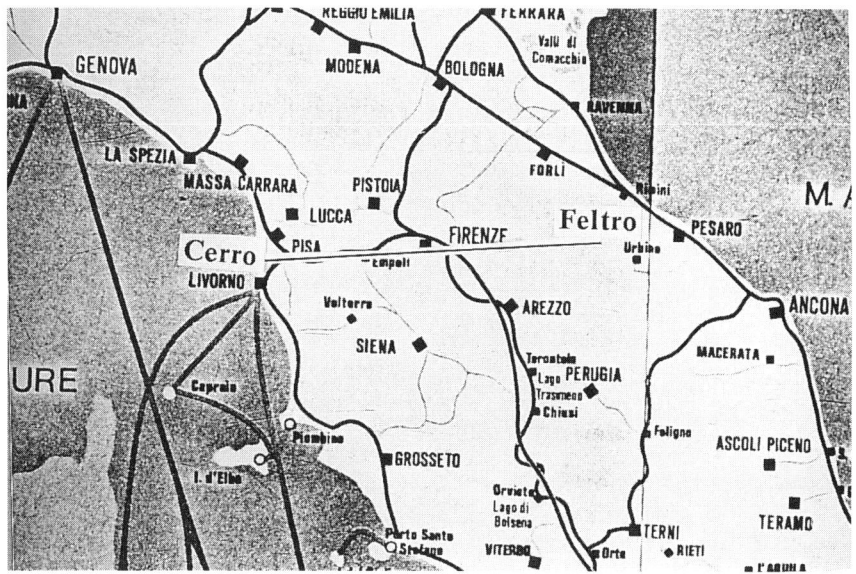

Figure 6.

NOTES

All photographs, including those deleted, were taken by Christopher Kleinhenz.

1. All passages from the *Comedy* follow the text established by Giorgio Petrocchi: Dante Alighieri, *La Commedia secondo l'antica vulgata*, 4 vols., Società dantesca italiana, Edizione Nazionale (Milan, 1966–67).

2. James Willis, *Latin Textual Criticism* (Urbana, 1974), p. 3.

3. Dante Alighieri, *Rime,* ed. Gianfranco Contini (Turin, 1965), p. 32.

4. "Il pendolino dice cercate a Pomposa," *Il resto del Carlino* (4 Nov. 1970).

5. Dante Alighieri, *La Divina Commedia: Concordanza, rimario, testo secondo l'antica vulgata*, 4 vols. (Turin, 1975).

6. St. Augustine, *Confessions* 8.12: "tolle lege, tolle lege."

7. For the discovery of the autograph manuscript of the *Decameron,* see the account by Charles S. Singleton in the introduction to his edition: Giovanni Boccaccio, *Decameron: Edizione diplomatico-interpretativa dell'autografo Hamilton 90* (Baltimore, 1974), pp. ix–x. See also the eyewitness account of Alberto Chiari in *Indagini e letture*, 3rd ser. (Florence, 1961), pp. 337–51. The first public revelation of Barbi's discovery was given by Chiari in the essay "Un nuovo autografo del Boccaccio?" which appeared in the *Fiera letteraria* (Rome) of 11 July 1948.

ARTORIUS REX BRITANNIAE FROM
A CONTEMPORARY WITNESS

Richard C. Hoffmann

Members of this *societas* will be interested to know that unknown agents have repeatedly thwarted this report to you. Travel plans have been disrupted and transcripts and draft papers have mysteriously vanished. Perhaps as I conclude, you, too, will ponder what mysterious forces are at work . . . and why.

My purpose this evening is to describe to the *societas*—and what group could more appreciate it?—the first clear evidence that King Arthur did live and rule! Not as the byname of some sub-Roman general or kinglet in Britain or the Continent but as, to use unimpeachable contemporary testimony, "Artorius rex Britanniae quondam rexque futurus." Yet the story of this discovery belongs not to the misty moors of the British Isles but to the chill gray of the bad old days in eastern Europe. Indeed, only recent events give me confidence that, with care, I can report it without risk to myself or others. But you will understand why certain particulars must still be passed over in silence.

As some of you are aware, I have spent years fishing about eastern and central Europe for late medieval economic records in local and regional archives. A while ago I traveled by train and bus—accompanied on the latter by crates of chickens and melons—to a small town off the beaten path near three then well protected international frontiers. Once a rich trade route passed that way, so a now-obscure and sleepy place early received a town charter and kept its civic autonomy. I was following a lead from an *Assistent* at the national library that books and archives from the long-secularized monastery of Saint Mendacionis had been moved in 1947 to the municipal library in the undamaged town hall, an early sixteenth-century structure with a nineteenth-century addition.

It was a dusty little place, with the one hotel not approved for foreign tourists, but a decent local beer. The municipal archivist and librarian was a minor party functionary with all the social graces of her class. She was duly impressed with my letter of introduction, which bore the seal of my university embossed in gold foil and the illegible signature of an engineer vice-president reputed once to have read a book without pictures. She was more impressed with a letter from one of her country's chief academicians, which bore several smudged imprints of rubber stamps. So she admitted me to the "Hall of Study," where two low-watt bulbs failed to enlighten one lower-watt "scientific attendant" asleep at his desk.

The attendant proved most helpful. After taking my signature and object of inquiry in an official ledger, he provided me with a typed list of holdings and some yellow forms. When I filled them out with the names of the files I wanted, he gently informed me that I had done them wrong. When I redid them, he gently informed me that foreigners were to use the pink forms instead. When I did the pink forms, he gently informed me that the typed file numbers were no longer valid and that I should refer to a handwritten sheet in the back for the new numbers. When I inserted the new numbers, he gently informed me that it was too late in the day to go to the *magazin*.

I was on a reconnaissance trip seeking administrative accounts and related records of quantitative serial data. These are not always easy to identify from perfunctory catalogue entries, but they are simply recognized once I can handle the object itself. Then I record a summary description and set especially suitable ones aside for microfilming or photocopying. Hence I rarely devoted as much time to each item as the attendant thought rightly proportionate to the interruption I had caused in his snooze with the soccer scores in the day-old newspaper from the provincial capital. I was sternly allowed but four items at a time, and I feared summary eviction when I first asked him to make a second trip to the *magazin* in a single day. Besides, the books and files were very heavy to carry into the Hall of Study. Yet this disdain for work habits appropriate to capitalist exploitation eventually proved to my advantage.

Some days of importuning inured the attendant to my persistence. Perhaps it also dawned on him that the sooner I had what I wanted, the sooner I would let the Hall of Study regain its normal somnolence. With the "lady comrade director" off to the provincial capital on "business of the state and people," he could even reduce short-term disruptions by having me carry the volumes myself. So help for a fellow worker thrust upon me access to the *magazin*—by an unlit circular wooden staircase up the very core of the old building. Huge tall shelves glimmered in the grainy light from small dormer windows last washed in honor of the visit of Count Anton the Pervert in 1587, but I could see more goodies than I had requested, or even learned about, from the catalogue. Surprisingly, among the bundles of files bound in now-faded red tape and the crumbling codices were some early printed books as well. One item caught my eye. I scribbled down its signature number. Before the next trip to the *magazin*, I filled out an appropriate form, and so we brought the volume down. It counted in my four. I stood on the shores of Serendip.

A sumptuous early eighteenth-century binding enclosed seven octavo gatherings on a paper bearing a watermark used in Savoyard mills ca. 1480–1540. The title page held two woodcuts. On the right, a man wearing a tall conical white hat sits on a stool in the corner of a room and contemplates the phrase "Me te mentirior?" (literally, "Would I lie to you?") written on the wall. On the left, a sumptuously dressed merchant tells a messenger, "Der Wechsel ist im Post" (literally, "The check is in the mail"). In gothic capitals of 3.2 mm., the title followed: *Epistulae sanctorum et aliorum innotae*. The printer's colophon was, as customary, on the final page: "In Konstanz: Einmal Undruck, MCCCCIIII"—probably a typographical error. The 110 intervening pages contained seventy-seven previously unknown letters from such familiar medieval personalities as Saint Patrick, Saint Bridget of Kildare, Saint Alban, Charlemagne, Wolfram von Eschenbach's friend Kyot, Geoffrey de Mandeville, and others. In a long dedicatory preface, the printer, Undruck (also known as Falscher von Schlaraffenland, and sometimes Subjectior), thanked his friend F. Abula (born Fritz Lugner), abbot of Saint Mendacionis, for allowing him to publish the letters from an ancient manuscript and consoled Abula for a recent fire in the monastery's library. The accuracy of the transcript was even verified by including a certificate from the local firm "Schlüpfrig, Zwirnig, Schlau, und Schlauer, consiliores in legibus," whose register, complete with special carbon parchments and disappearing ink, I had earlier seen in the provincial archive.

The house of Saint Mendacionis—now become a state hospital for the mentally ill—had a peculiar early history. Its founder and patron was among the first wandering Irish monks to penetrate the secluded hills of central Europe in the ninth century. He was originally called Blarneius Scottus. Following an unfortunate incident in which he pledged his right hand to a Viking that the cart horse he sold was guaranteed to be the son of Roland's Veillantif, he commonly used the byname *Sinistro,* or "Lefty." He then abandoned secular life and took the religious name "Mendacio." His house of refuge, also early known for its possession of the relics of Saint Poteen, whose blessed waters were well-reputed for their curing of mental ills and causing of wondrous visions, came under the protection of a powerful family of local barons, the lords Loozjorwitz. From the late thirteenth century, cadets of that house traditionally served as abbots of Saint Mendacionis, though none is known to have successfully completed so much as a year at their country's university. In the background of our abbot F. Abula, therefore, belong such neglected figures as Piotr the Dolt, Bernard the Power Forward, Engelhardt the Dubious, and his maternal cousin, the Blessed Credula. With such a background of learning and faith, we can place strong credence in our text.

Letter 22 is the one I draw to your attention this evening. It is from Saint Patrick to Pope Silverius and is dated 11 A.M. on 3 ides August in the year of our Lord 537. Patrick asks the pope when to celebrate Easter and quotes at length from an earlier letter by his unnamed "doctor pater noster in Britanniae" written "in tempore Artorii regis Britanniae, alias rex quondam rexque futurus." Plainly Thomas Malory or his source had access to this or a related text. Unfortunately, the passages from the earlier letter itself remain entirely in their original Pictish (with distinctive sixth-century grammatical forms) and hence unreadable, at least to a hurried specialist in eastern Europe. Personal names seemingly detectable, however, included *Gabanmaclot, Llankolet,* and *Ghanewera.*

Other items in the collection also caught my eye. Saint Brendan wrote of sailing westwards into the bay behind a long arm-shaped promontory, deciding not to land at a big shoreline rock, and coasting northwards to a harbor with islands and a river. The natives, he reported, called their village "Baastan," and they invited the Irish monks to settle on the south side. The bishop of Greenland ordered an engraved memorial stone for placement in Interior Vinland, a site in "Minnesota, where we can catch walleyes." The bishop of Winchester in 1426 censured an abbess named Berners for too much time spent fishing. The coroner of London in 1484 examined the bodies of two youths found in the moat of the Tower. As all these sources will shed light on important problems in medieval history and literature, they deserve treatment in future addresses to this society.

But was there more? Maybe clarification of Edward II's career after 1327? Perhaps solutions for the mysterious site of Great Moravia? I noted a carefully rubricated cross. Was there information on the ancestry of the Merovingians and the later role of the Templars? Will we ever know?

The afternoon hours ended before I could complete my look at the volume, and I knew better than to aggravate the attendant by asking him to let me stay on. We put the book with my other items on a special shelf in the workroom and I signed out, taking only my notes with me. When I returned the next morning there was a different attendant. I was told that the *magazin* was closed but that I could still work on items I had checked out. The book was not on the shelf. The entry sheet showed only my accounting files. I went to see the director, who had returned from the capital. As a special favor she agreed that I could have one more item, especially important for my scientific research, brought from the *magazin*. I submitted my request on the appropriate slip of paper and obtained a book with the very call number I had recorded—but it was a different book, a grammar of Old Polovtsian printed at Lwów in 1557.

"There must be some mistake."

"Oh, no, Mr. Doctor Professor. See, here is your request. It is the numbers you are writing down."

This was before the days of laptop computers. At least I still had my jottings in my spiral notebook. I finished my other research and returned to the capital, checking in to my usual hotel and, as always, surrendering my passport. I was given a room on a different floor and the opposite side of the building than in the past. The next morning a member of the hotel staff asked me to come to the front desk after breakfast. There I was told something was amiss with my visa and I must report to the special police for foreigners. My train left in the afternoon, so I raced to the address I had been given . . . and waited in line for three hours. When seen by an officer, I was told I should have reported to the police in the little town myself rather than relying on the hotel to do it, but that the omission could be solved with an appropriate stamp there in the capital. Profuse thanks to the "comrade officer." Back to the hotel, check out, hurry to the railway station, and win the debate for the seat I have reserved but someone else occupies. After minimal hassle traversing the border and a long journey, I reached my destination in the decadent West and late that night sorted out various papers to ship back home for the savings in weight. I reviewed the notebook to see if I needed anything there for the rest of my trip. There was no page on Undruck's volume.

THE LOST LETTERS OF
CHARLEMAGNE'S FIRST WIFE, AUTOSTRADA,
ALSO CALLED DESIDERATA OR DESIDERIA

Richard R. Ring

Some years ago—it does not matter exactly when—I stumbled (literally) on a book in the Oskaloosa, Kansas, Bookbarn, that last resting place for worn, torn, and hurt books from most of the libraries of northeast Kansas. This particular volume was printed on highly acidic paper, so that it was now yellowed and brittle; its covers—faced with what I took to be fake nineteenth-century vellum—were cracked and falling off the text block. Its crude title page read: *Le Désir, ou Mémoires d'une femme du plaisir* (Paris: Desmond Lombard & fils, 1891). It took only a few moments to realize that I had in my hands a French translation of that most famous of eighteenth-century libertine books, *Fanny Hill*. And I was instantly warmed by the thought that for a mere fifty cents I might improve my reading ability—if not my oral capacity—in French.

In this state of intellectual excitement, I almost overlooked the stained and smudged bookplate indicating that the volume had once belonged to the "H * * * Spencer Ash * * * Library." My first thought was that someone had stolen a book from the Helen Spencer Research Library at the University of Kansas. Quickly realizing that this was just about as likely as getting past Cerberus out of Hades, I considered the possibility that the book had actually been discarded—ferried out of the library on a dark night by some unknown Charon.

While I was musing on the volume's origins, I noticed on the back fly-leaf of the book a penciled name: "Pisanus Fraxi," followed by a number. Immediately an alternative explanation sprang into my head. I realized the source of the partially illegible bookplate and of the book itself: "Henry

Spencer Ashbee Library." Ashbee was the great Victorian collector and cat-
aloguer of erotica, whose bibliography of prohibited books was originally
issued under the name "Pisanus Fraxi." Now at least I knew the name and
provenance of this odd-looking rose, if not exactly how it got to Oskaloosa,
Kansas.

My subsequent examination of Ashbee's catalogue revealed no such
translation of *Fanny Hill* into French. Nor did inquiries to the British
Library's "private case" or the Bibliothèque nationale's "L'enfer" collection
turn up any hint that such a book ever existed. Moreover, the question
became moot when, while drifting on the Kaw River in a canoe with the
love of my life one fine spring afternoon, I accidently dropped the volume
into the water. I grabbed at it as it fell and managed to save only the fake
vellum boards. But these magic moments, involving great physical fatigue
and intense motor excitement, produced visions of people known in the
past and of books unwritten. For in my rough handing, the boards split
open to reveal a number of real parchment stiffeners.

When I got home and laid these out to dry—later examination showed
that the ink had blurred in only a few places—I discovered eight fragments
written in a crabbed cursive that could have been saec. viii or xiv (I make
no claim to paleographic expertise). The disjointed story told in these
fragments of what appeared to be one or more letters, however, was partly
familiar to me. After numerous trials of arrangement and painful hours of
squinting at the letters, I decided that this was the story: an old woman, evidently a nun, was writing to a much younger relative, and also perhaps a
nun, about some of the things she had experienced when she had been
young and married to a great king whom she called "Karlone"—"Big Karl."

I came to realize that this must be the Frankish monarch and emper-
or known to us as "Charlemagne" and that the writer must be Charlemagne's first wife, daughter of the Lombard king Desiderius, whose name
is sometimes given in the sources as "Desiderata" or "Desideria," and
hence in French, "Désirée." According to these fragments, her real name,
her Lombard name, was "Audo-rada" or "Audos-rada." These are perfectly
regular Lombard/Germanic name elements. I have chosen—and it is a
choice not an Eco—to think that she was "Audostrada," also named
Desiderata.

Now the sources tell us only that Charlemagne's mother, Bertrada, or
Bertha, traveled to Italy in 770 and arranged with the Lombard king to
have her son marry his daughter. One of Desiderius's daughters,
Adalperga, was already married to Arichis, the duke of Benevento, while
another, Liutperga, was married to Duke Tassilo of Bavaria. Still another

was the abbess of San Salvatore, or Santa Giulia, in Brescia, which had
been founded and endowed by Desiderius's wife Ansa. It looks as if Bertha
was trying to forge an alliance through marriage of Franks, Lombards, and
Bavarians, all of whom were enemies of the Lombards both before and
after. It didn't work.

Audostrada, or Desiderata, went to Francia, married Charlemagne
(probably in 771), but before a year had passed was repudiated by him and
sent back home to her father in Pavia. One source suggests that she was
barren, though nine or ten months seems too short a time for anyone to
be sure, while a very late and disputed source states that after she arrived
back in Italy, she bore a son who died at birth. Whatever the case, within
two years Charlemagne's armies swept into Italy and destroyed the
Lombard kingdom. Desiderius, his wife, and daughter were captured and
sent off into exile, presumably in Francia.

Such is all that the known sources tell us about this curious episode in
Charlemagne's life—sources known up until now, that is. For the fragments that I uncovered from *Fanny Hill,* read with a proper sense of meta-
linguistic submission and intertextual hermeneutic, will present the unpre-
sentable, the ontological transmission of "what is the case." (As Watson
asked and Wittegenstein answered, these Ecoes of "roses that bloom in the
spring have nothing to do with the case.") Disordered as they appear, I
have arranged them in an order in the elegant hope that the sheer narrative pleasure of the story they tell will gladden our several solitudes. "That
little life about which you asked tells how our Karlone liked to hear stories
read to him while he ate, stories of ancient kings and heroes and their
wars." Our lady is obviously referring to Einhard's *Vita Karoli* or *Life of
Charlemagne.* Since this was undoubtedly written in the 820s, we must infer
that Desiderata (1) was a very old lady, perhaps in her eighties, when she
wrote this and (2) had seen a copy of Einhard's work.

> . . . and even Augustine's *City of God.* I remember all too well those bar-
> barous songs of Ingeld and Siegfried, of dwarfs and their gold and of
> monsters and their mothers. He had memorized these when he was
> young, even more than the holy words of Scripture, and he tried to make
> me fill my mind with these foolish tales too. And dimly I still recall how
> the great child-king "made slaves of soldiers from every land, crowds of
> captives he'd beaten into terror; he'd traveled to Danemark alone, an
> abandoned child, but changed his fate, lived to be rich and much hon-
> ored. He ruled lands on all sides: wherever the sea would take them his
> soldiers sailed, returned with tribute and obedience. There was a brave
> king. . . ." And Karlone believed it too—believed that he should emulate
> the heroes of the pagans, that even I, raised in that most Catholic city of

Pavia, should act the part of his golden-ringed queen, raising high the flowing cup and drinking deep, and then "passing from warrior to warrior, pouring a portion from the jeweled cup for each, till I, the bracelet-wearing queen, had carried the mead cup throughout the hall."

Desiderata is here obviously referring to and quoting from the Saxon poem that we now know as *Beowulf*. And I think that we can be certain of this even though such characters as Beowulf himself and Grendel are not mentioned directly. How delightful, too, it is to note her slight distaste for her husband's favorite entertainments. Delightful also that we can now settle once and for all time the vexing problem of the date of *Beowulf* and place it no later than the middle of the eighth century! But in the same fragment she goes on:

As for Augustine—when I was borne over the Alps by Bertha and the handsome Breton Count Roland to become his [that is Charles's] bride, he could barely understand the Latin of the psalms and the prayers. It was I who urged on him the duty of learning the language of Our Lord, for He and He alone might prepare the true feast and bring enemies to sup like lambs. I told him of our most learned Paul [the Deacon] and his students from whom I and my sisters had learned not only Latin but even some Greek in the palace school. And I was pleased that he took up my suggestions. For though I never saw him, I know that Paul did come many years later to Karlone's court and that the king himself learned to read and understand even the most difficult of theological writings by the great Church Fathers. And as for Einhard's contention that Karlone could not write—I myself showed him how to form letters. And I know that he did not forget, for many years later after his wife had died [that is Charlemagne's last wife, Liutgard] and after he had restored the father lion's blindness instead of trampling on it along with the adder—as the psalm [90.13] commands—he wrote to me several letters in his own hand, passing them on to me through the good will of our abbess, his sister Gisela.

Where should I begin? The one obvious reference here—"the father lion's blindness"—is to Pope Leo III (Papa Leone), supposedly beaten and blinded by Roman thugs before Charlemagne rescued him and got himself crowned emperor. Beyond that—though we may believe that Charlemagne was less lettered and less interested in Latin in 770 than historians would have us believe—I do not think we need to credit Desiderata with singlehandedly beginning the Carolingian Renaissance. Charlemagne, however, was undoubtedly more information-literate than lettered, as the modern jargon would have it. She goes on in another fragment: "His man-

ners and ways of dealing with women were as rough and barbarous as his
Latin. I called him 'my Goliath' and told him that I would be his David, not
killing him with kindness but taming him with the slings and arrows of out-
rageous fortune. He said that his arrows of . . . — . . . desired to be David
. . ."Here there is a large gap in the text and several water-smudged lines.
But once again we learn that Desiderata is the key to understanding an
important element of the Carolingian mind: the use of biblical names later
reported among the *illuminati* at the court of Charlemagne. However,
Alcuin himself must still take the flak for the classical *nomina* (himself as
"Horace," Anglibert as "Homer," and so forth). It is possible though that
Desiderata and Alcuin may have acted in concert, since we know that he
had visited the court of Desiderius in the 760s, where he would have met
the teenaged daughter of the king. This may indeed explain Desiderata's
cryptic allusion to "the dawning of her little white dawns *(albescens aurorae
albinae albionis)*"—her angels—or is that her "angel of the morning?" The
fragment resumes: "If you were to protect the Holy Mysteries and unite all
of Christendom, especially those most perfidious and piglike Romans, I
would even call you 'my Hercules in Christ's struggle.'"

One comment should suffice: evidently the vulgar expansion of SPQR,
"*Sono Porci Quelli Romani* [those Romans are pigs]," was well known to
northern Italians as early as the eighth century. Perhaps it was even a
Lombard aphorism. Incidently this text in which Desiderata uses the name
"Hercules," thus revealing her knowledge of Virgil, if not Boethius, reads:
"Hercule in agathon Christi." This confirms Desiderata's earlier mysterious
statement that she knew some Greek.

In the second-to-last fragment in my ordering of things, Desiderata
explains to her young correspondent how she became the wife of
Charlemagne and then was divorced, apparently now in her old age showing no bitterness toward her husband:

> . . . bound himself to me and made me his debtor in his life and in his
> death. And I would gratefully pass over in silence all the benefits he con-
> ferred on me and on our family, were not his supposed deeds now glori-
> ously chronicled by that little one of almost nonexistent talents. He of
> course does not name me or describe the circumstances of our marriage
> for he was not there and the events were too shameful to be spoken of by
> Karlone in later years. And no one, if they had heard, if anyone remem-
> bered, dared speak of them. It was his own fault for sending that most
> handsome and brave Count Roland to accompany me to Frankland. What
> was I to do? I was so young, barely yet seventeen, and though well versed
> in the Roman tongue, I was unaccustomed to the clever ways of the

French. I fell in love with him, though I refrained from more than sneaking longing glances at his beauty. I loved my husband, too, and was true to him save for that one time. Roland without hesitation climbed into the cart in which I was riding and pressed himself against me and forced me to sit on his lap. They should have told me earlier that Roland was known as "the one who bears his javelin into the women's quarters *(gynaecei verutus),*" or sometimes as *gynaecei verres* or boar in the bedroom. The noble Karlone bore his shame silently. For he thought that it was perfectly all right for him to have many concubines but that women, especially his woman, should not be allowed even a secret lover. And when he and my father began to quarrel again, he took the opportunity to send me back to Pavia and marry the incomparable Hildegard. And I bore the pain of that journey across the Alps and bore the child, his first-born legitimate son, in pain; and in pain and sorrow, too, suffered the loss as he was snatched from me and borne back by the Franks. I have never seen my only son and never, save one time, heard of him. But my blessed abbess, Gisela, hinted to me that she knew my pain and sorrow and that the "little devil" had survived, though more I do not know. As for Count Roland, who can doubt that Karlone deliberately abandoned him and his men to the attack of the treacherous Gascons, just as that earlier David sent Uriah to his certain death before the walls of Rabbah. For I heard that Roland tried to seduce Hildegard as well.

This passage barely needs my commentary. For if Desiderata is to be believed, we have here the true origins and explanation for the *Chanson de Roland,* as well as, I would argue, part of the matter of Brittany, that is, the story of Lancelot and Guinevere. The whispered, distorted tales of Charlemagne's early days form the basis of these whole segments of medieval literature. And I would even venture the suggestion that phrase used by Desiderata of Roland—*gynaecei verres*—became by some twist of fate associated with his alleged lover and that she in the legends became "Gynaeceverres" or "Guineverre," while he in the legends recalled ever more dimly was still that gay blade "Lance-a-lot."

I think this is enough of our Lombard lady for this evening. Through her efforts, so oddly preserved, we have solved some of the major desiderata of medieval studies: the date of *Beowulf,* the true origins of the *Chanson de Roland* and of Roland's treachery, the real-life roots of that most charming part of the Arthurian cycle, the prototype of the stories of Lancelot and Guinevere, and of Tristan and Isolde, and how the worm of lust destroyed the Franco-Lombard alliance and Camelot. I will let our lady have the last word:

Now I am very old, and my inability to see in this post-Lombard world of fragments is perhaps the effect that the great shadow, the great darkness, as it approaches, is casting over this aging world. "Ubi est gloria nunc Babyloniae ac Paviae?" Where are the snows of yesteryear? The earth is dancing the dance of death. All I can do now is to be silent and to beg you to allow this letter to sink into the oblivion it deserves after you have read it. Soon I will be joined to my beginnings, as the abbesses of my order and the great Church Fathers have taught me. I shall sink into the divine shadow in a dumb silence and ineffable union and will not know the equal or the unequal, or anything else. And all differences will be forgotten in that place with neither work nor image. I leave you this letter; I no longer know what it is about. Yesterday's rose endures in its name; we cling to empty names *(stat rosa pristina nomine, nomina nuda tenemus)*. And I will no longer be the great king's desired one, his *desiderata,* as he addressed me in his last letter, but still his empty Desiderata named Autostrada. It is cold. A novice is bringing my supper. I have always depended on the kindness of strangers.

ON THE DISCOVERY OF A LOST MANUSCRIPT OF CHRÉTIEN DE TROYES: TOWARD AN APPRECIATION OF ITS VAST IMPORTANCE FOR THE STUDY OF MEDIEVAL LITERATURE AND CULTURE

Evelyn Birge Vitz

I am afraid that I must risk spoiling what should have been a most pleasant evening for you and for me by beginning on a very unpleasant note. I wish to express my indignation—nay, my outrage—at having my paper placed in this session, which, I am told, is devoted, not to true scholarship, but to mere parodies of scholarship. My having been assigned to this session—clearly by the phallocratic and phallogocentric organizers of Kalamazoo—as a subtle way of silencing me, a woman, is the straw that broke this camel's back. This injustice has converted me, at long last, to feminism (some will say I have been slow to see the light).

But here I am—here we are!—and at least I appear to have a somewhat larger audience than the one that generally attends the serious and scholarly sessions at which I present my papers. Let us begin. I have identified a major unknown manuscript of the great twelfth-century French *romancier* Chrétien de Troyes, the very parent of Arthurian romance. I should like at least to sketch out for you the vast—the truly incredible—importance of this manuscript.[1] (I can hardly scratch the surface here.) We have here nothing less than the entire oeuvre of Chrétien, including the romances that were thought lost.

Moreover, this is an author-supervised collection—the first, well before the compilation of the *Cantigas* by Alfonso el Sabio in the 1270s. Included in this manuscript is an author portrait, which I will show you. Parts of the

189

manuscript have musical notation—the earliest notation of any secular manuscript. You will see this notation. The manuscript also contains both exciting scribal marginal commentary and, in some places, full-fledged commentary. Finally, this manuscript tells us something we have all wanted to know: who Chrétien de Troyes really was.

First, let me describe the manuscript for you briefly: three volumes, of octavo format (135 mm. x 94 mm.), clearly made for private and personal use. The hand: early gothic, datable to the late twelfth century in France—but this merely corroborates what the manuscript itself says, for the manuscript was actually signed and dated by the scribe.

The manuscript is known to have been in the possession of Eleanor of Castile, who was the half-sister of Marie de Champagne and the daughter of Henry II of England and Eleanor of Aquitaine. The manuscript made its way into the treasury of a certain Spanish monastery—a monastery which does not allow outsiders to consult its books—where it lay hidden for centuries. (Its number has been largely scratched out, but appears to read "Mons [text here hard to decipher] Biblioteca de la Abadía, cod. fr. 1492"—a number resonating, surely, with other discoveries.) The manuscript left the monastery in the early 1970s when a monk stole it, one volume at a time, sold the books to a rare-book dealer in New York, defrocked himself, and married a former (similarly defrocked) nun. The first volume was purchased by a wealthy benefactor of New York University. It was, briefly, alas, the great jewel in our Rare Book Library's small crown; it was catalogued as New York University, MS Huebner 213. The other two volumes were bought by a Japanese industrialist—Hideaki Mitsubishi—who allowed me to examine them during a business trip he made to New York shortly before his death. (He assigned the number "C 22" to the volumes.)

Before I return to the scribe's contributions, let me speak briefly about the contents of the manuscript. As a literary scholar, I was personally thrilled to read the lost romances of Chrétien. Early in *Cligés,* you recall, Chrétien speaks of having composed a "Shoulder Bite," a story of King Mark and Iseut, and two other works as well. As Chrétien puts it:

> Et le mors de l'espaule fit
> Del roi Marc et d'Ysalt la blonde
> Et de la hupe et de l'aronde
> Et del rossingol la muance.

This manuscript gives us all these romances—and they are very surprising indeed.

In Chrétien's version of the Tristan story, Iseut eventually petitions the pope—successfully—for a divorce from Mark on the grounds of consanguinity: Iseut's mother's brother's godmother was the wife of Mark's maternal uncle's sister's half-brother's college roommate. Iseut is then free to marry Tristan, which she does. They have many children. Tristan however, turns into a rather tiresome middle-aged man. Not only is he jealous of Iseut, always locking her up, but also, unfortunately, matrimony has not quelled his fondness for illicit romance. To him, every cup of mead is a "magic potion." He eventually takes up with another maiden, Iseut *aux genoux roses,* who, he is forever saying (to the point of extreme tedium), reminds him of Iseut the Fair when she was fairer. In a word, Iseut's marriage to Tristan is no picnic, and when the story ends, she is thinking increasingly of a handsome older (paternal) uncle of hers—and even rather fondly of Mark. She is contemplating meeting one, or perhaps both, of them in the forest (the story line is not quite clear here).

The *Mors de l'espaule* turns out to be a highly erotic work—so bawdy that I cannot even describe it to this refined audience. I blushed as I read it! Suffice it to say, the "shoulder bite" appears to constitute our first literary reference to the hickey.

As to the work Chrétien refers to in *Cligés* as being "de la hupe et de l'aronde et del rossingol la muance"—"about the metamorphosis of the hoopoe, the swallow, and the nightingale"—this is, like Ovid's story, about Procne, Philomela, and Tereus. Chrétien's is a very violent work, about what we would term today the sexual harassment and disempowerment of women, and about their revenge through extreme forms of child abuse: the outraged women feed Tereus's son Itys to him for dinner (all this, of course, before they turn into various kinds of fowl). In a word, this is the story of men's oppression of women and women's tragic but understandable—indeed surely justifiable—revenge.

To return to our scribe, who did a great deal more than just copy Chrétien's text. This amazing scribe has signed her name—yes, *her* name— to the manuscript. She gives her name as "Hermengarde." She is, she tells us, the daughter of Jean and also of Rachel—"fille Jehan si de Rachel." She tells us that she made the manuscript for "cil qui se fist apeler Chretien" and that it was made for the countess Marie de Champagne. It is even dated Pentecost, 1191. Marie bequeathed it to her half-sister Eleanor of Castile, whom I mentioned earlier.

Here are a few of Hermengarde's extraordinary contributions to this manuscript: first, she provides an intermittent marginal commentary. From time to time, she has penned the words "a!" and "oi!" in the margin.

The spelling varies (sometimes the "oi" has an "l" at the end), and some-times the two words are joined together as a single exclamation: "aoi." These syllables seem to occur primarily when male characters do some-thing particularly stupid or unkind to women, or when they lie to women, or when they harass or threaten women—all of which, of course, occur quite often. Thus, when Erec first begins to torment his wife Enide, when Yvain leaves his wife Laudine, and then again when he fails to come back when he had promised, when Perceval kisses the maiden in the tent against her will—and so on, and on—Hermengarde has written "aoi" in the margin.

I have come to the conclusion that Hermengarde has given us the first feminist commentary on a medieval text! Let's look at her choice of the words "a! oi." The literal meaning of this is "oh, yes!"—"oï," of course, meaning "yes" in northern French. But, surely, the idiomatic sense of the words suggests the modern expressions "Oh yeah!" or "Yeah, sure!"—espe-cially when the man is lying to, or otherwise deceiving, the woman. This choice may also be related to the fact that Hermengarde appears to have a Jewish mother—"Rachel" being of course a Jewish name; thus her choice of the exclamation "oi!" may be, as they say, overdetermined, as well as being polysemic.

For all of us who work on the epic and who have long puzzled over the mysterious letters "AOI" at the end of some of the *laisses* of the Oxford manuscript of *The Song of Roland,* this is a very exciting discovery! It sug-gests that the scribe of the Oxford *Roland* may also have been a woman, indeed a protofeminist, disgusted by male behavior. This manuscript may have been for performance to a female audience: a rueful and sarcastic "aoi" ever answering back—giving the lie—to chivalric fictions: "Yeah, sure!"

Hermengarde has also given us, for at least parts of the romances, a full-scale commentary—such as, we have long believed, only the Bible received in this period. This commentary provides allegorical exposition—long before Dante and the letter to Can Grande. Here Hermengarde focuses not on just one romance but on the very role of Arthur, who by a pun is assimilated to the word "author" and to the very concept of "author-ity." Arthur is little more, here, than an allegory of the authority of Queen Guinevere.

Hermengarde also provides Aristotelian commentary for certain pas-sages—and I need scarcely tell you how astonishing it is for us to have such a commentary in the late twelfth century, and for a vernacular, secular text! To give just one brief example, Hermengarde defines King Mark's deficiencies as a husband in Aristotelian terms: too little substance and too many accidents.

Finally, Hermengarde provides musical notation for at least parts of the romances. It is not clear whether the romances were to be performed to music in their entirety or whether we are dealing with musical interpolations. Hermengarde refers to the music as "ours." Thus, she and the poet appear to have composed the music together. In any event, there are two distinct melodies here; one accompanies the octosyllabic lines themselves; the other seems to correspond to some sort of lyric refrain.

The melody is preserved in Boethian letter notation,[2] a notation used primarily for didactic purposes in the Middle Ages, but also occasionally for recording nontraditional sorts of music. While the letter notation permits an exact recovery of the pitches, it offers no clue to the rhythm of the melody. Luckily, however, a few snippets of mensural notation were added in desultory fashion to the first line at some time in the thirteenth century. This suggests not only that the work enjoyed a rather long transmission but also that at one point it was sung in the second rhythmic mode, a rhythmic idiom thought not to predate 1200. The second-mode rhythm of the octosyllabic lines would be as follows:

The rhythm of the seven- and six-syllable lines that make up the melody's refrain goes as follows:

The first melody is transcribed in the manuscript as follows:

G G G K K L L O
M K M K H N L I
K K L M M N M M
L M N N N O N M
[illegible, and in part cut out]
? ? ? ? ? N L K

As to the refrain:

> K K K L K K G
>
> H G H I K K

Thus, we have here, in a twelfth-century manuscript, in early medieval notation and in the second rhythmic mode, the melodies of "La Marseillaise" and "Good King Wenceslas"—melodies that were until now thought to be "modern." Chrétien de Troyes, in collaboration with Hermengarde, appears to be the author of both of these melodies.

But let me turn now to the question: who was Chrétien de Troyes? You all know that the identity of this poet has long puzzled scholars. The vast majority of medievalists have believed that Chrétien was a *clerc,* schooled in Ovid, Virgil, the Bible, and rhetoric. I—along with, I believe, virtually no one else—have recently come to believe that Chrétien was a high-class minstrel, rather than a *clerc.* But at any rate, Chrétien's identity has long eluded us—and (as is ever the case) the very lack of firm evidence has invited the proliferation of hypotheses.

This manuscript can put all speculation to rest. Here Chrétien's identity is revealed. But it is revealed in a sequence of enigmas that I have had to resolve; I invite you to retrace my steps with me.

First, as I mentioned earlier, this manuscript contains an author portrait—the first known author portrait of a *romancier* (figure 1).

I am sure you will agree with me that it is beautiful. Here the poet is shown in a letter *A*—which is surely a bit curious, since the text itself does not begin with that letter. Here we see Chrétien very much, it must be said, in the guise of a *jongleur*—a gracious, slender, rather feline *jongleur.* The figure wears a curious coronet-shaped headdress. We should recall that several minstrels were known as, or referred to themselves as, "king," such as Adenet le Roi. The figure is, as you can see, also carrying a *viele.* Beside the miniature are the words: "li conteor ki se fist apeler Chrestien" ("the story-teller who had himself called Chrétien").

Incidentally, this manuscript also has an image of a musician carrying a small—long, thin—rather mysterious instrument that we have finally been able to identify as a kazoo.

While I was, I will confess to you, relieved to find that Chrétien was not a *clerc,* I was no nearer to knowing who Chrétien was. But as I was reading Chrétien's conclusion to the *Perceval*—the last work in the manuscript—I fell upon the following lines:

> Qui de moi veut connaissance
> Montez dix vers, sans decevance.

Figure 1. Author portrait: Crowned *jongleur* playing a *viele*. Formerly New York University MS Huebner 213, fol. 2r. (Image by Elliot Nesterman, used with permission.)

That is:

> The person who wishes to have knowledge of me
> [Should] go up ten lines, without trickery.

Up I went, and here is what I found. The lines read:

> Li reis partit en terre aliene
> Or triste en est remaint la reine.

That is:

> The king left for a foreign country,
> Now sadly the queen remained behind.

These lines were not surrounded with other lines of text as would normally be the case, but were set off from their context: surrounded only by several centimeters of empty but eloquent parchment—and an empty cartouche for an illumination that was never completed.

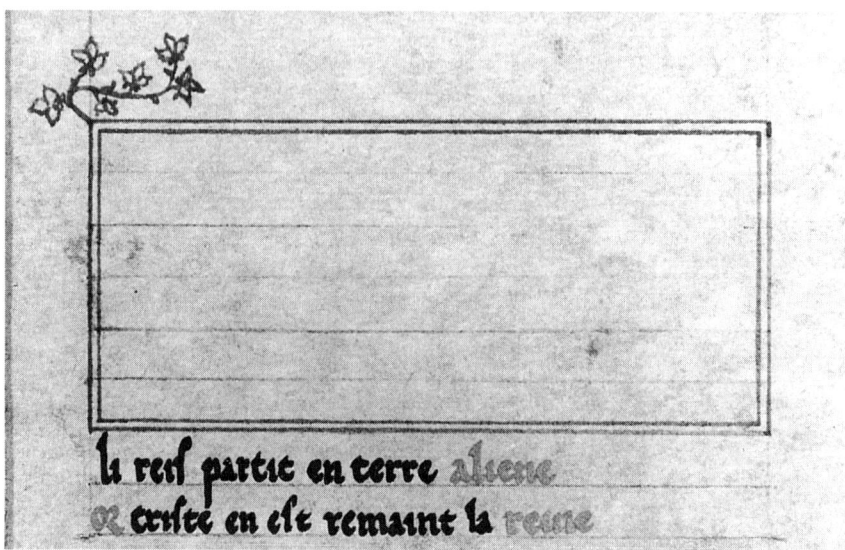

Figure 2. Textual enigma, below floriated but empty 6-line cartouche. Private collection of Hideaki Mitsubishi, Fr. C 22, vol. II, fol. 112r. (Image by Elliot Nesterman, used with permission.)

Here is a picture of these lines (figure 2), and here you can see how the author set up the enigma.[3] Not all the text was written in black ink; certain letters were done in silver. When I rubbed the manuscript gently, very gently—the Japanese industrialist watching nervously over my shoulder—the tarnish of eight centuries vanished, melted away, revealing this message.

> Li reis partit en terre **aliene**
> Or triste en est remaint la **reine**

The silver letters spell out "Alienor reine"—Queen Aliénor! No Queen Aliénor is even conceivable other than the great Eleanor of Aquitaine herself! As I finished deciphering this enigma, chills ran up my spine. And yet it all made perfect sense!

Who was Chrétien de Troyes's greatest patron, or rather patroness? Marie de Champagne, Eleanor's own daughter! Why did she give the divorced and remarried Iseut a whole gaggle of children and, more importantly, an old bore of a lover turned jailer and middle-aged, lecherous bogeyperson? What could be more like Aliénor/Eleanor's own relationship with Henry II, who perhaps eventually made even the tame and tepid Louis VII look good, and who would certainly have made her think back fondly on her uncle Raymond, with whom she had had such scandalous fun while she was party to the Second Crusade. Why else are so many of Chrétien's stories—the ones that men presumably have wanted lost—about men's ill treatment of women?

But what about all the learning in those romances? Aliénor was, indeed, "learned"—in Ovidian stories, for example—but she was no clerk. She was an intelligent, cultivated woman who was born and raised in one of the most exciting courts of medieval Europe—that of the dukes of Aquitaine—and she spent the rest of her life in a succession of royal and other noble courts. In a word, throughout her entire life she rubbed elbows with learned men and women. No wonder she was knowledgeable!

But *can* Aliénor have been Chrétien de Troyes? Let's look at the historical facts, at dates: Chrétien's career began sometime after 1164, when Marie de Capet, Aliénor's daughter by Louis VII, married Henry the Liberal, count of Champagne. Most of the romances are thought to date from the late 1160s and 1170s. In 1181 Henry of Champagne returned from the Holy Land and died shortly thereafter. Chrétien is then known to have had as patron Philip of Alsace, count of Flanders. It is during this period—in the late 1180s—that *Perceval* was apparently composed. Chrétien died sometime after 1190, though we do not know when.

And Aliénor? What was she doing during these years? In the 1160s Aliénor moved about freely—and she is known to have been on cordial terms with her daughter Marie. It may well be that during these happy years Aliénor got the idea of dressing up as a *jongleur* and performing romances incognito to the accompaniment of a *viele*—which she is known to have played beautifully—at festive gatherings. Is such an idea—or dressing up as a *jongleur* and acting out the part—out of character for her? Hardly! Let's not forget that Eleanor of Aquitaine was a role player, and even a bit of a cross dresser, from way back, decking herself up as an Amazon on the Second Crusade.

For fifteen crucial years—from 1174 to 1189—Eleanor was out of circulation, thanks to Henry. Would her imprisonment have kept her from her poetic activity? Hardly! What better way to while away the hours than to compose romances—and arrange to have them performed at her daughter's court. Whether she sent copies of the romances, or arranged for *jongleurs* to learn them by heart, remains unclear. (One small miniature in the manuscript shows a woman writing, but it is not clear whether this is a self-portrait of Hermengarde or a picture of Eleanor writing.)

Incidentally, it does make sense that it is during this period of her captivity that Eleanor composed *Lancelot*—which, precisely, begins when the queen is stolen away and kept in captivity; it ends abruptly with Lancelot still imprisoned, perhaps because it may all have been too painful for the poet to bear. This romance clearly provides a *mise en abyme* of Eleanor herself, who clearly longed for some faithful servant—or lover—to come rescue her. But she was only freed on, and by, the death of Henry.

After her release from captivity Eleanor was deeply involved in political and diplomatic missions—in statespersonship—and presumably had little time for the composition of romances. It is therefore not surprising that she falls silent—or puts down her pen—within a year or two of her liberation. The very fact that she has organized the compilation of her entire oeuvre can be taken as an indication that, in her eyes, it is over: closed, complete. (Eleanor died at the age of 83 in 1204.)

Why did Eleanor choose to adopt the name "Chrétien"? A number of lines from *Perceval* (Chrétien's own version of the ending) explain this— and these lines make sense if, and *only* if, Chrétien was Eleanor. The name "Chrétien" is, the lines say, a joke, but is justified by Chrétien's having been on a crusade. Well, Aliénor was indeed, in her own fashion, a crusader: she had been to the Holy Land all right! In this same passage, but in lines from two different couplets, Chrétien speaks of being from Troyes:

> Sui de Troyes, si com Helene
> Ki fit tant noise et disturbance

That is:

> I am from Troyes, just like Helene
> Who caused so much trouble and discord.

Chrétien-Aliénor is from Troyes in the same sense that Helen was! That is, she is another troublemaker—just like Helen! In a word, the choice of the name "Chrétien de Troyes" was apparently based on a couple of in-jokes that Aliénor had with herself and with others in the know.

It is, then, not only possible for Aliénor of Aquitaine to have been Chrétien, it is true. It is even (if I may speak thus) historically necessary.

This identification allows us to explain, to understand all manner of details that had hitherto been inexplicable.

There are other advantages as well—and here I speak not merely for myself (though I do hope to be awarded a chair for this discovery).[4] No, I speak for all of us who love Chrétien. And I speak for those of us with a commitment to feminism, to which I am, as I said, a recent convert. (I may even rejoin the MLA.) We can confidently affirm that Chrétien, instead of merely being, as a *man*, on *most* academic reading lists, will now be—as a *woman* writer—on *each* and *every* reading list, for the M.A., the Ph.D., the M.Phil., the D.Phil., the M.B.A., the D.S.T., the LL.D., and the L.S.D. We will all raise our scholarly glass to Eleanor of Aquitaine, the Parent—nay the *Mother!*—of Arthurian romance, and to Hermengarde, her scribe. We have given Aliénor back her tongue, and Hermengarde her quill.

But, alas, I cannot close on this triumphant note. I must shift to an elegiac mode and speak of the destruction of these manuscripts—for all of them, by some strange and cruel twist of fate, were destroyed last week in the space of three days, just before I was able to make a microfilm of the manuscript. I am still in shock!

I have been teaching a graduate course on Chrétien this semester, and I revealed to my students the true identity of the poet. One student—of an antediluvian male chauvinism—was very distressed to discover that his favorite poet was in fact a poetess. My discovery was all the more painful to him as he was just completing a dissertation on gender in Chrétien, with emphasis on the "problématique de l'écriture masculine dans le roman médiéval," and this new information would, of course, have necessitated an entire rethinking of his topic. It would also have made it impossible for him to go on the job market in January. One night last week as he worked in the Rare Book Room of Bobst Library, he simply went berserk. He ate the manuscript, moaning as he doggedly chewed the untenderized calfskin, "No, no! He, not she! She, not he!! Never again!" We had his stomach pumped but, unfortunately, he was stronger dentally than mentally. Nothing worth preserving emerged from that ghastly gastrointestinal dig.

As to the other two volumes, their fate is scarcely less tragic (if less revolting). Mr. Mitsubishi, the Japanese industrialist who bought them, was already in ill health. When he died, also last week, the two volumes of Chrétien, along with a small but lovely Van Gogh and some other objets d'art (little Etruscan statues, I believe) were buried with him. He may not truly have been able to take it all with him, but he has taken our precious manuscript away from us.

But let us not end on this tragic note. We (I!) have made a major discovery: we know both Eleanor and Chrétien in an exciting new way, not to mention the wise and witty Hermengarde. Let us rejoice, and not weep!

NOTES

1. I wish to thank a number of scholars who have helped me decode and fully appreciate the great importance of this manuscript. I am deeply indebted to Elliot Nesterman, formerly a graduate student at the Institute of Fine Arts of New York University, for his valuable help with the images (he created them). I thank my colleague Edward Roesner of the Music Department of New York University for his learned advice (he provided the music and the notation, and had many entertaining suggestions). I particularly thank two friends who were at the time colleagues at NYU for their many useful contributions (and we shared lots of laughs): Kathryn Talarico and Karen [Katherine] Duys. Julian Onderdonk (then a graduate student in music at New York University) recorded the music, and Emily Sue Pinnell played the *viele* at my presentation at Kalamazoo; my thanks to both of them.

2. The letters *A* through *P* connote the two-octave gamut, extending from low *A* to *a'*. *I* and *J* are the same in this system.

3. Blessedly, I took photographs of these two images on the spot!

4. As this volume goes to press, I am happy to announce that I have just been named the Gould and Silver–Aliénor d'Aquitaine Femme de Lettres Professor of Medieval French Literature at New York University.

SUE DOE'S SOCIETY:
A RECENT ARCHIVAL DISCOVERY

Janetta Rebold Benton

While doing archival research, I recently came upon an evidently un-noticed folio from a late tenth-century English manuscript tucked into the binding of a later work. The text, written in rhymed couplets, reveals the sense of hysteria that gripped the populace as the demise of civilization at the turn of the millennium was anticipated. The writer, perhaps adding to the interest of the document, an intelligent observer and articulate author, ancestor of our celebrated John Doe, was the abbess Susanna Doe. This document offers extraordinary insight into Sue Doe's society.

The text reads:

In a vision, I received a visitation—
An angel flew to me, without hesitation.

And while his wings were still fluttering,
He began his awful uttering,
Of the most dreadful devastation,
That would befall all civilization.

The angel then drew back his cloak—
At this movement, Sue suddenly awoke.
Terrified by the words he spoke,
Hyperventilating, she began to choke.

"How will I know when the end is near?
What will I see? What will I hear?"

The angel said, "I will make it very clear,
Just when you should be *filled with fear!*

"The onslaught of disaster will begin when,
Two or three thousand women and men,
Delude themselves into thinking they can,
By typing on computers or writing with pen . . ."

"On *what?*" queried a confused Sue.
"I fear I do not understand you."

The angel gasped, "It flashed before my eyes!
A premonition of the scribes' demise!"

The angel continued, "And on the dreaded day of doom,
People will be found, two to a room,
Bartering for bathrooms and making deals,
Using tiny tickets to receive their meals.

"Finally, they will perform a ritual dance,
Feet freed by alcohol, as they leap and prance,
Claiming to all that 10 P.M. is midnight,
And this lie put in print, without a fight.
But several among them, able to tell time,
Will maintain, this is the devil's crime.
Others mutter, 'We are being punished before our time,
By being compelled to hear this rhyme!'"

Sue cried, "Angel, tell me, *when* will this be?"
The angel replied with gravity,
"The year of our Lord, nineteen hundred and ninety three,
Will mark the onset of this depravity."

Said Sue, "Whew! What a relief, for, luckily,
This will not have any effect on *me.*"
It is not in *my* lifetime that disaster will come,
I am safe by a millennium.
I live in the year nine hundred and ninety-three."
And thus was spared Sue Doe's society.

REGISTRUM INVENTIONUM OMNIUM, COMPLECTENS ANNOS 1986~2002

una cum relationibus de Jutis anno 1976

1976

Dennis W. Cashman. Jutish Studies: Introductory Remarks

Jo Ann McNamara. Saint Withelas, Mother of the Jutes

Jan Malcolm Phillips. The Travels of Winnles the Jute: In Fact, in Legend, and in Reliquary. [Announced but not presented.]

Vern L. Bullough. What Happened to the Jutes: A Possible Sexual Explanation

Dean Ware. The Jutes and the Bayeux Tapestry

Jeanne Krochalis. Notes on the Unique Copy of the Jutish National Epic. [Announced but not presented.]

Frederick H. Russell. The Medieval Hunt and Some Modern Survivals: A Jutish Perspective

1986

James A. Brundage. Inventing the Past: The Methodology of Pseudo History

Bernard S. Bachrach. A New Portrait of Charlemagne

R. Dean Ware. The End of the Bayeux Tapestry

Vern L. Bullough. A Newly Discovered Medieval Redaction of a Previously Lost Section of Soranus Which Amplifies upon the Abbreviated Translation of Caelius Aurelius

James Muldoon. Richard I at Vienna: New Interpretation

John F. McGovern. The Account Books of Saint Francis of Assisi
James D. Ryan. Chastity Belts and Technology
Richard Kay. The Latest Invention of Leonardo da Vinci

1987

James A. Brundage. *Peccata papae:* The Secret Diaries of Pope
    Innocent III
William Calin. Or/ordure: From Gold to Garbage, or Deconstructing the
    Anglo-Norman Romance *Topas et Pleindamour*
Albert C. Leighton. The Original Patent Application for the Pivoted
    Front Axle
James F. Powers. Saintly Interventions on the Medieval Battlefield: A Newly
    Discovered Hagiographical Tract

1988

Charles T. Wood. Joinville's Secret History
David Parry. Grafton's Bill: Necromancy and Food Fetishism in the
    Dramatic Records of Medieval Europe
Maureen Fries. Boethius on King Arthur: A Newly Discovered Text

1989

Thomas F. X. Noble. *Libri pontificales extravagantes*
William Cook. The San Gimignano Dossal: A Thirteenth-century Image of
    Francis Rediscovered
Christopher Kleinhenz. Newly Discovered Danteana from the Biblioteca
    Bengodiana

American Historical Association, December 1989

R. Dean Ware. Inventing Our Motto: Introductory Remarks at the AHA
Jo Ann McNamara. The Engendering of the Franks: The Methodology of
    Urkonstruktionismus
Thomas F. X. Noble. The Name Game
Richard Kay. The Badman of Bossy-sur-Inept: Memoirs of a Medieval
    Peasant
James A. Brundage. Final Comments at the AHA

1991

Richard Hoffmann. *Artorius rex Britanniae* from a Contemporary
Witness
Charles Bowlus. The Ethno-genesis of Greater Lower Moravia
Richard R. Ring. The Letters of Charlemagne's First Wife, Audostrada,
Called Desiderata

1992

Evelyn Birge Vitz. On the Discovery of a Lost Manuscript of Chrétien de
Troyes: Toward an Appreciation of Its Vast Implications for the Study
of Medieval Literature and Culture
Marilyn Jane Stokstad. The Paradise Garden: The Fruits of Post-
Processual Approaches
Karl F. Morrison. Re-figuring Enigmatology

1993

Adam Knobler. You Can't Get There from Here: An Eastern Pilgrim's
Guide to Western Europe (ca. 1295)
Thomas Izbicki. How the Neo-Goths Came to America
Janetta Rebold Benton. Sue Doe's Society: A Recent Archival Discovery
Richard R. Ring. A Medieval Surprise Visit from C. D. Oleander,
Professor Emeritus, Collegium Durictuum, Near-Here, Kansas

1994

Susan E. Farrier. A Paleographical Description and Literary
Consideration of the "Buttcabbage Codex" (Manchester Industrial
Consortium Library, Stig Futterman Collection, Add. Cod. 14, CRP,
791, AT.4)
Katherine Emblom, Linda R. Gray, and Jennifer C. Vaught. *Ultra atram
viperam:* Slipping between the Spirit and the Flesh
Lee Francis Sherry. Popular Continuation of the Middle Ages: The
American Popular Press

1995

William W. Clark. The Divorce of Eleanor of Aquitaine and Louis VII:
Some Unexamined Evidence

Steven H. Silver and Valerie J. Gulick. The Spiritual Effects of the Black
    Plaque in Europe
Janetta Rebold Benton. Sue Doe's Society Recordata et Renovata
Fred Cheyette and Bailey Young. Pre-Columbian Hiberno-Irish
    Settlement in New England

1996

M. D. Edwards. *Monstra et Narra: Mea Peregrinatio recens . . .*
Mike Bailey. On the Medieval Origins of Modern Underwear: Leutard of
    Chalons and His "BeeVDs"
Constance B. Bouchard. Deconstructing the Gendered Silences on the
    Body's Margins: Genealogy in Burgundy

1997

Charles Bowlus. The *Vita Razzonis* and the Light It Sheds on the Rise
    and Fall of the House of Andechs
E. M. Orsten. Odium Poeticum: Chaucer's Views from beyond the Grave
Richard R. Ring aka Vulgus Promiscuum et alia. The (not long so) Secret
    Diary of John Kempe

1998

Kelly DeVries. Cuthbert's Victory: A New Interpretation of the Battle of
    Neville's Cross
Constance Hoffman-Berman. The Women in White: A Reconsideration
    of the Evidence for a Little-known Religious Order in the Twelfth
    Century, the Tartines
Thomas F. Head. The Piece of God: The Rise of the Cult of the Holy
    Foreskin

1999

Mary D. Edwards. The Exceptionally Large Person of Cerne Abbas
    (Dorset)
Ann W. Astell and friends. A Double Discovery: The Yeoman's Tale of
    Robin Hood and Friar Tuck
Carl F. Barnes, Jr. Villard de Honnecourt, Cannabis, and Cross-dressing
    in Thirteenth-century France

2000

Christine Meek. How the Irish Saved Medieval History: Progress in Insular Studies, 1964–1999

Siobhan Nash-Marshall. Boethius' Very, Very Mysterious *Desolatio theologiae*

Richard Landes [in absentia]. Manic Depression at the Millennium: Newly Discovered Fragments from Adémar of Chabannes' Lost Pilgrim Diary with Entries from 1033 and 1034

2001

Bret Kramer. The Role of the *Megadux* in the Byzantine Military, 330-1453: Reimagining a Synthetic Hypothetical Supposition

Elinor Nauen. Piers the Batsman: Baseball (and Other Games) in the Middle Ages

Paul E. Chevedden. Climax at Long Range: The Male Member and the Crusades

2002

Lloyd Laing [in absentia]. A Discourse upon Divers Ancient Signifiers Attributed to the Cruithnic Nation of Alba, Vulgarly Call'd Pictish Symbols . . .

Hagith Sivan. The Secret Diary of Galla Placidia

Bonnie Wheeler, Jeremy duQ. Adams, and Richard Kay. The Unexpurgated Love Letters of Heloise and Abelard

CONTRIBUTORS

JANETTA REBOLD BENTON, Honors Program, Pace University

JAMES A. BRUNDAGE, emeritus, Department of History, University of Kansas

VERN L. BULLOUGH, emeritus, California State University–Northridge

WILLIAM CALIN, Department of Romance Languages and Literatures, University of Florida

DENNIS W. CASHMAN, Department of History, Quinnipiac University

WILLIAM COOK, Department of History, State University of New York–Genesco

MAUREEN FRIES†

RICHARD C. HOFFMANN, Department of History, York University

RICHARD KAY, emeritus, Department of History, University of Kansas

CHRISTOPHER KLEINHENZ, Department of French and Italian, University of Wisconsin–Madison

JOHN F. MCGOVERN†

JO ANN MCNAMARA, emerita, Hunter College

THOMAS F. X. NOBLE, Department of History and Medieval Institute, University of Notre Dame

JAMES F. POWERS, Department of History, College of the Holy Cross

RICHARD R. RING, Department of History and Library, University of Kansas

JAMES D. RYAN, Department of History, City University of New York

EVELYN BIRGE VITZ, Department of French, New York University

R. DEAN WARE, emeritus, Department of History, University of Massachusetts

CHARLES T. WOOD, emeritus, Department of History, Dartmouth College

Medieval Institute Publications is a program
of The Medieval Institute, College of Arts
and Sciences, Western Michigan University

Typeset in 10/12 New Baskerville
with Dwiggins Uncial display
Designed and composed by Linda K. Judy
at Medieval Institute Publications
Manufactured by McNaughton & Gunn, Inc.

Medieval Institute Publications
College of Arts and Sciences
Western Michigan University
1903 W. Michigan Avenue
Kalamazoo, MI 49008–5432
http://www.wmich.edu/medieval/

 WESTERN MICHIGAN UNIVERSITY